Praise fo

In a world where loss is an inevitable part of the human experience, *Goodbye for Now: True Stories of Life, Love, and Loss* offers an insightful exploration of grief. Each narrative, woven with honesty and vulnerability, illustrates the diverse ways we cope with the absence of someone loved. Through shared experiences of heartache and resilience, the authors of each story invite readers to reflect on their own journeys of mourning and transformation. The editors skillfully organized a range of authentic voices, with each story exposing the universal themes of love, grief, and strength. A must-read for anyone navigating the complexities of grief or trying to support someone through it. *Goodbye for Now* reminds us that while our stories may often differ, the threads of shared humanity unite us all.
—*Dr. Laurel Elizabeth Hilliker, Sociologist and Fellow in Thanatology; author of Grief-Stricken: Stories of Altered Loss in a Pandemic Haze*

These stories of love and loss offer readers a way into the depths of their own feeling. They give that rare and longed-for permission to experience the heartbreak and vulnerability that come with being human. Bearing witness to the stories of others can support the difficult work of remembering ourselves in the wake of loss, gradually gathering the pieces together in new and unexpected ways.

—*Patrick Huston, Psychotherapist*

This beautifully crafted book is a heartfelt journey through love, life, and loss, offering gentle guidance for those facing the depths of grief. With profound sensitivity, it explores the various stages of mourning, providing readers with tools and insights for coping with diverse losses. From the heart-wrenching grief of losing a baby or a teenager to addiction, a beloved friend, or a parent, each chapter resonates with empathy and understanding. The book also provides a poignant look at the resilience of an ill parent who embraced positivity and hope even in their final days. Through each story, readers find comfort, perspective, and a reminder that, in the face of loss, healing is possible.
—*Jeanne L. Surface, EdD, Professor, Educational Leadership, University of Nebraska at Omaha*

Goodbye for Now is a heartfelt tribute to the strength and resilience found following the loss of a loved one. I have worked in the field of grief for over forty years, and countless individuals have described the value of stories in helping them move forward. Through deeply personal stories, this collection invites readers to share the authentic, unfiltered emotions of individuals navigating their grief. The contributors' courage in revisiting and sharing these moments is both moving and inspiring, offering readers a unique opportunity to reflect on their own relationships and losses. This book is an invaluable resource for individuals who are seeking comfort, connection, and understanding on their own grief journey.

—*Camille B. Wortman, PhD, Professor Emeritus of Psychology, Stony Brook University*

Goodbye for Now is a rich collection of grief stories describing the loss of a parent, spouse/partner, sibling, child, grandparent or other relative, a friend, or a pet. For readers on a personal grief journey, the book provides opportunities to compare and contrast possible paths through loss and find validation for the unique ways that people grieve. For readers who are hoping to support the bereaved, this resource will facilitate understanding and empathy for people who are learning to balance the pain and challenges of grief with the joy that comes with having loved.

—*Carla Sofka, PhD, MSW, Professor of Social Work and Public Death Educator*

We are invited into the painful grief journeys of family and friends by these stories. Each setback leads through overcoming challenges to reach hope. The reader connects with the deep emotional core of their messages while their pain and pleasure deeply resonate within us. The writers offer us insight, courage, and strength while we realize that one day we too will say goodbye for now. The stories lead us from where we've been to where we are going, as they build a bridge connecting us to one another. Thank you for your honest courage and vulnerable transparency about your loss. Your path has been messy, full of confusion, yet there is deep meaning fueled with passion and love. You give us hope and we are grateful.

—*Dr. L. Keith Taylor, DMin, Adjunct Professor of Thanatology, Tyndale University/Seminary; Consultant, Tyndale Centre for Grief and Loss; Member of Association for Death Education and Counselling; Author, Seminar Speaker*

Goodbye for Now is an amazing and eloquently established personal account of the loss of loved ones that anyone that has experienced loss due to death will relate to. I find the personal stories within to be an invaluable source of inspiration derived from times of devastation. I believe every reader will find this book a relatable yet beautiful source for which to carry on in the now, knowing loved ones will be embraced again. Simply a beautiful must-read!
—Isaac C. Carrier, PhD, Assistant Professor of Educational Leadership, University of Louisiana at Monroe; Co-owner and Principal Consultant of Carrier Instructional and Leadership Consultants

Goodbye For Now is an amazing piece of literature that reaches across all of humanity. Everyone in life has felt a part of their soul disappear when a loved one leaves us forever. Embracing those losses are hard. But, having a safe space to express those emotions and have those stories told is therapeutic, for not only for the contributors but the reader as well.
—Korwin M. Jean, Author and Educational Consultant

Goodbye for Now

Goodbye for Now

True Stories of Life, Love, and Loss

Edited by:
Sandre Griffiths and Darrin Griffiths, EdD

Goodbye for Now

True Stories of Life, Love, and Loss

Edited by Sandre Griffiths and Darrin Griffiths, EdD
Copyediting: Emily Bradley (chaotix inc.), Steve Viau (Pointed View Editing), Sandre Griffiths (SJE Editing), and Jennifer Holmes-Dziuba
Book design by Jim Bisakowski – www.bookdesign.ca

ISBN 978-1-9994224-5-5

Word & Deed Publishing Incorporated
1860 Appleby Line, Suite #778
Burlington, Ontario, Canada, L7L 7H7
(Toll Free) 1–866-601–1213

Visit our website at
www.wordanddeedpublishing.com

Contents

Part 1 *Child*

Part 2 *Friend*

Part 3 *Grandparent*

Part 4 *Other Relative*

Part 5 Parent

Part 7 *Sibling*

Dedication

For my dear sister Pauline. Much loved, much missed.
~ Sandre

For John Alexander Roberts: A great friend and mentor who passed in 2018.
~ Darrin

Foreword

<blockquote>
Hope is being able to see that there is light despite all of the darkness.

—Desmond Tutu
</blockquote>

A central need of authentic mourning is the instinct to "tell the story." Stories of love and loss. Stories of pain and joy. Stories of hope fulfilled and dreams lost. The stories in this compilation are beautiful reminders of our shared humanity.

While the word "bereavement" literally means "to be torn apart," it is the art of re-telling our stories that supports us on the path to healing—"to become whole again." As we tell how our grief impacts our lives, we allow ourselves to come to know who we are in new and unexpected ways. We allow ourselves to be vulnerable and that contradicts the isolation that all too often exists when we experience grief in our lives.

Because stories of love and loss take time, patience, and unconditional love, they serve as powerful antidotes to a modern society that all too often is preoccupied with inviting us to "carry on," "keep busy," and seek "closure." Yet, we are well served to remember that closure is for windows and doors and not some goal to achieve when someone in our life dies.

Before you begin to reflect on the stories contained in this book, allow me to gently remind you of how actively remembering helps us integrate loss into our lives. When we tell the story, we allow ourselves to do the following:

- Search for wholeness among our fractured parts.

- Come to know who we are in new and unexpected ways.

- Explore how love experienced and love lost have influenced our time here on Earth.

- Discover how a life without story is like a book without pages—nice to see but lacking in substance.

- Journey inward and discover connections previously not understood or acknowledged.

- Create an awareness of how the past interfaces with the present, and how the present ebbs back into the past.

- Understand that the route to true healing lies not only in the physical realm, but in the emotional and spiritual realms.

- Discover that in our pain and suffering lies the awareness of the preciousness of each day on this Earth.

When we are in mourning, we heal ourselves as we tell the tale. This is the awesome power of the story. Yes, it takes time and a true commitment to heal during times of loss and change. As you read this poignant book, I encourage you to set your own intention to befriend your life losses. As you tell your story, make a true commitment to positively influence the course of your journey. Make a commitment to be an "active participant" in your grief, not a "passive witness."

No, our life losses cannot be fixed or resolved, but they can be soothed and reconciled through re-telling the story and honoring those that go before us. In attempting to set your intention to live your life with purpose and in love—not despite but because of your losses—you can turn to the virtues modeled in this extraordinary book. If you read closely, you will discover not just profound grief, but love, faith, hope, and courage.

Alan D. Wolfelt, PhD
Author of *The Paradoxes of Mourning: Healing Your Grief with Three Forgotten Truths*

<h1 style="text-align:center">Introduction</h1>

This book is a labour of love; love, of course, being the starting point for grief. It has been a few years in the making, always on my mind but needing time to come to fruition. I had just retired in 2019 and was thinking about the people I had lost. I was especially reflecting on the loss of my father in 2003 and wishing that I could have another minute or hour with him to tell him how much I loved him; I still miss him every day. I recalled us watching the movie *Field of Dreams* together when I was much younger, and both of us having tears in our eyes when the father and son reconnected at the end; in essence, we all want that experience with those we have lost, even if it is just for a moment.

This led to my reflecting on the many people I had met throughout my years as a school principal. I have always been fascinated with people's life stories and experiences, and my role as a principal afforded me ongoing opportunities to serve and support students, their families, and my staff. A critical component of this involved listening as people shared their concerns, general thoughts, and, more specifically, private components of their lives. Often, I would hear stories about people (and pets) they had lost and the impact this had had on their lives.

Other people's experiences can become an integral part of our own journey. Grief stories, in particular, are unique and a part of the human condition. In reflecting on my own losses and those of others, I realized that a book sharing stories about life, love, and loss would be something that could connect with anyone. The title, *Goodbye for Now,* reflects my hope to one day reconnect with my father as I believe our separation is only temporary. The cover makes me imagine two people sitting together watching a sunrise or sunset and leads me to ponder these questions: What would you tell someone you had lost if you could reconnect? What would it feel like to have another moment in time with them beside you?

As we begun work on the book, Sandre and I were fortunate enough to attend a session with world-renowned grief expert, therapist, and author,

Dr. Alan Wolfelt. Listening to him provided us with the stimulus to move forward with our work on this book. One of the many critically important points he made was the importance of "looking backward before you can go forward" (Wolfelt, 2023, 69). In other words, people need to return to their memories, thoughts, and emotions first before they can truly begin moving forward in their lives (Wolfelt, 2003, 2023). As he explains:

> *Because stories of love and loss take time, patience, and unconditional love, they serve as powerful antidotes to a modern society that is all too often preoccupied with getting you to go forward. Whether you share your story with a friend, a family member, a coworker, or a fellow traveler in grief whom you've met through a support group, having others bear witness to the telling of your unique story is one way to go backward on the pathway to eventually going forward. (Wolfelt, 2023, 79-80)*

The stories in this book are raw, heart-wrenching tributes about life and loss, examining both the power of love and the finite time we have with those we love. I applaud the contributors for their vulnerability in sharing both their joy and their pain. Wolfelt (2003) states that people "telling their stories" is an integral part of the mourning process:

> *Telling the story isn't a sign you're going crazy; in fact, it's a sign that you're doing your work of mourning ... you tell yourself the story, and you tell others the story, in an effort to integrate it into your life ... telling the story helps bring your head and heart together. (73)*

This book has allowed the contributors to do just that, thereby fulfilling an essential part of the work needed to work through their grief.

I shed many tears reading these stories, marvelling at the people whose lives were showcased; I also learned many lessons about love, commitment, and life that I believe will make me a better person. Reading them also helped me realize that I need to devote more time to going backward for my own healing. I hope this book helps you on your own journey of life, love, loss, and healing.

Darrin Griffiths, EdD.

References

Wolfelt, A. (2023). *The Paradoxes of Mourning: healing your grief with three forgotten truths.* Companion Press.

Wolfelt, A. (2003). *Understanding Your Grief: Ten Essential Touchstones for Finding Hope and Healing your Heart.* Companion Press.

Part I

Child

Born Still

By Heather Lewis-Barchue

Early in the day, your heart beat strong within me.

There was no sign of the terror that would unfold in the hours ahead.

Contractions began slowly in the evening.

Your daddy and I walked together with a shared innocence and lightness in our hearts.

I laugh now at the way danger never crossed my mind back then.

By 10 p.m., the contractions were coming at a fast and furious pace.

Guttural moans, blood, water, and pleads for it all to be over came pouring out of me.

Around 3 a.m., my midwife toyed with the idea of heading to the hospital.

She didn't disclose this information until the following day.

I was dilating, yet you were not descending through my body as anticipated.

I now wonder if your brain was already dead then ...

At 3:35 a.m., they tracked your steady heartbeat with the Doppler.

At 3:40 a.m., I screamed to get you the fuck out of me.

I still regret those words today.

My midwife manually maneuvered you down from outside my belly.

At 3:45 a.m., I squatted in our old living room, and you finally appeared in our world.

You were the little brother we had all been waiting for.

There came a cheer of joy from your daddy and a cry of relief from me.

Then, an eerie silence enveloped the room.

"

At 3:46 a.m., I scooped your perfect body to my chest and desperately patted your back.

At 3:48 a.m., my midwife pulled you from my arms, leaving them with a perpetual feeling of emptiness for years to come.

At 3:50 a.m., she began pumping on your tiny chest—counting the beats of the compressions.

I lay there listening silently and staring at the clock ticking ahead as if in slow motion.

I watched your daddy crying and begging above me.

I was frozen in place.

No one knew what had happened.

At 4:05 a.m., flashing lights appeared outside.

They took you to the ambulance, and Daddy followed.

I still cannot listen to his experience of what he witnessed outside.

I lay there and delivered your placenta.

I knew in my heart you were dead.

Today, I regret not having kept you in my arms.

At 4:30 a.m., your daddy and I were driven to the hospital by a police officer.

I scream-cried the entire ride there.

The police officer sat next to me in silence.

At 4:40 a.m., I was wheeled into the sterile room where they tell you the worst news of your life.

It was as if I were watching myself from above.

At 4:45 a.m., I walked into the room where you lay in your daddy's arms.

I cried in a sickened way I had never heard myself cry before but have become very familiar with since.

I told you I just wanted to be your mommy.

I begged you to come back so I could feed you my milk and change your diapers and swaddle you in blankets.

I was like a small girl who had lost her favorite dolly.

I pleaded for you not to go so I could hear your cries and see your eyes and feel your touch.

At 5:15 a.m., I could no longer handle holding your dead body, covering it with my tears.

That body was not my baby.

My baby was gone from me forever.

At 5:30 a.m., your daddy and I arrived back home, and I crawled into bed with your big brother and fell into a deep sleep through silent tears.

At 8 a.m., I awoke to the reality that you were still dead.

At 12 p.m., your big sisters arrived back home and shook in my arms with broken hearts.

I sobbed at the truth and newfound knowledge that I could never really protect any of you from life's pain.

We slept and wept and went to playgrounds and kept on living because what else could we do?

There is a hole in my heart that will never be repaired.

I will always miss you.

You will be four this year.

You will be my sleeping baby forever.

Elijah's Goodbye

By Katrina Voshall

I found out I was pregnant while I was seventeen and homeless, yet for the first time in my teenage life, I wasn't hopeless and suicidal. I was excited to meet my baby. I cleaned up my life, moved in with my sister, decorated the nursery, and waited with so much joy and anticipation. Finally, the day arrived.

On December 12, 1996, a massive ice storm rolled in, and I went into labor at 8 a.m. By 2 p.m., I was holding my son, Elijah. My birth was perfect, and so was he. After my family came to meet him and everyone was gone, I sat staring at him. He opened his eyes, and our eyes met. An overwhelming sensation of déjà vu rushed over me, "Oh my gosh, I know you, how had I forgotten you?" I knew instantly that this wasn't my son but a very dear teacher of mine on a soul level. I then said, "Crap, you're here to teach me a huge lesson, aren't you?"

As Elijah grew, he confirmed my belief that he was not an ordinary child. He was wise beyond his years and taught me to be kind, loving, and authentic. I wouldn't be the person I am today without him. Being a single mom and so young, we were extremely close and raised each other. I chose to fill his life with adventures. We didn't have much money, but I sacrificed new clothes and lattes and used my money to take him to Belize and Mexico, ski lessons, and concerts. Raising him was the most amazing and fun experience of my life. He was so full of joy that it was hard to have a bad day around him. He wasn't perfect. He loved to lie and exaggerate, he was *always* right, and he would become obsessed with strange things like politics or high fructose corn syrup. He wandered the house making weird screaming dinosaur noises or tried to be annoyingly funny on some level, which could get overwhelming. But he was never mean or angry.

I was shocked at the age of thirteen when his whole personality changed, and he became depressed and angry about humanity and life in general. He struggled with drugs as a teenager and eventually became a meth addict. Our lives were crumbling around us. My heart broke watching him struggle. With a lot of unconditional love and support, he finally got into recovery around the age of twenty-one. He would slip up occasionally, but we stayed close, and he was somewhat honest with me. We weren't as close in his adult life, but we remained tight. We texted weekly and saw each other a couple of times a month. My favorite times were about once a month when he would sneak away from his controlling girlfriend and call me, and we would talk for hours, solving all the problems of the universe. I was proud of how he remained kind and honest despite his struggles. He loved misfits and took them all in; the more misunderstood you were, the better in his eyes.

Ironically, on December 21, 2022, another huge ice storm was about to hit the Northwest, and my car was being packed to drive to my sister's house and hunker down for Christmas. Elijah had texted at 3 p.m. that he had time off work and would be joining us. On December 23 at 6 a.m., there was a loud knock on my door. A chaplain stood on my porch, a massive dark storm rolling around behind him.

"Are you Katrina? I have sad news about Elijah."

My world sank, my heart shattered, my life was over. I had seen him a few days earlier, and I knew he was back in his battle with meth; he was confident it was just a slip-up, and he was determined to get back on track. But he had done some cocaine at work, and it was laced with fentanyl.

Time stopped, my heart stopped, my life was over. At first, I couldn't feel anything. I was cold, numb, my ears were ringing. The chaplain offered to stay with me, but I excused him. It felt like my life was a picture, slowly crumbling to the floor. I looked to my left, and Elijah was in the corner of the room, clear as day, with his back to me, looking over his shoulder, afraid of my reaction. I dropped to my knees and screamed. I now had to tell my family. I would have to say it out loud. *How the fuck am I going to say it out loud?* There were screams and panic on the other line, my mom, my sister, my niece all sobbing. This is what hell feels like. My heart won't make it. I'm having a heart attack. Please, God, let me die. Please!

It didn't take long for Elijah to visit me. On the evening of January 5, I was alone in my room bawling, and he started flickering the lights. I could feel him telling me that he was free and felt amazing. I started screaming at him, "But I'm not free. I'm in hell. Take me with you!" I was crying, yelling, and pleading that I needed to be free. Then, suddenly, I was floating in space. I was free and felt ultimate love. I had no body, no pain, no time. I'm not sure how long it lasted, but when I woke up from the experience, I felt calmer and ready to receive whatever God/spirit/the universe/source had for me.

Elijah always has the same message for me: that he has finished his time on this planet, and he is exactly where he needs to be. He wants us to know that all this pain is an illusion. We are simply souls having a human experience. In a sense, we are lucky to have had the opportunity to love so deeply and powerfully that we also get to grieve so deeply and powerfully.

The Glass Partition

By Catherine E. Zeisner

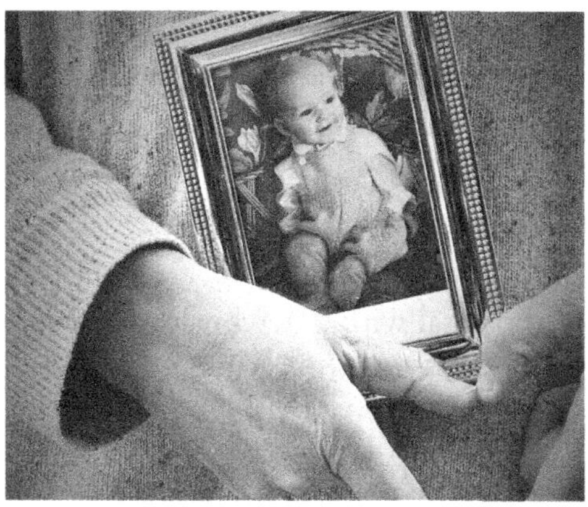

They come in waves. Roll in and wash out. Sometimes they come from a far-off place. Mostly, it is just a flash. A thought, name, smell, or a scar felt. Often, the flash turns into minutes, sometimes hours, staring out a window wondering and crying uncontrollably—even thirty-two years later.

Why? Why grieve for someone you have never met? Why cry on a birthday for a person you do not know? How can you love someone who is not yours? Is it because you feel pain so deeply that you know healing is not possible? As a teen mom who signed her baby boy over to a lawyer and the Children's Aid Society the day after he was born, life, love, and loss were all experienced in a twenty-four-hour period.

I never saw him. I purposefully kept my eyes closed as he came into this world and was handed to a nurse to be cleaned and weighed. She eventually asked if I wanted to hold the baby, but even at nineteen, I knew that I needed to decline because I knew I would not hand him back. Later, a candy striper took me to take a shower. We walked by the nursery where all the newborns were swaddled and sleeping in their cribs. I had no idea which one he was as I stared at them through the glass partition. I leaned on the glass wall not being able to see through my tears as a nurse approached to ask if I wanted her to hold up one of the babies. I shook my head and walked back to my room.

Loss encompasses so many pieces to a birth mom. Not only do you lose your baby, but also you lose your sense of innocence, self-esteem, friendships, respect, and figure. Decisions for a lifetime must be made and adhered to. Lies are told for years and need to be remembered. What makes healing so difficult is the everlasting presence of both physical and emotional scars. Giving birth produces an incredible assortment of marks to the female body that no garment can hide, no pill can delete, and no amount of counselling can erase.

Never having had another baby, I do not know the love and joy of driving away from a hospital with a newborn to start your lives together. I drove away with my dad to return home to act like nothing ever happened. "Why did you leave high school?" "Why were you living with your grand-parents?" "Why are you fatter?" The questions have never stopped. "Why did you quit the curling team?" "Why do you have stretch marks?" "Have you ever had a baby?" So many questions results in a lifetime of lies. Lies to friends, family, and yourself.

The struggle for a birth mom is living with the secrecy and unknowns. Where has your baby gone, who they are living with, and how they are doing? Are they healthy, progressing, and happy? The wondering never stops. And then, the birthday. A day normally spent celebrating, honoring, and acknowledging a great event. A day you must survive, often alone, confused, and not with your child.

What many do not know is that while you have left the hospital to return home to heal, tangible reminders never stop. Just when you are starting to come to terms with the situation you created, a letter arrives for another lawyer visit and more paperwork to sign. This cycle of reminders continues for years, the system needing to confirm that you agreed to hand your baby over for another family to raise, forever.

Ironically, talking about it helps, but since being a woman who has given a baby up for adoption continues to be somewhat of a taboo in our society, whom can you trust to keep your secret? You lose your opportunity to heal without talking. You lose your ability to move forward without reliving the experience. You can pretend it never happened—until the birthday comes around again and you are thrown right back into the feelings of life, love, and loss. You lose so much time and energy wondering, worrying, and hoping. Hoping to hear news of your baby. Was it ever your baby if you never met or held them? You truly love them unconditionally, but the conditions in which they were born are so hard to confront.

As a person taught to identify the bright side in any situation, I found numerous silver linings to make sense of this difficult experience. Happily, I have lost many things through the years. I have lost the sense of shame I have carried for the past thirty-three years. I am no longer embarrassed to call myself a birth mom. I am not afraid to show off my scars, both inside and out, from giving a baby up for adoption. I did not ruin my life, but in fact, gave the gift of life and love to others for a lifetime. Recognizing how lucky I am through this selfless act of giving life and love to others, I now feel I have tears worth shedding when the waves roll in. Instead of the tears being those of sadness, they are tears of pride, life given, love found, and loss worth having. Goodbye for now baby boy.

Ocean Man

By Shannon Coburn

He was my blonde-over-blue, sushi-eating, video-game-playing, outdoor-loving, hard-working Ocean Man. He was my second-born and the most like me in more than just looks. Born February 29, 2000, Alex was the first in our hospital to claim the title of "leap day baby" for the new century.

When he was little, he was this happy little ball of energy. His smile was contagious. He loved going to school and looked up to his big brother. He slept on the bottom bunk, so I was able to get extra cuddles at bedtime, and he was the one who still gave me hugs before heading to school after his older brother gave them up.

He loved playing in the water. He learned to water ski, rode wave runners with me, and couldn't get enough time on the inner tube. We spent the evenings on the lake relaxing in the back of the boat while his grandfather took a leisurely drive around the coastline.

As he got older, we slowly drifted apart, but our family still cheered him on from the sidelines as he excelled in the drill team for JROTC in high school. During this time, he met the love of his life, dating her on and off for four years, and got his first job as a tour guide at a local cave. Alex's adventurous spirit was brought out while working there as he decided to take a spelunking tour in the cave where, because of his height—over six feet—he got stuck for several hours until they could figure out how to get him out.

Alex expressed an interest in SCUBA diving in high school, so I took him to our local dive shop to check into lessons. The price was a little too high for us at that point, so when he decided to go to dive school after he graduated, it was not a surprise.

I spent two amazing days driving him to Seattle, where he would attend the Diver's Institute of Technology, and then two more driving home with him nine months later. We were smarter on the way there as we stopped halfway and stayed in a hotel. On the way home, however, he wanted to push it. So we drove eighteen hours straight, taking turns sleeping while the other tried to keep the car on the road. It was probably the dumbest thing we ever did, and were lucky to be alive, but I wouldn't trade the time we spent together for anything. The conversations we had during those drives are long forgotten and probably not so important, but we had an amazing opportunity to reconnect in ways we hadn't in years.

After graduating, he bounced around for a few months, looking for a stable job before COVID hit and shut things down. At the time, he had just driven down to Florida for a series of interviews for SeaWorld. Not knowing how long the shutdowns would last, he came back home until he could find a job. In the summer of 2020, he finally landed one with a diving company in Louisiana.

He sent us photos of the oil rigs his company was working on, highlighted by the sun setting behind them or lit up at night. He sent videos of his and other people's dives so we could see into his world. It was fascinating to see, and I shared his stories and talked him up to anyone who would listen. I was so proud of him.

Alex managed to come home several times a year, although he missed a few holidays, and stayed with us occasionally for months at a time while trying to commute to work on the coast to save money. Almost every time he came home, I made sure we had lunch together. We grew even closer with these meals, talking about various topics, including his work, over our favorite sushi. When he was away and able, he would hit up sushi restaurants and send me pictures of his meal and the menu to make me jealous. I never got sushi without him.

The last time he was home was over Christmas 2022. He stayed out late at the bars with his friends and slept until after lunch. We usually had dinner as a family. I never got my sushi date. Not to worry, there would be a next time. Except the next time never came.

At 9:25 on the morning of April 30, 2023, I received a text from my oldest. It was a screenshot of a text Alex had sent to a friend at 5 a.m. telling him goodbye. This text was so unlike him that I went into panic mode. It was Sunday, and the main line for the police station in Lafayette, Louisiana, was closed. I couldn't call 911 from South Dakota. I called his father, begging him to call the police for a wellness check. I was at work, pacing frantically in the office, waiting for someone to replace me as I was the only one there.

It took hours for them to get into his apartment, and by then, he was long gone. Alex had been suffering from depression far more than anyone had known. We knew he was having trouble at work. We knew he hated his job. He was alone, far from family and friends. We had asked him to come home many times. I told him to switch companies so he wouldn't have to deal with the HR lady who was frustrating him. He chose a different path. My little boy was gone.

We never had the chance to say a proper goodbye. His father, older brother, and I cleaned out his apartment and fit the pieces of his life into two vehicles to drive home. We had our own private viewing and the public one, but Alex wasn't there—not really—only a body that vaguely resembled his.

The year 2024 was another leap year. Alex would have been twenty-four years old. I threw a sixth birthday party for him at the last restaurant I saw him at—looking for a happy memory, looking for one more reason to celebrate his life. His friends met at the same restaurant for the anniversary of his death and invited us along.

Alex had a beautiful spirit but a broken soul. No, we didn't get to tell him goodbye, but he lives on in the memories we share and the stories we tell, and I am happy that he touched so many lives.

To Be a Father

By Joseph Ferrier

My first son, Elliott, died the week before he was due. There was no warning. The pregnancy wasn't high-risk, there were no complications, and the tests showed no signs of birth defects.

We found out during a routine appointment, a final checkup before the impending labor. We were so excited; I was practically floating. Every appointment leading up to this one, every test, measurement, and milestone had been passed conclusively. All signs indicated we would have a healthy baby sometime in the next seven to ten days, and I would get to be a dad.

When the nurse-midwife couldn't find his heartbeat, I didn't panic. There was no reason to. We were in the clear. Obviously, the Doppler wasn't working. They'd get a replacement, find the heartbeat, and we'd be on our way.

Ten minutes and one ultrasound later, the OB-GYN told us our son was gone.

No words can adequately describe the sense of loss and bewilderment I felt that day. For thirty-nine weeks, we had joyfully prepared to be parents for the rest of our lives. We had money saved, and I had taken time off work so we would have no distractions—just him. In a single moment, it was all over.

I felt like reality was unraveling around me, that I was coming untethered from the world. It was such a sudden and cruel turn that I no longer trusted my senses to tell me what was true. I was dreaming or hallucinating because surely this couldn't be happening. We couldn't be saying goodbye to our son before we even had a chance to say hello.

I remember walking like a zombie out of the office to call my mom to come and get us. She knew something was wrong, but I struggled to put the words together.

"Mom... we lost the baby."

And then it was real. I wasn't going to be a father anymore.

For nine months, all I did was daydream about being a dad. Nine months of ultrasound images, of watching him grow, feeling him move, looking forward to a future of joyful purpose and fulfillment. And then there was nothing ahead of me—just an unending, excruciating present and a future forever out of reach.

In the days after, our families became our life support. There was always a parent, sibling, or in-law to do what was needed as we had all but ceased to function. All we wanted to do was lean into the grief we were feeling because we weren't ready to let go.

We didn't work, we didn't leave the house. We slept, cried, sometimes ate, sometimes bathed, and cried some more. Our families handled everything else. They cooked, cleaned, did our laundry, hugged us tight when we needed it, and left us alone when we wanted it. There were no hollow encouragements to get back on our feet or misplaced reassurances that we could try again later. We held fast to the pain while they held fast to us.

Weeks went by, then a month or two. Slowly, things began to change. We went for walks, distracted ourselves with TV, joined my parents for meals, and even smiled sometimes. We began to talk about our lives after loss—our future. We had been allowed the time and space to be broken, but it was time to put ourselves back together, though some pieces would never fit right again.

Before Elliott died, we had planned to move to Maine and live with my wife's parents while we went to school. We decided to stick with that plan, and when we had recovered enough, we planned a three-month road trip. It was a long, meandering drive with many stops because the grief would come on us again in sudden waves. But we were moving again, moving forward into a visible future for the first time since we lost him.

Before setting out, we scattered Elliott's ashes in a meadow in the Sierra Nevada foothills where other family members were laid to rest. My parents had planted a young cherry tree there as a memorial to him. We sat in the grass, listening to the wind in the pines, and said our goodbyes—in pain but healing slowly.

I don't think it would have been possible without our family's unconditional love. Their understanding, respect, and care allowed us to take in the magnitude of what we had lost and comprehend it instead of drowning in it. We'll never be completely free of the pain, but with their help, we survived it and found new life after.

My second son, Judah, is fifteen now and a miracle in many ways—living proof of our recovery. The joy I felt when we brought him home was like the closing of a ring, like I was finally living the life I was meant for. Every diaper change, every sleepless night, every breath he took was a treasure.

The love I feel for Judah is tied to the love I feel for his brother. In his short life and loss, Elliott revealed to me what I wanted most in life: to be someone's dad. When I look at Judah, I feel joy and grief mingled, but not regret. I'm glad we were brave enough to try again.

Losing Kaylee

By Tiffany Neal

Losing a loved one to cancer is a harrowing experience that leaves an indelible mark on those left behind. My stepdaughter Kaylee, a vibrant and compassionate young woman, succumbed to stage 4 metastatic colon cancer, a result of familial adenomatous polyposis—a battle she fought for ten long years. My family battling cancer, compounded by the physical distance and the isolating grip of the pandemic, led me through a profound journey of grief and healing. This journey, marked by spirituality, ultimately catapulted me into a renewed zest for life—a life I chose to live fully in her honor.

From the day I met Kaylee, her warmth and kindness were unmistakable. She was a teenager and could be a handful, but she had an innate ability to make everyone around her feel loved. Her laughter was infectious and could brighten the darkest days. Kaylee was a passionate advocate for anti-bullying and animal rights. She was found cuddling with our dog Charlie or being a friend to anyone who needed one. Her love for others was just one aspect of her generous spirit. She was also incredibly artistic, often painting and drawing. She would create worlds as beautiful as she was.

One of my fondest memories of Kaylee is our conversation after school one day about my relationship with her mother. Though I was new in her life, we bonded over our shared love for her. The night before her mother and I married, I was upstairs when I heard Kaylee screaming. I rushed downstairs to find her and her brother soaking wet, falling all over each other and laughing as they ran around to avoid the spraying water from a busted pipe in the bathroom. The next day, Kaylee was adamant that she be allowed to come with us to the courthouse for the ceremony instead of going to school. She had missed several days of school already due to her FAP, but we agreed, and she stood as her mother's witness.

Kaylee was always by my side when I was cooking a big meal for the family for the holidays. I couldn't have asked for a better sous chef. She was always so helpful. When we moved to our new house, we decided to host a St. Patrick's Day party. Kaylee was a whirlwind in the kitchen. Her laughter echoed as we chopped veggies together, and I taught her how to plan a party on a budget. When she wasn't helping, she would be looking over my shoulder. "What's in that?" she'd ask—an annoyance I greatly miss. She had a forgiving heart and saw beauty in the simplest things—she taught me to do the same. Her enthusiasm for life and dedication to cultivating connection, even in adversity, was truly inspirational.

The diagnosis of stage 4 metastatic colon cancer after the birth of my granddaughter was a devastating blow. Bridget was about two months old, and the subsequent year and a half was a rollercoaster of hope and despair. Despite countless treatments and hospital visits, Kaylee remained optimistic and never let her illness define her—she was a mother first. She continued to care for her family, albeit with increasing difficulty. Her strength and resilience were a testament to the remarkable woman she had become.

Saying goodbye to Kaylee was the hardest thing I have ever had to do. The pandemic had forced us into physical separation, and the distance between us felt insurmountable at times. We relied on video calls, messages, and small gifts to stay connected, but it wasn't the same as being able to hold her hand and comfort her in person. When her condition rapidly deteriorated, I knew I had to see her one last time. I made the journey to her bedside, my heart heavy with sorrow.

Our final moments together were a blend of pain and peace. My wife and I held her hand together, feeling the fragility of her life slipping away as we whispered words of love and reassurance. It was a very hard day. As Kaylee took her last breath, I felt a profound sense of loss mixed with a strange sense of calm. She was no longer in pain, and I took comfort in knowing that she was at peace.

Grieving for Kaylee has been a multifaceted process. An impending divorce isolated me from my in-laws, leaving me to navigate my sorrow largely on my own. I found solace in creativity, channeling my emotions into writing. This creative outlet became my sanctuary, a way to express my grief and keep Kaylee's memory alive. I also turned to spirituality, seeking comfort in the belief that Kaylee's spirit is still with me. Through meditation and prayer, I began to heal, finding a sense of peace and acceptance.

This journey of grief and healing led me to a profound realization: I only have one life to live, and I must live it fully for Kaylee. She had so many dreams and aspirations that were left unfulfilled, and I felt a deep responsibility to honor her memory by pursuing my own passions and living my life to the fullest. I started to take risks, step out of my comfort zone, and embrace every moment with the same enthusiasm Kaylee had.

Kaylee's passing was a turning point in my life. It forced me to confront the fragility of life and appreciate the time I have. Her strength and resilience continue to inspire me every day. I strive to live a life that would make her proud, one filled with love, compassion, and a relentless pursuit of my passions. Kaylee may no longer be with us in body, but her spirit lives on in everything I do.

Patrick's House

By Kelly McCoy

atrick Dillon Mack McCoy was an exceptional young man, as distinct as his name. When choosing his name, his mother and I tossed Patrick and Dillon around before deciding to keep both. Since he was my only son, he was also christened with my name, Mack. Kelly was already taken by one of my daughters.

When I walked by with Patrick on my shoulders, people did a double take because, when they looked at that happy kid, they saw a smaller version of the man who carried him. He was my spitting image and my biggest fan.

When Patrick was given money, he gave it to me because he didn't want to bother with it. My son knew I would provide whatever he needed. Isn't that a perfect picture of how we should trust God to supply our needs? I've carried that lesson with me throughout my life, and have sought to have that kind of open heart and trust with my Father in Heaven.

After he grew into a young man and started working, his co-workers lovingly called him Paddy because of his name and Irish heritage. He was an old soul loved by everyone who crossed paths with him. Why did they love him so much? He was full of empathy, which allowed him to connect with everyone regardless of their age or position in life.

Patrick loved Hank Williams as much as he loved Bob Dylan, the Beatles, classical music, old Christian hymns, or more modern music. Oh—and the blues! When I grabbed my guitar and started belting out our favorite blues song, Patrick rolled on the floor in laughter.

When I came home from work, Patrick wanted to know about my adventures on the road that day. We then settled in for the night and watched black-and-white episodes of *The Twilight Zone* and *Alfred Hitchcock Presents*. Sometimes, I would reluctantly play video games with him. He felt terrible for me because I played so poorly. He encouraged me to keep at it, assuring me I would eventually become skilled at the games. I didn't.

According to family lore, Patrick's great-grandfather, a coal miner from Virginia, had his mine illegally taken from him. The elder McCoy died in poverty, leaving my dad and uncle orphaned at six and nine years of age. This happened against the backdrop of the officially ended but still simmering McCoy-Hatfield feud. Patrick was so incensed by the injustice, and fascinated by the history, that he wanted me to help him with a school project about the story. We spoke of writing a book about it one day.

At twenty-two years of age, after going missing for a couple of days, Patrick was found dead. He died of an overdose of street drugs mixed with his mom's legal prescription drug, fentanyl. Shocked? I learned of his death when I received a note of condolence from a counselor who presumed I knew. I was so shocked that I shook uncontrollably after reading the note. Patrick? Gone? Not Patrick! Noooo!

Patrick was not the kind of kid that you would in a million years expect to die from drug use. But his story has been repeated almost a million times since 1999—a million deaths. A million sons or daughters, leaving behind brothers and sisters, and moms and dads, all lost to the epidemic of drug overdose.

No, Patrick was not the kind of kid you would expect to die like that. Neither are most of the others. Those who do fit the profile have often suffered such horrific abuse that they deserve our compassion as well.

I said goodbye to Patrick at his gravesite, where I ripped off my leather jacket and threw it atop his ashes. He dearly loved that jacket and wore it often, even though it was way too big for him. Why did he love that jacket so much? Because it looked cool? He wore it because he thought his dad was cool and he wanted to be cool, too.

Patrick was cool. He was just a cool kid. I had hoped to say goodbye to him on my deathbed, where I would encourage him to live out the calling God placed in his heart. I would close my eyes and die in peace, knowing he would carry on the McCoy name and legacy.

But instead, the name dies with me. We only get to control the endings of our stories when we write books or screenplays. Real life often ends in ways we never expected. Life is not fair. Not this side of Heaven.

My faith and the knowledge that I'll see Patrick again on the other side have kept me going through it all. There will always be a Texas-sized hole in my heart—one that won't be filled until that day. Any parent who has lost a child can relate.

The pain of losing my only son is not something I would wish on anyone. But through the pain, I find purpose. If sharing his story helps to prevent the loss of another Patrick or Patricia to a grieving parent, it will be worth it all. I hope that by sharing Patrick's story, I can contribute to a dialogue that leads to meaningful change in the way we allow dangerous drugs to be passed out like candy by people who should know better.

Patrick's legacy lives on. He deserves to be remembered as one who brought change, compassion, and hope. My dream and vision is to create a home for boys like him, boys who may have their lives turned around instead of turning to drugs. I have a name for the home—Patrick's House.

A Son

By Aiza Claire P. Jamisolamin

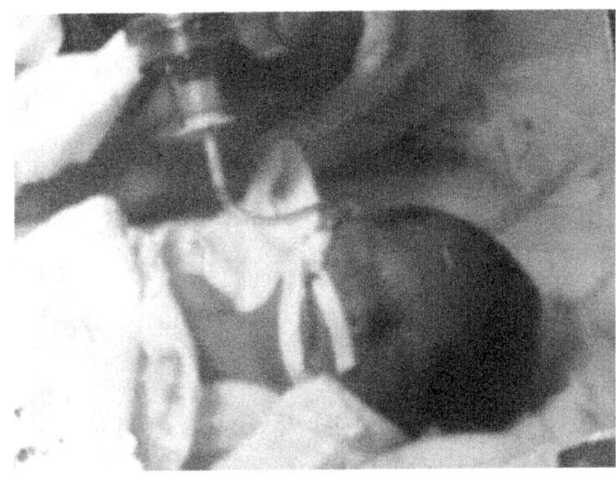

They say no parent should outlive their children. Losing a child doesn't go away. I never imagined I could love someone as much as I love my children. My eldest, Joseph, was born prematurely on March 18, 2011. I wasn't ready to be a mom, but I was even less prepared to bury my son. I kept asking my son for guidance and strength. Because I was young, I was still trying to figure out life and the strength to face the challenges I knew I would deal with once I became a mom. The first time I felt my son growing inside me, I knew I loved him more than my life. He made me a better person and changed my perspective on life. I stopped thinking about myself and started thinking about how I could support my child.

March 17, 2011. The night I never imagined would happen. Around midnight, I felt uncomfortable and started feeling pain. At first, I thought it was just a cramp and would go away by morning. But it became worse. We decided to go to the nearest hospital. There, the medical staff said that I was in early labor. I felt dread; my whole body went cold, and I couldn't think anymore. They gave me medicine they thought would help stop the contractions, but my water broke soon after. I slowly realized that my biggest fear was coming true no matter how hard I prayed and hoped it wouldn't. I felt relieved when I heard him cry and saw his little fingers, but

I did not have the chance to hold him. He had to be transferred to a bigger hospital because they did not have the right equipment for his little body. His first cry and those little hands were my first memory of Joseph. I was hopeful. I kept telling myself that he was going to be okay because I heard him cry.

The next day, I was allowed to visit him at the hospital where he was transferred. Nothing is as painful as when you see your child gasping for air inside a machine, with tubes attached to his tiny body. It felt like I was being poked with a million needles, and I couldn't think properly. Watching him, I knew he was in pain. I couldn't stop blaming myself. I hated myself. The doctor explained that since he was born prematurely, his organs were underdeveloped. If he survived three days, his chances of surviving would increase. My son was fighting for his life, and all I could do was watch, wishing I could suffer in his place.

On the second day, they allowed me to hold him for a bit. He held my finger and squeezed it so tight. I kept talking to him, begging him to fight, and I felt like when he squeezed my finger, it was his way of saying, "I will, Mama."

On the third day, I was excited because, in my mind, he made it through the third day. When I arrived at the hospital, he was out of the incubator and on a bed with a tube. My hand was shaking, and I touched the bag and compressed it as I breathed. I wanted to believe that it was all just a bad dream. I was crying so hard that I felt like my chest would explode. I was so helpless. A parent would do anything for their child, but we can't take away death. I whispered to my son that I would go home for a bit and come back, and he squeezed my finger again. I knew he was trying to fight.

Just as I arrived home, I received a phone call with crying on the other end. I knew it already happened. I wanted to cry and scream, but nothing came out. I felt like I died that day too. I wanted to kill myself. When you lose your parents, you become an orphan. When you lose a partner, you become a widow. But when you lose a child? Nothing. And so is the pain; no words can describe it. It stays with you. It is a wound that will keep bleeding no matter how much you try to heal it.

They wrapped Joseph in a white cloth. I did not dare to look at him one last time; I did not have the strength to hold him. They put him in a small box, wrapped comfortably. Saying goodbye to him was the hardest thing I've ever done. I will never see him grow. I question everything. Why me? What is the purpose of losing him? I wanted to take him out from the ground. The pain doesn't get easier with time; you just get used to feeling it. It will make you strong, or it will break you. We must feel and go through that grief and the pain. Most importantly, we must accept it. It will take a lot of time. Only when you accept that they are gone can they truly rest in peace. Joseph made me who I am today—strong, resilient, and doing my best to be a better person every day.

Part II

Friend

My Fifth Sister

By Jimica Howard

It was Friday, January 9, 2009, and I had just arrived home after a very busy day. I hopped out of the car and mustered my last bit of energy to run up the stairs. My phone started ringing as soon as I hit the top step. I saw that it was one of my girlfriends and I answered the phone with a jovial tone and a joke. When she didn't laugh, I became concerned and asked her what was wrong. She paused and told me to sit down and then she said something that would change my life forever. She said, "Mica, Nemit is dead."

I was speechless. I sat there silently shaking my head while I listened to the details of the sudden death of one of my best friends in the world. There had been a terrible accident and while her stepfather left the scene with minor injuries, Nemit had died on impact. My friend ended the call by apologizing and saying all of the things people say when someone passes away. I squeaked out, "Thank you for the call." and sat where I'd landed for some time; numb and silent. I don't know how long I sat there replaying the call over and over again in my mind; it is still a blur. But I do know that on that day, a piece of my soul was wrenched out when I lost one of my closest and dearest friends.

I moved to Kentucky in 2003 to be a teacher. I didn't know anyone and had no family there, so I picked a church at random and joined. I made a few friends, but while it was cool to sit with them at church, I didn't want to hang out with married women in my free time so I continued seeking out single women my age to get to know.

One weekend, I was sitting alone and noticed a svelte woman with gorgeous dark brown skin who was also sitting alone. She had shoulder length locs, wore all white, and had an RBF that wouldn't quit!! So naturally I went over and sat behind her. I leaned forward and whispered, "I like your dreads."

She turned sideways to look at me with one eye and said, "They are locs. There is nothing dreadful about them."

I was taken aback at her candor and let out a loud laugh. She glared at me through that slitted eye and turned back to face the preacher. I knew right then that I was going to make it my business to get to know this woman. Her air of confidence and cavalier demeanor was my kind of carrying on.

To my surprise, after church Nemit came up to me and asked me if I had a place to eat. I didn't and she invited me to join her. This was the first of many meals we shared. Eventually I introduced her to the other young women I'd met and connected with and we became nearly inseparable.

Every weekend we would spend time together, sharing meals, going dancing, and engaging in other twentysomething shenanigans. Nemit was three years older than me and seemed to feel responsible for me, like an older sister. She was a natural caretaker and could be counted on to watch your back if you'd had too many drinks but also just as likely to make you dinner and scold you about not properly washing the dishes.

Nemit, the youngest child and only daughter in her family, adopted me as her younger sister. She invited me to spend time with her mother and brothers, and even took me to her hometown of Kingston, Jamaica to get to know her extended family. As a woman who already has four biological sisters, you would think that I wouldn't need any more. I thought that too until I met Nemit.

One of my favorite "Big Sister Nemit Moments" was when she decided that she was going to braid my hair because she was tired of me cutting it.

She goes to part my hair and says, "What is going on here? What color is your hair anyway? It's not black, it's not brown. It's gray!!!" This was hysterical for several reasons. First, my hair is not gray. It is a conglomeration of sandy brown, red, brown, and blonde called, "dishwater hair" because it has everything but the kitchen sink. Second, it sounded so mean but she was absolutely not trying to be insulting. Third, it was just *so* Nemit; caring, kind, hilarious, and brutally honest.

The weeks after she died were a blur. I remember speaking with her mother, brothers, and her fiancé and refusing phone calls from my other friends. I remember the nightmares and not being able to drive the stretch of road where the accident happened. I remember looking at my beautiful friend in her white dress in that casket and refusing to leave her by herself because she would have never willingly left me. But I also remember her laugh, that infamous side eye, the taste of her delicious vegetarian cooking, and the peace of mind I had knowing that she was always looking out for me.

It has been fifteen years since I lost my friend and each day as I progress in my life and career, I carry her memory with me. I think of things that I would tell her, technological advancements that she would enjoy, how much she would love my children, and how much I would have loved hers. I also consider what it would be like if we had really gotten to grow up together the way we'd planned.

Saying goodbye to Nemit was one of the most difficult things that I've ever had to do. I don't know if the hole in my heart will ever heal. But, I am beyond grateful for the time I had with her. I am also grateful that she shined so incredibly bright that my memories of her remain as vivid as she was.

Borrowed Time

By Lizbeth Meredith

"What's your pleasure, miss? Pizza or a burger?"

Before I could open my mouth to object, my new friend Mike interjected, "And it's my treat. *Seriously. I'm not kidding.*"

Both phrases would be repeated often over the next many years.

I was eighteen at the time. Mike was twenty-one.

We first met at the cafeteria at Western Washington University, and even before he introduced himself, I knew he was a jokester. Was it his pinstriped vest, parachute pants, and fedora that he wore like a uniform amidst a sea of hoodies and tee shirts? Was it his prominent nose and wild brown curly hair that completed the look? I wasn't sure, but what was clear to me was Mike's confidence and acceptance of who he was.

"I was born with a lot of health problems. No one expected me to live so I inherited a lot of money when my older relatives died," he had said with a shrug. "So, here I am. Still here. And I'm buying."

That explained why he had a large hump on both his back and rib area, which affected his gait. And it explained why he felt compelled toward generosity.

My still-developing brain at the time could not imagine how wonderful it would be to have intermittent piles of money for any reason. What a lucky guy he was, my new friend Mike, I thought then. Not me. Born to two high school dropouts, I was pleased to get a student loan and a job as a dishwasher at night to keep me afloat. The offer of a complimentary burger or pizza was huge.

Mike was generous with his time, too: walking my roommate and me to dinner a few nights a week; inviting me and our other friends to study with him once he had gotten his own place; and listening as I prattled on and on about my youthful insecurities on weight, grades, and whether I would ever find a boyfriend. But he had his own uncertainties. Mike indicated feeling like a misfit at times. And while the steady stream of money coming his way from dead relatives afforded him a fancy truck and great trips, it also served as a reminder of his shorter life expectancy. Would he ever find love? He mused about it without bitterness or obvious expectation, but it weighed on him.

Yet he kept moving forward. Mike earned a degree in marine biology, leaving me behind to blaze a trail to Kenya with his church, and then landing a job in the Dominican Republic as a schoolteacher.

We stayed in sporadic touch from that time forward. While Mike got his teaching experience thousands of miles away from home, I returned to my home state after bombing out of school and marrying the first man who showed interest.

After that man wrung the air from my neck, four years into marital bliss, it was Mike that I called when the immediate crisis abated. He invited me and my daughters to visit him at his new home in Seattle, offering to help defray the costs. *"Seriously. I'm not kidding."* In no time, we turned his home upside down—toys strewn all over the living room as he played the role of uncle and I got a much-needed reprieve.

I envied the way Mike didn't worry about his future. I worried enough, however, for the both of us—willing him to invest money into a retirement account, to trade Ramen for an occasional salad, and to embrace more structure in his life. But Mike was content to live life on his own terms.

After that visit, we traded occasional phone calls and handwritten letters, reconnecting more regularly once Facebook was launched. It was 2011 when Mike let me know that he had met someone. Now pushing fifty, Mike was engaged to his first girlfriend, and he could not have been more excited.

"I can't wait for you to meet her."

Months after their wedding in 2012, I called to let Mike know I had a long layover in Seattle on my way to Vietnam. He and his new bride arrived in an old truck that was dented so badly on the driver's side, we all had to cram into the passenger side door. Mike had lost his teaching job and they were struggling financially.

From the outside, one might have thought that he had worked his way down the ladder of success. But both Mike and his wife were radiant, looking as though they had won the lottery and couldn't wait to see what came next. Love looked good on him. Mike's hair, now graying on the sides, combined with his glowing skin, made him look like an enhanced version of Bruce Springsteen. I had adored watching them on Facebook: snorkeling, dinners, walking hand in hand—savoring love the way that only two people who knew not to take life for granted would. Life appeared to be one long honeymoon. I learned that he and his bride were moving out of state for new job opportunities. I congratulated him, and we promised to keep in touch.

And we did. Sort of. I admit I mostly watched his social media as he blossomed into his new life, celebrating his students, the first ripened tomato in his garden, and—above all—his wife. But in 2014, he began to post about health.

It was July of that year when Mike's bride texted me, urging me to say a final goodbye. Mike had a cancerous tumor that was exacerbated by some of his congenital health problems. He could barely breathe.

I called Mike, grateful to have the chance to say farewell. He couldn't speak. Soon after, he was gone. While my soul was crushed at the loss, Mike had far exceeded his life expectancy, showing everyone around him how to live with joy, courage, and most importantly, love.

Then, Now, and Forever

By Bijaya Giri

Time does not heal; it only makes the pain bearable.

September 18, 2016. A day that broke a part of me that would never mend again. I received the call: "Amina is no more with us ..."

Born and brought up in a lovely station of Darjeeling, a town in West Bengal, India, I had completed my education and started working as a high school teacher. Life was simple and good. Being a typical Capricorn, I was not much of an extrovert and, therefore, did not have many friends; I couldn't make friends easily but once I did, we would be friends for life.

It was the spring of 1997. The new academic session of the school where I worked had just begun. Our principal entered the staffroom one day, followed by a young woman, and introduced her to us. She was the new geography teacher, Miss Amina. Amina flashed a striking smile at all of us. Little did I know then that she would become an integral and irreplaceable part of my life. As she went from one teacher to another, shaking hands, I watched her from afar. The shy, introverted me would not go up to her. So, I just kept watching until she turned around, walked up to my table, and plonked herself in the chair beside me.

"I'll sit here. Is it okay?"

I nodded my head in response.

Amina was a fiery, vivacious woman oozing with confidence. She proved to be an excellent teacher and soon became the favorite of many students. She was always full of life and loved adventure. She must have noticed the quiet me and decided to be my friend. She would force me to go for long walks in the hilly terrains, watch movies, and drink wine. She had a lovely voice and sang occasionally. I slowly opened up to Amina, and over time I would share everything with her—my passions, my dreams, my fears, and my pain. Rock solid as she was, she would listen with rapt attention, giving me advice or her shoulder to cry on. In Amina, I found the kind of friend I had never had.

It was the last week of January 2016 when I received a call from Amina.

"I am going to CMC Vellore tomorrow."

Amina's voice did not sound like hers. The Christian Medical College in Vellore had a multi-specialty hospital that catered to the treatment of all kinds of diseases. The modern-day facilities, latest equipment, and technologies made CMC Vellore one of the best options to treat grave illnesses.

"Vellore? Why? What happened? Is anyone in the family sick?" I bombarded her with questions with an uneasy feeling in my stomach.

"I have been diagnosed with cervical cancer …"

I couldn't believe what I was hearing. I sat down on my bed, my heart beating rapidly. However, collecting myself together and trying to sound very strong, I talked to her for more than an hour, telling her to remain positive while I was breaking inside. I was feeling scared.

Amina left for Vellore with her husband. I did not call her often as she would be undergoing multiple medical tests. She called me up one day to say that the oncologists had confirmed her disease to be stage 2B cervical cancer. There would be no surgery but she would be undergoing chemotherapy and radiotherapy over the next three months. Days passed. We didn't talk much. Then one day, in the month of May, Amina's husband called me to say that the treatment was over and they were back home. Amina was fine. My happiness knew no bounds. The very next day, I decided to visit her.

Amina looked thinner and paler but her striking smile was the same. We hugged each other and talked for hours. She had undergone rigorous and painful treatment and had braved it all. I left her house promising to visit her again. I silently thanked God for saving my friend. Two days later, however, Amina suffered a stroke in her sleep and had to be rushed to another hospital in a nearby city. After a month, she was brought home. I was planning to visit her when I was informed that she had to be hospitalized again as her condition had deteriorated. The series of bad news was putting a weight in my heart.

That very day, I went to the hospital to meet my friend. As I entered the cabin, I saw Amina lying on the bed, immobile. My vision blurred. She had lost her speech and could barely lift her left hand. There was no movement in any other part of her body. She looked at me with teary eyes. I moved closer and held her hand. She made an animal-like cry that wrenched my heart. I turned my face away and began sobbing uncontrollably.

Amina was kept in the hospital for a week but the doctors told her husband to take her home as there was no further treatment they could offer. I visited Amina once in a while. I couldn't bear to look at my friend, now reduced to a vegetable. Flashbacks of the times we had partied, walked in the rain, sang endlessly, and laughed together tormented me.

September 18, 2016. "Amina is no more …"

Death is such a final word. I felt helpless and cheated. I lost my friend, my confidante. Amina didn't stay with me to become friends for life, but I know I will meet her someday on the other side. Till then, I carry her inside my heart and relive the beautiful memories we created together.

The Last Renaissance Man

By Karl W. Gruber

ONG LIVE THE WIZARD! The Wizard of Clio, Michigan, that is—Riley McLincha.

The internet was in its infancy in 1996. Yet somehow, a guy named Riley from Clio, Michigan, found out about me via an internet search. In 1996 and 1997, I was on my own adventure and mission of running fifty-two marathons in fifty-two weeks to raise money and awareness to find a cure for leukemia. I called it my "Super Run for the Cure." Somehow, Riley McLincha stumbled across my effort while cruising the internet. There was an instant connection between us—we were both born in the same year of the post-World War II era, lifelong runners, and lovers of good beer. Although we lived about 250 miles apart, we became fast, virtual friends because of the internet. Riley was one of my biggest supporters during my year of running 26.2 miles once a week.

After our connection in 1996, it didn't take long for me to realize that Riley was a one-of-a-kind man who thrived on exploring and pushing the limits of every ounce of talent and ability he had. I call Riley one of the world's last Renaissance men. He grew up in a rather impoverished home setting, and much of his adult life was spent working in a General Motors

"

factory. Riley shunned a mundane life and went on to invent two previously unheard-of sports: "Drubbling" and "Runyaking."

Drubbling is the art and ability to dribble three basketballs while running. It is a combination of the words dribbling and running. Riley ran many races and miles while bouncing three basketballs for the entire distance. He once drubbled the entire 26.2 miles of the Boston Marathon.

When it came to his invention of runyaking, this is how it was performed: He would drop his kayak (a 9.5 ft. kayak he called Swiftee) at a launch point along a waterway, then drive his vehicle to another spot miles downstream. He would run back to Swiftee, kayak back to his vehicle, and land. Thus began his initial runyaking adventure on April 27, 2009, where over a four-year period, segment by segment, he successfully runyaked the 1,400 miles from the Flint River all the way to Niagara Falls. However, that was not enough; Riley continued his journey for a couple more years to successfully runyak all the way to the Statue of Liberty in New York City. Along the way, Riley made up rules for both of his sports for future participants. Drubbling and runyaking—only the genius and innovative mind of Riley McLincha could have invented them!

Over those twenty-seven years that we knew each other, we only met up physically four times, and, of course, our meet-ups revolved around running and beer drinking! With both of us being lifetime runners and beer drinkers (Riley personally visited over one thousand breweries in his lifetime!), it was only natural for it to play out as it did. Our first meet-up was in Toronto in 2007 when we both ran the Scotiabank Toronto Waterfront Marathon. In 2008, he was kind enough to invite me to speak at the Crim 10 Mile pre-race expo. Considering he was a Michigan grad, and I was a graduate of Ohio State (they are football rivals), it indicated that he was willing to forgive me for being a "Buckeye" and have me join him in his element. In 2014, Riley published a book he wrote called *The Runyaker's Journey.* Inside the cover of the book he sent me, he wrote, "To Karl, who has been one of my heroes!" I was deeply humbled because I felt he was one of *my* heroes!

On June 18, 2024, at the age of seventy-three, he was on yet another runyaking mission on the Illinois River—this time with the St. Louis Arch as his destination—he was navigating his kayak through a series of locks.

Unfortunately, he was pulled underwater by the current of a nearby barge. A few days later, I saw a social media post about it, and of course, I immediately thought it was a joke. After a few moments, I realized it was all too true. The board members of the Crim 10 Mile—Riley's all-time favorite race—posted this, which struck a beautiful chord in my heart: "He was a man of amazing talents and great generosity and was a person who lived life beautifully and enthusiastically." When I found out about Riley's passing, I immediately felt a void in my heart as my kindred brother in spirit and zest for life had left the planet. This is what I wrote on an online community posting:

> Riley, we met virtually twenty-seven years ago while I was doing a year of marathoning for charity (you were one of my BIGGEST supporters!) … I felt like we were kindred spirits and brothers cut from the same cloth! Love you, bro! Thank you for all you did in your lifetime and enriching all our lives by showing us all that there are NO LIMITS! You are a shining example of that! Love you Riley, my friend! At least we know you went out doing what you loved!

It is with great sadness but ultimate respect, gratitude, and love that I say, "LONG LIVE THE WIZARD! The Wizard of Clio, Michigan, Riley McLincha!"

Gone Too Soon

By Sarah Hahn

I attended my first funeral when I was thirteen years old. It wasn't the funeral of a grandparent or even a parent. It wasn't for a distant relative or any other family member. It was the funeral of my best friend.

I'd been friends with Tanya for as long as I could remember. We met in elementary school in the first grade. Both of us—two shy souls—somehow found our way to each other. Along with our friend Amanda, we were the three musketeers. Inseparable. We sat together in our little portable class-room, ate lunch together, and climbed the play structure together during recess. We giggled as we talked about our crushes and laughed until our bellies ached, and we were gasping for air.

I gravitated to Tanya like a magnet. She had a gift for making us laugh every time we hung out. She vibrantly recounted stories about her family, especially her two younger siblings, whom she deeply cared for. Raised in a Christian home, on Sunday she brought Amanda and me to her church, where I witnessed a group of people dancing and singing at the top of their lungs. This experience felt illegal compared to my own conservative Korean church, where we tended to stand in the pews like we were statues. I watched Tanya clap excitedly and sing hymns in a soft but enthusiastic voice. To our peers, Tanya was quiet and reserved, but to me, she was animated and full of life.

Tanya always stood out. The tallest one in our class, year after year, she stood in the back row of every class photo. At only eleven years old, her height had already reached six feet. Whenever I caught sight of her face in the schoolyard, looking above everyone else without having to try, I beamed at her.

In Grade 8, while sitting in health class, our teacher started sharing a story about Tanya from the night before. At first, I was confused about why she was bringing up a student who wasn't even in our class. She spoke to us in English, which was surprising since we were enrolled in a French Immersion program—we weren't allowed to speak in English during class. But I quickly learned that what she had to share was too important to risk getting lost in translation. Our teacher said something about Tanya collapsing on her kitchen floor.

Is she okay? I wondered. *Perhaps I'll see her tomorrow.*

As I sat in the uncomfortable, orange plastic chair with my right elbow resting on the desk in front of me and my chin leaning on my right palm, tears began to well behind my eyes. I finally understood what our teacher was announcing to us. A similar announcement had been made by my Grade 5 teacher about another classmate of mine who had been hit by a car. Tanya wasn't okay. And now, neither was I.

My tears escaped from their ducts and fell fast and hard down my face. I didn't wipe them. Snot trickled out of my nostrils. I let it. Not wanting to draw attention to myself, I sat motionless with my eyes fixed on my teacher, who was still talking. She said something about Tanya's heart not having grown at the same rate as the rest of her body. Eventually, with her heart no longer able to keep up, it failed her. In my peripheral vision, I could see Josh Bouchard, who sat to my right, looking at me. I was the only one crying. "Her best friend …" he whispered with a frown on his face. As a painfully shy child, this was the first time my classmates had seen me express so much emotion.

Tanya died on December 16, 2001, nearly one month after her thirteenth birthday. She was outlived by both of her parents when she should have been the one to outlive them. She would never experience all that

Goodbye for Now

there was to experience in her youth. Everything that the rest of us got to experience. She would never ride another roller coaster. Develop another crush. Tell us another joke. Celebrate another birthday. Attend prom. Graduate university. Get married. Pursue her dreams. Or have children.

I'd never lost a friend before. I'd never lost anyone, really. Maybe a great-grandmother whom I barely knew. Losing Tanya was like losing a limb. Her death altered the trajectory of the rest of my life. After Tanya's passing, Amanda and I hung out less and less. In high school, we drifted apart and found ourselves in separate social circles—our interactions were mostly reduced to faint smiles at each other across the hallway. It seemed that Tanya was the glue that held us together.

Today—twenty-three years later—I wonder what my life would look like if Tanya were still around. Would the three of us have stayed in touch? Would we be raising our kids together? Would I be laughing more often? I will never know all the ways in which her death impacted my life. But I know that the void she left will never truly be filled.

As I grow older, I will continue to cherish Tanya's memory: her laugh, her smile, her friendship. It's been said that none of us are indispensable. But not everyone can be replaced.

For My Friend Sandi Kelly

By Em Del Sordo

As a secondary school principal, I regarded the office staff as the front-line staff to connect with students, staff and community. The office staff helps create "the weather" of the school and hence why it is super important to have an office staff that always makes people feel understood and valued. Focusing on students, the school receptionist is always the first friendly face that serves the needs of our students. I needed someone whose disposition speaks to servant leadership and service. Enter Sandi Kelly.

Sandi's disposition was all about being a caring-adult to our students. Kindness and compassion were her guides. She became a partner in co-leading the school with love, compassion, kindness, understanding, and empathy. She led with character and left a legacy that speaks to the Vision and Mission of our school: "Responding empathetically and filter our learning through a Human Rights lens." She illustrated in action the power of one!

What I loved most about Sandi Kelly was how she worked for the betterment of humanity. She always saw and treated everyone with the dignity they deserved. Sandi knew the power of love. She gave it so freely and so frequently. I remember how Sandi would see a lonely student and connect with them. She would learn their story and do her magic. She made sure every human-being was treated with dignity. People felt seen and valued.

"

The students felt "Sandi love." Sandi worked for the most vulnerable and marginalized and she did it without recognition or reward. To recognize or reward Sandi Kelly would be the very opposite of what she wanted.

Without ever asking me or telling anyone, Sandi would bring in food for those who were hungry and struggling. She bought shoes for students in need, made birthday cakes for the lonely, sat with those who felt unseen, and laughed with those who needed joy. She would purchase clothing and toiletries for those in need. She always checked in with kids with whom she connected. She made the lonely feel wanted. She would drive staff home if she saw them walking after work or if they were waiting for the city bus. She was a gentle reminder that we create the weather in our lives.

She created an atmosphere of joy! Her disposition always centered on you as the "be all and end all" of her time. With Sandi, any problem could be solved and anything could be possible. She made you believe in you. She would be there for you and I knew it. She would *always* make me feel like I was the priority. She made all of us feel the greatest that lies within us. *And*, I came to understand that Sandi Kelly was always about "the other" … the other person, the marginalized, the broken, the downtrodden … and the unloved. She would love them all and call them "sweetie." Oh, how I long to hear her calling me "sweetie" while gently placing her hand on my heart.

Early in September of last year, Sandi and I met at her favorite breakfast diner and she told me she had been diagnosed with cancer. She was planning for her funeral … even though we knew there was a lot of hope and optimism in her diagnosis. She asked me to speak at her celebration of life. I told her that I would but it would probably be fifty years from now and that I might be suffering from dementia. She needed to know that I would be there for her. I reassured her that I would speak and brag of her love, laughter and light.

Over our scrambled eggs and stacked pancakes, we spoke about dying and our fear that there was still so much to do with life. We talked about our lives and the fragility of it all. We laughed at our memories and pranks. We planned travelling together and touring countries just for the street food. All the while, I was falling apart inside, trying so hard to pull a "Meryl Streep" and pretend that all was well and would be well. And, I knew that Sandi was scared herself. She spoke with a tone in her voice that had never been there in the past. She seemed to know that somehow her time was limited. She knew or felt that something was not "sitting right." I felt it in our breakfast chat. I pretended not to pick up on that … I wanted to be there for her as she had been for countless people … giving hope and optimism.

Weeks later, Sandi went in for a "simple" procedure that spoke to the hope and optimism we had chatted about. I texted her just to check in and got a text from her that spoke about being in the hospital for six days and that the side effects of the treatment had been horrendous. She texted, "I am extremely weak, and my concentration is almost nonexistent. That doesn't mean to say, I haven't thought of you." Two days later Sandi died from complications from her treatment.

My world fell apart. My heart ached, my legs gave way, and my eyes filled up. I had lost the greatest human being to ever cross my path. I had lost a support that had buoyed me up, supporting my spirit, goals, dreams, and belief in myself. I grieved for days.

Her family was destroyed by her passing. I was destroyed.

Sandi Kelly was a *beacon of light*. Darkness had no power over her! I know I told her often how much I loved her. I still tell her! I know she knows. That is why we live … to love and be loved.

Echoes of Friendship

By Talha Raja

I met Ahsan on a seemingly ordinary day that would become one of the most significant of my life. We had just moved to a new city, and I was grappling with social anxiety, making the prospect of making new friends daunting. On my first day at school, as I nervously found my seat, Ahsan approached me with a beaming smile and introduced himself. That simple act of kindness broke through my anxiety, and a friendship was born that would shape my life in ways I could never have imagined.

Ahsan was an identical twin, and soon, his brother became part of our trio. The three of us became inseparable, navigating the ups and downs of adolescence together. Ahsan had a way of making people feel at ease. He once told me, "I might not know the right thing to say when you're sad, but I'll always be by your side." His words were always a comfort, and we would often joke about him being a total goof. Despite this, Ahsan had a depth of character that I greatly admired.

Our friendship grew stronger with time. We would routinely ditch class to lie on the grass behind the campus basketball court, talking about life. Ahsan was strong with immense willpower. He made time for his friends, excelled in his studies, and was always there when I needed someone to talk to. I found myself spending more and more time at his house, where his family welcomed me with open arms. His parents treated me like their own, offering a sense of stability when things were rough at home.

Ahsan had an infectious energy and loved sports. He would often tease me for being lazy, urging me to shoot some hoops or play catch with him. His enthusiasm was hard to resist, and over time, our bond deepened. I remember our first hangout vividly. We decided to try a Chinese restaurant, but it was so bad that we left halfway through the meal and got burgers instead. We spent the rest of the day playing video games at my place. This spontaneous adventure was just one of many.

We had a tradition of driving around the city after exams, discussing literature, life, and the future. Ahsan was a great listener, absorbing my stories with genuine interest. He had a unique ability to make every moment memorable. He was like the brother I never had, and his family became a second family to me. Through his support, I gained confidence and began to tackle my mental health challenges, including depression and borderline personality disorder.

Ahsan was always there with mature advice whenever I had a fight with my girlfriend. He was my rock, with abundant emotional intelligence. Our late-night escapades often involved sneaking out to smoke on park benches, talking about everything and nothing. I introduced him to new music and shows, and he became a big fan of the anime *Haikyuu*. His enthusiasm for the show led us to attempt playing volleyball, which we quickly realized we were terrible at, but the laughs and memories were priceless.

Ahsan remained a major part of my life until January 2024. On the day of my medical school exam, I noticed several missed calls from his brother and father. When I finally called them back, my world came crashing down. His brother, crying hysterically, told me that Ahsan had been in a car accident and didn't make it. The shock and grief were overwhelming. I rushed to their house, my legs trembling as I witnessed the burial. Those days were a blur as I struggled to process the loss of my brother and best friend.

Ahsan, you were one of the most important people in my life. You taught me how to be confident and mature. I'm happy to report that I've lost a lot of weight and am focusing on my mental and physical health, just like you always encouraged me to. I still stay in touch with your family, though there's always an emptiness when I walk into your room. Your mother has kept everything the same, a shrine to your memory.

Helping your family settle after your passing was one of the hardest but most necessary things I've done. Nothing anyone says can ease the pain of losing you, but it brings me comfort knowing you're watching over us. You were a role model, a source of strength, and a great friend. I love you, man. Let's shoot hoops and talk more about our favorite anime when we meet again in the next life.

If someone asked me about my favorite memory with him, it would be when I was invited to his hometown for a family wedding. We spent two days wandering aimlessly through the rural areas of his hometown, playing, laughing, and having a blast. I got to meet his extended family and attend the wedding of both his older brothers. It made me feel like I was a part of his family. That was when Ahsan told me that I was like a brother to him. I don't think he realized how precious those words were to me. Stuffing our faces with kebabs and making jokes about my new hairstyle was one of the few mundane memories his shining soul made priceless.

In remembering Ahsan, I'm reminded of the power of kindness and friendship. He was a beacon of light in my darkest times, always there with a smile, a listening ear, and a willingness to help. His legacy lives on in the hearts of everyone who knew him. Rest in peace, my dear friend. You are missed every day.

A Bond Beyond Words

By Olubukola Awodamila

Ruth burst into my life like a ray of sunshine. She was not just a friend to me, but a soul sister and a confidant. We had a lot in common, from being course mates and seamstresses to our aspirations to become fashion designers. Our dream of building a brand together seemed within reach. We were inseparable, and our bond grew stronger with each passing day—until I had to say goodbye on March 27, 2020.

I met Ruth on my first day at university in 2018. Our paths crossed and we almost walked into each other. After we each apologized, I quickly asked her for directions to my lecture room, and she showed me the way. Little did I know that I had just met the friend of a lifetime.

Ruth was vibrant and compassionate; our conversations flowed effortlessly, like we had known each other for years. Her dedication and optimism drew me in—she was like a breath of fresh air in my life, always encouraging me to step out of my comfort zone and reach for the stars.

Our friendship was a beautiful tapestry woven with threads of laughter, adventures, and memories. We explored our creativity together, sketching designs and sewing for customers, sometimes even falling asleep at our machines.

One of my fondest memories was our late-night study sessions before exams. We would stay up until the early hours of the morning, pouring over textbooks and notes, quizzing each other, and offering support and encouragement. Our shared determination and perseverance during those challenging times solidified our connection and friendship.

The first party we attended together was our departmental dinner night; we were excited and eagerly planned for it. We designed and made matching dresses, complete with intricate details and sparkling accessories. We were so excited to show off our design, let loose, and have some fun. When we arrived at the party, the music was popping and the energy was electric. We danced the night away, laughing and singing along to our favorite songs. And we received so many compliments on our outfits! It was such a carefree and joyful night.

Ruth lived with her mom and sisters off campus, and I was welcomed into their home with love. Countless times, she would bring food from home to my place so we could dine and share moments together. She was full of love, and her sense of humor and ability to make me laugh was a gift. We had plans to spend our six-month Students Industrial Work Experience Scheme (SIWES) program together, seeing it as a great opportunity to explore a new city, and launch a ready-to-wear brand for our fellow students when we returned to school.

Unfortunately, fate had other plans for Ruth. She was diagnosed with diabetes, and our world was turned upside down. Despite her struggles, she never gave up, always pushing forward with strength and resilience. She continued to sew and attend classes, never letting her condition hold her back. She would sometimes discuss her fears with me as her health began to decline—I was always a shoulder whenever she needed one. Our bond grew stronger even in the face of adversity.

On that fateful day we had a test, and I noticed that Ruth hadn't shown up, which was unusual. I sensed something was off and I was worried; my intuition was unsettling. I couldn't reach her or any of her family by phone. I was devastated and confused. Suddenly, my phone rang. It was a call from her neighbor who told me that my friend had passed away.

The news was like a crushing blow; I felt like I had lost a part of myself, leaving me with a deep sense of loss, of grief—saying goodbye was the hardest thing I could do. How could I say goodbye to Ruth?

Ruth's passing left a void in my heart that seemed impossible to fill. The memories of our time together flooded my mind, bringing a mixture of joy and sorrow. I remembered the late-night study sessions, the laughter-filled moments in her home, the good times and the dreams we had shared. It was difficult to accept that she was no longer here, that our plans for the future would never come to fruition.

I felt broken and lost without my dear friend by my side. The world seemed darker without her infectious laughter and unwavering support. Consumed by anger and hurt, my impulsiveness led me to delete our entire shared photo album. The pain of seeing her face and not being able to touch or hold her was too much for me to bear. I was furious that she had left me behind. Today, I deeply regret my actions. Fortunately, I recently stumbled upon a few remaining photos in my old Snapchat memories. Even though Ruth will always live in my heart, these precious images have become my lifeline, allowing me to hold on to the memory of her face.

I find solace in the support of family and friends, and in the shared memories and stories of Ruth that keep her alive in our hearts. Although Ruth may have left this world too soon, she lives on in everything I do. Her passion for fashion and design was contagious, and she encouraged me to pursue my creative interests. I graduated as the top female student in our department in 2023; I dedicate every achievement, every success, to her memory. Her unwavering optimism and resilience in the face of adversity taught me to stay strong and focused, even when the road seems unclear. She taught me the true meaning of strength, perseverance, and love. She will always be a part of me. Goodbye for now, my dearest friend, Ruth.

Part III

Grandparent

Cane Poles and Shock Theater

By Darian Jones

" Grandma, are you still awake?"

She had her eyes shut, her hand resting atop her belly, and her pocketbook clutched under her arm—even in her own house.

"Yes, just resting my eyes," would be her response in the middle of the best part of *Shock Theater*, the greatest set of black-and-white horror films from the 1950s that aired for the first twelve years of my childhood on Saturday nights in Mebane, North Carolina, on Channel 8. It was my first introduction to Dracula (the Bela Lugosi and Vincent Price versions), Frankenstein, The Wolfman, and more. Here was this amazing little old lady with a little pot belly, a jolly laugh, and a snuff dipper who loved horror movies. You could find us on the couch, just her and me, her seven-to-twelve-year-old grandson, deep into the scare of those classics before bedtime.

I spent countless Saturdays of my childhood with my maternal grandmother, affectionately named Maggie Moo by me. Most of those Saturday mornings you would find me cajoling her to take me to the pond in the back or one nearby. She would finally agree most of the time—if I could pry her away from that old rotary dial phone (she would sit and talk for hours to two of her friends). It got so bad at one point that my grandfather, out of frustration, put a little lock on the dialer so it could not turn. I learned to pick the locks so he turned to collecting all four phones and taking them in his truck whenever he left the house.

On those fishing mornings, right after breakfast, she would grab her favorite cane pole from beside the house. Yes, that bamboo, five-foot, non-casting hotness with the orange cork. She would stand on the bank, fishing in the shallow water.

"Grandma, why don't you use one of these reels? You're barely in the water. There are no fish that close and that shallow."

But without fail, she always caught her fish first, and usually caught more than I did. With a wink, she'd say, "Sometimes, it's the simple things."

The lessons she taught, the stories she told, and oh—how she could hum.

"Grandma, why do you hum all the time?"

"Not sure, just something I picked up from my aunts and elders."

Little did I know at the age of nine that humming was a form of ancestral mindfulness that centered one, brought peace, and connected past and present. Today, it makes sense—all that she endured and carried with her words would never say—that a familiar melody would echo from her throat in the form of a powerful hum.

After we almost lost her to a stroke and she spent weeks in a coma, she made a remarkable recovery with only one noticeable change: she started wearing knit hats all the time—even in the house—and stopped dipping snuff (for the most part—she didn't think anyone knew she was still sneaking it but I knew). Seeing her with her pocketbook under her arm, a knit hat on her head, and sitting on the couch, I would ask, "Grandma, where are you going?"

"Nowhere, I just need to be ready."

Cane pole fishing … you never know when it will be the last time. *Shock Theater* … how I yearn for one of those nights on the couch.

Grandma, are you still awake?

Yes, just resting my eyes.

Those Saturdays of my childhood, unknown at the time, would shape my adult philosophy about appreciating and honoring the simple things. They also ignited my passion for living intensely—believing that if my

Goodbye for Now

heart is not on fire, in my throat, and beating 500 beats a minute, I haven't lived. She is with me on every roller coaster, every bridge I bungee from, and every plane I jump out of. The need to feel deeply, passionately, and with a quickened pulse is all her legacy.

I would tease her mercilessly. "Go on," she'd say, "you get that from Marvin (my grandfather). You just love to ag (a term for teasing)." Then, she would belt out a laugh. What I would give for one more Saturday with my Maggie Moo.

Years later, my kids—her great grands—adored her. Whenever we got in the car to leave, baby girl would always ask, "Daddy, why does Maggie Moo always have a hat on in the house?" I never had a good answer other than she just really liked her hat. At her homegoing service, I sat up front with my mom and aunts. Her sons, Roy Campanella and Charles Allen, had died before her. My girls were sitting with my father midway back in the chapel. She looked so peaceful, much like those Saturday mornings on the edge of the pond with her cane pole and those Saturday nights watching *Shock Theater*.

Grandma, are you still awake? I thought as I said goodbye to her in my head. This time, the response never came back. Rest, sweet lady, rest.

At that moment, with a church full of tears and deep sadness, my three-year-old beautiful, amazing baby girl shouted, "Daddy, Maggie Moo don't have her hat on now!" Laughter erupted for five minutes; even the pastor was tickled.

Grandma, are you still awake? I will let you rest. Goodbye, for now, Mary Magdalene Warren Bradshaw.

Mamie's Way

By Michelle Patrovani

Like the burnt brown sugar, capful of Johnny Walker rum, and dash of Angostura bitters Mamie always added to her stew chicken, making the air aromatic and tastebuds gleeful with anticipation, Mamie flavoured everything she did with lessons in love and living.

Mabel LeGendre née Steele (May 7, 1915–December 27, 2020), or Mamie, as her grandchildren knew her, was the matriarch of my maternal family and the only grandmother I ever knew.

Both names, Mabel and Mamie, mean lovable. Spiritually, Mabel means "to carry on for others or bear their burdens with joy"—this is the Mamie I knew, the Mamie I remember, and the Mamie I carry with me always. Mamie defined and redefined love, selfless giving, strength, and resilience in every season of her life.

When I was young, Mamie would often tap the back of my head to nudge me not to stick out my tongue—remembering that now makes me smile. As much as I didn't like those taps, they were love lessons I eventually appreciated: Work consistently to cultivate good habits and overcome. Do what must be done—remember, restart, and relearn.

Mamie lived through the 1918 Spanish Flu and the 2020 COVID-19 pandemic with childlike peace—no fretting or complaining about the world, politics, people, injustices, ugliness, or limitations. In the former, at three years old, I imagine she played and did whatever her mama allowed. During the latter, her second childhood due to age and a stroke, she needed constant care and rarely remembered her children or grandchildren. But the Mamie I knew entered this second stage in life with the long-held understanding that life was short and with arms open to embrace whatever came next. In her melodic island accent, she often said, "My time comin', yes."

Mamie raised her three girls alone. They were aged three, two, and one when her husband left Trinidad for Venezuela and never returned. She cared for her aging parents and three babies, working daily in customer service until retirement and tending to her prized hanging ferns, crotons, hibiscus, and other tropical plants around the home.

Mamie was stoic and a giver. I never knew if she wanted anything for herself or thought about her exhaustion and life's hardships. I never heard her complain. Mamie taught and reinforced lessons of sacrifice and long-suffering and remains my role model today. Despite abandonment and loss, I saw the laughter she demonstrated daily, giving without expecting anything in return and always having some joke to share. Mamie established that legacy.

In her last years, Mamie continued to give. When she needed full-time care, she provided her youngest daughter with employment, income, and housing. When her wallet was empty, her eldest daughters (my mom and godmother) and their children opened their pockets to cover the cost and provide for her care. Like Mamie's stoic resolution not to complain, not once did anyone grumble about having to contribute. Her legacy of self-lessness continued through to her children and grandchildren.

Mamie lived courageously. Her speech was never poisoned with resentment that her husband left or that life was punishing. Her favorite expression was, "Ça pour faire" or "What to do?" It was a rhetorical question. It means tackle it, let it go, and go with the flow. This was Mamie's way—quitting was never an option. Embrace whatever life sends. Challenges are obstacles to overcome. Take action with determination, patience, and without complaint.

Mamie celebrated the simple satisfactions of life. She never sought material possessions and made do with what she had. A rum and coke each evening and the occasional toolum (a sweet Trinidadian molasses and coconut delicacy) were her only vices. Her richest treasures were sitting in her white rocking chair on the front porch, enjoying the cool evening breezes, tending to her many plants, having her family visit, and feeding them.

At seventeen, I asked to go live with Mamie, and she agreed. I thought I would keep her company and help in her later years. Looking back, I see that she was saving me. Having experienced a traumatic childhood, Mamie allowed my first passage away from a place of pain to a place where I could begin healing.

I said goodbye to Mamie twice. The first time was on June 13, 1988, when I left Trinidad to build a life in the United States. Mamie was seventy-three then and knew how much I wanted to go to New York. She helped me get my visa and sent me off with her blessings. I sometimes wonder if she wanted to facilitate my passage to the land of opportunity because, silently, she only knew a life of responsibility.

The second time I said goodbye was on December 27, 2020, when I got a phone call saying Mamie had passed peacefully in her sleep. That day, and during her funeral three days later, I said goodbye as I walked through the park near home filled with peace, talking with, touching, and tenderly loving every plant I could. For me, each bore Mamie's spirit and legacies of love and living—rooted strong, green, and giving, and always reaching toward heaven.

Mamie remains my cap full of rum and a dash of Angostura seasoning every day as I witness the rejuvenation of life and flowers that bloom in the spring in the north and remain all year in the south.

Mamie is with me each morning. I choose to walk bravely in life as a human, a woman, and a mother who has raised two adult sons living with chronic, incurable, progressive illnesses. Daily, I clothe myself in her legacy and honor her with courage, laughter, gratitude, and love. Long ago, I quietly resolved to teach my sons not to quit because quitting was not in her DNA, and it is not in ours.

Grampy D

By Mary Hallarson

Blood may be thicker than water, but love is thicker than both. Family isn't defined by genetics but by the bonds we nurture and the memories we create together. Grampy D entered my life long before I was born. He was married to my grandma when my dad and aunt were kids, practically raising them as his own. Although they eventually divorced, they maintained a civil relationship. For reasons I never fully understood, Grampy D moved to Florida. Despite the distance, he remained an integral part of my life.

Grampy D was an adventurer, a storyteller, and a man of many talents. He'd been a park ranger, a limo driver, and even served in the Coast Guard. His love for the ocean ran deep, manifesting in his passion for scuba diving. Movies, history, and adventure were the cornerstones of his interests, each feeding into his vast repertoire of stories that would captivate me for hours. But beyond his varied experiences, what defined Grampy D was his unwavering support. No matter the path I chose or the dreams I pursued, he was there, cheering me on and making me proud of every step I took.

My memories of Grampy D are like a collection of vivid snapshots, each filled with joy and laughter. One summer, my sister and I stayed with him in Florida for a week. One morning, Grampy D, an early riser due to his love for fishing, decided to wake us up in a unique way.

"Three … two … one …" his voice boomed through the house.

Suddenly, a water balloon landed on us. The shock quickly turned to laughter when we realized it was filled with air, not water. It was quintessential Grampy D—playful, unexpected, and full of joy.

Grampy D's love for the water was infectious. He would take me out on his boat or canoe, introducing me to the world he adored. While he couldn't name all the birds we saw, his enthusiasm for nature was unbounded. He taught me to appreciate the quiet moments, to find beauty in the stillness of a lake at dawn or the approach of a storm on the horizon.

As the years passed and I grew older, my trips to Florida became less frequent. But Grampy D had a gift for making distance disappear. His phone calls became a constant in my life—on birthdays, holidays, or any day that ended in "y." These weren't quick check-ins but marathon sessions filled with conversation, laughter, and love. Grampy D had a way of making me feel like the most important person in the world when we spoke. He remembered details about my life that I had forgotten sharing, asked about friends I'd mentioned months before, and celebrated my smallest victories with genuine enthusiasm.

My last call with Grampy D came just after my engagement in 2021. We laughed about the ups and downs of relationships, with Grampy D sharing stories from his own experiences.

"Love isn't always easy," he said, his voice growing serious. "But it's always worth it. Remember that, kiddo."

His words were not just advice but a reflection of the wisdom he had gained from his own life. We talked about the future—my hopes, my fears, the life I was planning to build. As always, we ended the call with "I love you" and "I miss you." And, as he had done countless times before, he told me how proud he was of me.

I didn't know then that this would be our last conversation. I didn't know he was sick, that the clock was ticking faster than we realized. The news came early one morning. When I called my dad at 6 a.m., just before starting work, the world shifted on its axis. Grampy D was in the hospital.

I was on a plane within hours, a whirlwind of worry and disbelief. At the hospital, COVID protocols meant we couldn't all be with him at once. The room was quiet except for the occasional sniffle and Grampy D's labored breathing. There were no monitors, no tubes—he had signed a DNR. I took his hand, feeling the weak flutter of his pulse. At that moment, all the miles that had separated us over the years and all the time that had passed seemed to disappear. We were together, and that was what mattered.

As Grampy D's heartbeat grew fainter, I was struck by an overwhelming gratitude. I leaned close, my lips nearly touching his ear, and whispered, "Thank you." Thank you for the summers full of laughter. Thank you for the long phone calls. Thank you for showing me what it means to be a family. I like to think he heard me. It wasn't more than two minutes later that I felt the last beat of his heart, a moment forever etched in my memory.

In the days that followed, I honored Grampy D in the way he would have wanted. My fiancée and I took the canoe out on the water one last time. The sky was overcast, a storm brewing on the horizon. We barely made it back before the rain started—one final adventure with Grampy D. His ashes were buried at sea in a salt urn by the Navy, a fitting tribute to a man who loved the ocean and adventure in equal measure. He taught me to embrace life with open arms, to find joy in the simple things, and to never stop exploring. He showed me that family is defined not by blood but by love, time, and shared experiences.

Grampy D may be gone, but his impact on my life remains. He lives on in the lessons he taught me, the love he shared, and the memories I cherish. And in that way, he'll always be family—the family I chose and who chose me right back.

A Goodbye Postponed

By Chris Angelis

The late afternoon sun is hot in Greece, but the soft pelagic breeze makes it a bit more tolerable. The little village cemetery is peaceful and serene, with nothing interrupting the pleasant monotony of the cicadas' song. It feels weird being here after all these years. It feels weird staring at a humble, unadorned grave displaying a name ignored by virtually everyone else, yet one that means so much to me.

Is this all that remains of you? A memory? The regret of not having been there to say goodbye? Or (truly an unbearable thought) the relief of having avoided such pain?

My grandma, Vasileia, was as typical as Greek grandmas come: loud, gossipy, superstitious, and occasionally obscene. Yet, at the same time, she was caring and infinitely patient with me, an unruly little rascal who took radios apart just to see how their innards looked. Growing up with only one parent—my mother, who worked long hours—I was basically raised by my grandmother. Not only did she cook for me, spend time with me, and tell me stories, but perhaps above all, she was an adult I could depend on, a rock-solid presence in a childhood sorely needing assurances and stability.

You were already ill when I left, with the disease that insidiously took away your mind, the very thing that made you the grandma I grew up with. Would you have understood me if I'd said goodbye face-to-face?

When I grew up a little, my grandparents moved back to their house on the island. They had given everything and certainly earned the right to spend their final years the way they wanted. Even so, I was lucky enough to spend summers with them, and Grandma's flair for village gossip and funny stories offered me an inexhaustible supply of entertainment. Even today, several decades later, I recall those times as if they happened yesterday.

Remember that July night when you woke us up claiming there was a mouse under the bed? We spent half an hour looking for it, and when you saw it on Grandpa's shoulder—the disrespect!—you were a little too eager to try and smack it. I think it was my laughter that chased it off.

Without the passage of time, our lives don't exist; yet it's time that brings us closer to our inevitable demise. That's the price humans have to pay for the insolence of existence. My grandparents did enjoy several happy years in the village, but eventually, time—which, as Sophocles wrote, sees all things—arrived one evening in the form of a phone call. Grandpa had died; his heart had simply given out while he was walking. It wasn't surprising, given that he was over ninety years old, but it was a shock still.

You still smiled and laughed, yet even a naive young man like I was could see that something had changed. You were absentminded, lost in thoughts, and focused on meaningless details. Who knows, maybe losing Grandpa was what triggered the disease that would later claim you.

Eventually, we all moved to the village so my mother could care for my grandma, who was well over eighty. The still-naive young man almost thought we could pick up where we'd left off, telling funny stories, gossiping about the village idiots, or reminiscing about old times. Pretty soon, I discovered that I'd lost that time, and it would never come back.

We found you in the garden in the middle of the night, looking for your rubber boots. You had to go to work, you claimed. There must be an absurdist universe where I considered this yet another of your little pranks and laughed about it. But in this one, there were only tears and a sense of despair.

It didn't take long for the doctors to discover the cause of this bizarre behavior. The news was delivered (and, dare I say, accepted?) with clinical precision and an air of practicality: My grandma's mind was disappearing, and there was nothing to reverse the process. Her memories and sense of reality would vanish, and she would eventually not even recognize people, the doctors said. Not long after, I moved out. I left behind not just the village or the island but the entire country, moving two thousand miles away.

I remember leaving, though I can't remember realizing it was the last time I would see you alive. Isn't that a bit ridiculous? Wouldn't you call me an impudent, foolish child for such a thing? Actually, no; you wouldn't. You didn't. You smiled, perhaps realizing—even in your condition—the repercussions far better than I consciously did. "This is goodbye," your tired smile said. "Enjoy your life, you crazy kid who set the carpet on fire and broke our LP records using them as frisbees."

Months later, I received a call from my uncle. Grandma was no more. The emotions I felt were complex. I was sad, certainly, but it was a sadness less personal and more collective. I was upset not just because I'd lost my dear grandmother but because life was flawed. Ironically, it was this imperfect life that got in the way and kept me away from the island for many years. I focused on studying, meeting people, creating something of my own. Those summer nights when we laughed with Grandma at the neighbors' expense seemed so far away.

When we exist, death doesn't; when it does, we do not. And yet, there are states that are more problematic. So here I am, so many years later, to say goodbye to you. After all, there is a "you" that will continue to exist in my memories, like a poem murmured in a dream.

Goodbye in Slow Motion

By Eileen Cullen

Alzheimer's is a cruel disease. It destroys the mind, slowly erasing memories until nothing is left. And the worst part is, there is no cure—once Alzheimer's has its grip on you, there's no going back.

My grandma, Maureen Cullen, has late-stage Alzheimer's. Physically, she's still alive and breathing. But the woman I knew and was so close to for my entire life is gone. I watched as the strong, fun-loving, and independent woman I loved so much faded away as her memory deteriorated.

I was always especially close to my grandma. I was her first grandchild, so when I was born, I had her undivided attention. As I got older, it became clear that we shared many similarities—we were both shy, a bit socially awkward, and happy to stay in our own little bubble. My grandma had a very difficult childhood and was raised in a particularly cruel foster home. But rather than break her down, that hardship instilled in her a deep dedication to her family.

My grandpa, her husband, couldn't have been more different. He was as outgoing and sociable as a person could be. We'd always laugh at how easily he could strike up a conversation with just about anyone. They were opposites but complimented each other perfectly. My grandpa passed away after a battle with lung cancer when he was only sixty-four years old. But as hard as this was on my grandma, it didn't dampen her desire to live a fulfilling life. She lived for her grandchildren.

Sleepovers at Grandma's house were frequent and exciting events throughout my childhood. We'd go to shows, participate in art activities, and frequently take the train into Boston to find something new and adventurous to do. Following my grandpa's death, she remained fiercely independent.

Her home was our family's hub. Whether it was for a holiday or because she wanted everyone to get together, she'd invite everyone over for dinner, with more food than we could ever need. I'll never forget the way that it always went: after dinner, the adults would talk in the kitchen, and the kids would play in the living room. My grandma would keep bouncing between the two, making sure that she was spending enough time with everyone.

Some of my fondest memories are from sleepovers at her house when I was a child. We'd go out for pizza, paint at Plaster Fun Time, and pick out a movie at a video rental store near her house. We'd watch a movie, and I'd stay up late with her long after my younger cousins went to bed. From a very young age, she was someone I could trust and confide in.

When I was a teenager, I started attending high school very close to my grandma's house. I was there after school almost every day. I have fond memories of sitting at her kitchen table, doing my homework with NPR playing in the background. My grandma was someone I could talk to about *anything*. Politics, school, family, pop culture—no matter what, she would always listen with genuine curiosity and care. Before her memory was gone, there weren't many things I *didn't* talk to her about. She was always there for me.

When her memory started fading, it was easy to chalk it up to simple signs of aging. Things like misremembering dates, forgetting where she left things, or repeating the same question. She was becoming forgetful, but she was still the same woman I knew and loved. But things got worse very quickly. She began forgetting what year it was and who people were. She forgot that my siblings, cousins, and I had grown up and, in her mind, still thought we were children. She was becoming a danger to herself if left alone.

At that point, our family recognized that she needed care beyond what we could provide. She moved into a memory care unit. I continued to visit her, but I could tell her memory of me was fading. She would ask who I was and briefly recall when I explained, but then she would get confused again. Now, she doesn't recognize me at all.

For the last several years, I've been experiencing the loss of my grandma in slow motion. Rather than an illness that ravages the body, she's afflicted with an illness that ravages the mind. Watching her slowly fade away has been difficult and painful.

In this case, "goodbye" wasn't so much a moment as it was acceptance. It started with accepting that she was getting older when her memory lapses could more easily be attributed to "senior moments." As her memory deteriorated, I needed to come to terms with the fact that she was declining. For years, I reminded her of the things that we used to do together and the memories we shared. I tried so hard to ingrain these things into her mind. But eventually, I needed to accept that I couldn't. She has a disease she can't fight, so I've had to mourn the loss of who she was.

She's still alive, but she doesn't know who I am. And I've had to learn to accept that and be grateful for the many amazing years and precious memories I had with her.

Grandfather's Legacy of Wisdom

By Halid Tarakčija

I used to hate taking pictures—a lifeless piece of paper that reminds me of something that once was but never will be again. I guess now I don't mind them as much. Looking at people who are long gone feels captivating, even though I know it won't be long until I feel their absence again.

One person whose presence I feel most strongly is someone who shaped and guided me since I was two years old, crying over my broken toys. It was my grandfather, Uzeir.

Uzeir was a military veteran, a cold steel type of guy. You could see it in his hazel eyes—something that silently said, "I'm prepared to suffer for my family."

Due to harsh living conditions in a developing country, I lived in my grandpa Uzeir's home for over seven years. I grew to love the old interior and often thought about the symbols so neatly arranged to create such a captivating picture. Grandpa Uzeir told me that what I was looking at was a lawha, an Arabic painting centered around religion and beautiful calligraphy. He taught me to care for those close to me, appreciate nature and all it offers, and—probably most importantly—never to eat all the sweets when guests are around.

Due to my father's occupation, my family had to live away for several months. Uzeir had to hide his tears when he saw me sobbing on the floor, wanting to see my parents. Grandpa Uzeir welcomed my family with open arms when they decided to also move into his home—a decision of kindness that grew in my grandfather's heart. It was often mentioned, but people never discussed the intention. From what I know about my grandfather, and I know only a little, he left home when the war in Yugoslavia ended. He lived in Cairo as a construction worker when earning an income was difficult. My grandfather decided that the bread his family ate would be earned through courage and dedication to a righteous goal.

I don't think I was the only person who loved who my grandfather was. However, I think very few understood him. There had to be something behind the smile of an old man who went out in the morning and returned in the evening with his tractor, white circles around his clothes from sweat and hard work. Yet he would laugh, talk, and advise us all. I wish I could hug that man one more time to let him know I am grateful for what he taught me. In a world filled with darkness, his character was a beacon of light and a safe house, prepared to do anything for his grandchildren.

Uzeir often spent time with people from his town. Laughter was a common sound around the house, as he would often tell jokes and make sure others felt welcomed in his home. Most of his friends described him as a man who valued leisure, but when work was being done, he would encourage others to be steady and give their best.

When I was little, he promised my grandma and me that we would travel through Bosnia, see all the riches, and hear all the stories of our famous historical monuments. I still remember his laugh when I tried swimming in one of the waters, looking like a little fat seal that wasn't supposed to be there.

Years passed, and our healthcare system developed enough that my grandfather was scheduled to have a heart operation. All his life, he took chances, and with bravery, he asserted dominance over any life situation. Telling him not to go would be like trying to force the river to flow against the current. And he did go. Near the doors, he kissed us all goodbye. I hugged him and watched him leave.

Uzeir died on the operating table in April 2016. I still remember my mother's phone ringing and the doctor telling her that her father, my grandfather, was gone and that he was sorry for her loss.

In a home centered around a belief in the afterlife and cemented in faith, the loss of our grandfather was a strong gust of wind, but it did not break our spirit. I wasn't heartbroken, and I accepted that he was gone. Now that I think about it, little me was brave for doing so. My family taught me about death and its role as the only absolute truth, but at that time, I also experienced its chilling cold in my bones.

Years have passed, and I still grieve. I still look at their photos, and day by day, I feel less hate toward these lifeless pieces of paper that remind me of something that once was but never will be again. I'm a little older now, and I think I understand why goodness, honor, wisdom, kindness, and strength were my grandfather's points of interest and why he spent so much time telling me to be a good man. He knew that no one would live forever and that the only things that stay with us are our character and the things within us that make our world a better place.

Granny

By Lloyd Wilkinson

My Granny was a young grandmother at forty-one. I was the first grandchild on my father's side of the family, and she spoiled me. My earliest memory of Granny is driving up to her house when I was four or five. She couldn't wait for us to knock on the door, couldn't wait even a second to see us. Running out of the house and down the sidewalk, calling my name, with her arms wide open and smiling with her whole being is how I'll always remember her.

She and my Papa only lived three miles from us, so my brother, Lyn, and I spent much of our childhood at their house. It was a wonderland of adventure for a couple of active boys. Apple trees in the backyard for fruit and climbing, a grapevine along the back fence, plum trees in the front, and a black walnut tree whose fruit we used for baseballs in the summer.

And Granny was right in the middle of our sandlot games! When we started gathering up to pick teams, she would come around the corner of the house, barefoot, asking whose team she was on! We loved it. No other adults in our family ever played with us like that. She loved going barefoot. I don't ever remember her wearing shoes around the house. And she could hit. Her form wasn't great, but she would whack that walnut and, with the biggest laugh, take off for first base.

Granny never did anything halfway. Her Thanksgiving meals were epic: a huge turkey; ham; half a dozen different kinds of vegetables; pickles of all kinds (including pickled peaches!); salads; that horrible Southern concoction, ambrosia; and the most delicious desserts I've ever had! I don't even eat dessert anymore because nothing can touch my Granny's home-made coconut cake and lemon meringue pies. These were the days before shredded coconut in plastic bags in the baking section. Granny cracked her own coconuts with a big mallet, or by slamming them on the counter, as she held court in her kitchen. Then she would let us drink the coconut water out of the shell.

She never loved halfway either. Her faith was strong. She was a devout Christian, and she believed strongly in unconditional love—not only believed in it, but lived it. I learned unconditional love by watching her live her life. She always wanted to know what was going on in my life. And not just by asking me about it when I visited. She came to every Little League baseball and basketball game I played for seven years. I'm sure she must have cheered for my whole team, but I only remember her loud, clear voice cheering me on as I came to bat or struck out a batter. And I'm not talking about polite clapping. Like everything else in her life, she was all-in at that moment and place, with a body full of joy and love, and I knew it was all for me.

When I was a teenager, I was not happy at the church I was attending. Granny, ever attentive to my adolescent moods and general state of hap-piness, is the only one who picked up on it. She sat me down and asked about it one day. I poured out my frustrations and feelings of dissatisfac-tion to her; she listened patiently and quietly and let me finish. Then she told me about a church with a dynamic new pastor, who could answer all my questions, and a young congregation, where I could find some friends. I started attending there and it changed my life—all because Granny knew me so well and cared.

After I was grown and married with five kids of my own, I didn't see Granny and Papa as much as I wished. They would sometimes babysit our children so we could work on Saturdays. They were active great-grandpar-ents in their sixties and seventies. Granny loved her great-grandchildren with the same unbridled joy she had always shown. When they got to be

          Goodbye for Now

in their eighties, their life slowed considerably, and they moved in with my parents.

Mom and Dad traveled a lot in those days, and when they were away, it fell to me to take care of Granny after Papa had passed away. Those are days I treasure because I got to repay, in a small way, the love and care she had always given me. We had some great conversations; unfortunately, some of them were by her bedside in the hospital.

We would occasionally talk about death during that time. She knew she was going to see Papa again, but she was still afraid of getting sick and dying. I tried to comfort and assure her, as she had done for me so many times.

The end came not long after that. Her big heart was finally wearing out, and she slipped into semi-consciousness in the hospital. My dad called and said I should come to the hospital. I held her hand for a long time. She never opened her eyes. Mine were blinking back tears, and I was afraid she would wake up and see me crying. The time came for me to leave—I leaned down and whispered in her ear, "No one has ever loved me like you have. I love you."

Losing Granny was the first time in my life that I felt like I lost a part of myself. When Papa died, I was sad. I had learned much about being a man from him. But when Granny died, she took something of me with her that I would never see again. She knew me in a way that nobody else did. She loved me in a way that nobody else ever would. It may sound selfish, but I cried at the loss of that. But most of all, I'll miss seeing her run towards me with open arms, shouting my name, and shaking with joy. That's how I'll always remember her.

Grandma's Song

By Myriah C. Boudreaux

On a bright summer morning, I rose from my computer and solemnly strode to my bedroom. My fingers caressed the ornate wooden doors to the wall-mounted music box my grandmother had bestowed upon me years ago. Opened doors revealed the endearing picture within. Steadying the box, I tugged the stringed ball to wind the pegged cylinder. The golden sphere rose as tinkling notes played Schubert's "Ave Maria."

This music box accompanied my earliest memories, originating in my grandparents' house. My parents' teen marriage had been tumultuous and brief, so my mother had soon returned to her folks' home. The chaotic life with my parents was forgotten. My memories began with the security of my grandparents' home. My mom's long work hours meant Grandma provided wholesome shows, snacks, and playtime before reciting bedtime prayers with me. Upon my waking, she would reach above her bed's head-board to wind the music box, which displayed a young Madonna nestling a sleeping Christ Child.

My mom soon found an apartment for the two of us. Still, I eagerly awaited returning to Grandma's house. Grandma listened to my stories, taught me crafts, and played card games with me. My single mom seldom engaged in such interactive pastimes after working long hours. Most of all, Grandma demonstrated how to live as a devoted wife.

Her frequent banter with her husband taught me that loving a spouse doesn't mean agreeing on everything. Surely, marital squabbles didn't compare to the difficult Great Depression era of my grandparents' childhood or the troubling World War II years of their young adulthood. Nevertheless, Grandma did disagree with her husband at times. Yet even when my grandfather's chuckles deepened into grumbling, Grandma quickly offered a kiss and hug to make amends. As I matured, I understood that her prevailing contentment resulted from a firm commitment to weather life's storms with this man she trusted wholeheartedly. Having experienced my own fatherlessness and being from a generation of broken families, I looked to Grandma's marriage as the sole model of selfless dedication, proving that marriage could endure years and decades. Furthermore, the spousal union could even become richer through the wear.

I valued Grandma's example tremendously upon marrying and starting my own family. Grandma transformed from my childhood caregiver to my mentor in marriage and parenthood, and I frequently called her for domestic advice: *What goes well with ham? Do you know a home remedy for earaches? How can I help my toddler not be jealous of the new baby?* Grandma always had an answer.

As she neared her eighties, Grandma's memory began faltering. Raising my growing family out of state, I called regularly but couldn't visit much. Her deterioration spanned several years. Grandma eventually struggled to recognize family members, suffered diminishing mobility, and lost most of her speech. Still, whenever my grandfather would walk into the room, she would announce, "My husband!" He diligently tended to her day after day.

By the time I last visited Grandma, I had been married for over a dozen years and had five children—the same number she herself had raised! As I approached her bed, arranged in the living room, she awoke, eyeing me with surprise and confusion. My grandfather lifted her into a chair and wheeled her to the dining table. An aunt was joining me in bidding Grandma (her mom) a final goodbye. We shared photos of ourselves to remind her that we had been a vital part of her life. We were among the visitors she should have rejoiced in seeing, even though we now lived far away and hadn't seen her in a long time. For me, it had been four years since I'd last seen her. Grandma could walk then, at least while leaning on a walker. She could name each of my aunts, uncles, and cousins who had gathered for a family picnic that year, even if she had often stuttered to get them right. Sure, we had noticed she was a bit sillier than usual, but she was still our beloved Grandma.

This woman I struggled to recognize. The feeling appeared mutual. She peered at me as though I resembled someone she once knew, someone tapping into a memory she couldn't quite retrieve. Conversation seemed futile yet ignoring her felt worse. I pondered how to bless her. Remembering the music box, I told my aunt, "Let's sing some hymns."

As our voices filled the room, joy filled Grandma's face. With child-like delight, she smiled at her husband. I imagined her saying, "Honey! Listen to the girls singing! How lovely!" Like the Little Drummer Boy's gift to the newborn Messiah, this *musical* moment enveloped all I could give Grandma during our last visit together.

Although I sensed the hour of her death would soon arrive, grief swelled when reading the email announcing the hour had indeed passed. Knowing I wouldn't be able to attend her funeral, I lamented the vast distance separating us. Even so, her spirit felt closer than ever. My great fortune enabled me to know my grandmother well into adulthood. She had flown across the country to attend my college graduation. She had danced with my grandfather at my wedding just months before celebrating their golden anniversary. Through my sporadic visits, she had met each of my children.

Truly, her life had been a blessing to mine. Though my children did not know her as the same woman I had known, I wanted to emulate her spirit for them. I wanted to replicate her calm and forgiveness in my own marriage. I wanted to provide a peaceful house that my family would ever consider home. And I wanted to spend my last moments the way I later learned that she had spent hers: cradled by her husband as he assured her, "It's okay, honey. I'll see you again soon."

I called my children over as the song slowed to a stop. "Let's say some prayers for Grandma Marie. I just learned she died this morning." Making the Sign of the Cross, we began: *Hail Mary.*

King of the Montiaghs:
A Love Letter to My Grandfather

By Anna Frances Conway

A rusty tin: the most precious thing my grandfather left. My dad dug it out carefully. Inside were yellowed, handwritten poems by my great-grandfather. My own grandfather had acknowledged it nonchalantly.

"Oh aye, I've had them for years."

I realize now that this wasn't indifference. The poems penned by his father, wrought with the importance of family, were second nature to him.

James Conway—Jim to everyone. My Granda Jim. Born and raised in Derrytrasna, County Armagh—the land of the "Montiaghs" (pronounced "munchies"). As a child, I thought this meant country people were always hungry. The Irish *Mointeacha* refers to moss lands and bogland, and this is where I grew up—teetering on the edge of Lough Neagh.

The Montiaghs were good, practical, family-orientated people. My Granda Jim had a big purple car, a deep plum color. It was always full of sweet wrappers, and I thought if I licked the outside, it would taste like a big juicy grape. He wasn't tall, had the same nose as my dad, and wore the type of jumpers you saw men wearing in American films about Irish people.

He brought everyone everywhere. He picked me and my brother up from school, took us to appointments, and went to the depths of South Armagh to see my cousins. He didn't need to be asked. When I was five, a farmer brought his ducks into my class. I dragged my granda in to see them; they were everywhere, running over toys, textbooks, and the table. It was a mess. There's a picture of the two of us and one of the chicks, his mouth open in an O shape, cautiously holding my back to prevent me from falling off the chair in excitement.

I don't think he liked the ducks very much, but he pretended for me. In those long car journeys, he'd get me to count the streetlamps. The sickeningly sweet taste of panda pops he'd get me from the shop. Like many of the men in my family, he wasn't a man of many words. He didn't need to be. I'd spend the afternoon sitting with him, watching football, rugby, and the horses. He loved the horses. He was never noisy with sports like other men but quiet, listening to my worries for the week. These silences were comforting, welcomed, and simple. As I grew older, I realized how much he was like my dad in showing love. I learned that support, acts of kindness, and being there for someone were forms of saying, "I love you."

As I grew older and went to university, I moved to Belfast. My social life took off, my studies took over, and I wasn't worried about silently watching sports. Even in his old age, he'd give me lifts here and there when I was home. I used to hate it when he showed up an hour earlier than he needed to, but now I know he was making sure I was on time. It was the type of love that fell on the deaf ears of a girl in her twenties discovering herself.

Then he crashed his car. He came out of it with some bruising but a prognosis of pancreatic cancer. After that, the silence between us scared me. I didn't know what to say, didn't know how to comfort him. In 2020, he developed dementia. I rationalized the situation, thinking it could take years to get really bad—but it didn't. He deteriorated rapidly. The living room I'd spent hours playing in was transformed into a hospital room. A bed the length of the room sat at the far side, heavy like a slab of granite. It's as if once he was diagnosed, all of the symptoms and deterioration came at once. He didn't know me. He shouted at me when I tried to change his urostomy bag. His face was gray. There was no recognition in his eyes other than the feeling of fear.

    Goodbye for Now

In that tin, his father's poem "The Old Hearthstone" talked about family togetherness. The hearthstone was a centerpiece of the home, now in the living room that was converted into a hospital bed. We all gathered around him, and for a few months, we agonizingly cared for a loved one who no longer knew us.

> Now that Hearthstone and me will be parting,
> For I feel the time ticking away,
> No more will I roam through the country,
> Or around by the shores of Lough Neagh.

His broad shoulders had sunken in, and the nose like my dad's was as pale as a corpse. He stared at the wall. It was a silence I hope brought him comfort in his confusion, in his pain. Then all of a sudden, like the fire had been lit in the hearth on my great-grandad's verse—he winked at me. He knew me. Or he knew someone who looked like me. Or he thought I was someone else. Maybe it was his way of telling everyone this was all a big joke. That was the last time I saw him alive.

> Although I have got old and feeble,
> I can still hear the little birds sing,
> And those song in my heart they do kindle
> The thoughts of some years long ago.

The poems penned by his father were beautiful. I imagine him as a little boy, scruffy like me, listening to these words. Knowing the importance of family. Knowing he was loved. Knowing this love would be passed down for generations to come.

I love you, Granda.

Invisible Ink

By Jo Lavender

You were an incredible woman, Grandma. Among the first to wear trousers, drive rally races, and set foot in China when it reopened. A dentist against the odds, a widowed mother raising four children single-handedly. The best grandma with the bubbliest laughter in the world. Mummy Ho Ho, Marmaduke—many names, but at the core of them all, you were Grandma.

The world took a lot from you. It took your stability, your sight, your mind. It took your sense of where you were and who you were. We watched, sometimes able to help—but mostly not. We laughed when we got you to laugh, and we cried with you, too. As little pieces of who you were and what you could do flaked away, we watched them pass through our fingers, and it seemed a few tears were justified.

Dentistry, motherhood, grandparenting, golfing, traveling … one by one, they peeled back and disintegrated. We hugged what was left of you closer, held it tighter, and tried to smooth the shedding fragments back into place.

And we all sat around and watched as the world took what we thought was the last of you—your life. At 1 a.m. on August 10, 2017, in a dim room. After many hours of watching, you left surprisingly quickly. It was a greater struggle than we thought it would be, though. You held on tighter. Perhaps you heard the music we played. Maybe you were listening as we all thanked you in broken voices and insufficient words. Maybe you were enjoying a few last moments in the body you'd had for ninety-one years, sorry to leave it after all the fun you'd had.

But leave you did, while we stood and sat like a symbol around your bed—a ragtag symbol of two generations of love brought together by you. I remember watching the last breath go out of you and waiting for the next, but it never came. Your room was dark and still, and we all just sat, waiting, numb with exhaustion. Time had muddled together into one long, confusing day. We didn't know how to handle a sunrise without you.

We'd had so much fun. Your soup was the first meal with vegetables I would touch. We'd arrive late at night, tired and longing for bed, and it would be steaming on the stove—just time for a hot bowl before stumbling upstairs to clean, soft beds. It wasn't like going on holiday; it was like coming home.

When I was seven, you took us to Disneyland Paris and the cutest hotel, where we had croissants and jam every morning—rides, candy floss, and rollercoasters with you next to me. When I was nine, we went to Florence and ate two ice creams in a row because they were just that good. When I was eleven, it was Australia, and we were holding koalas, swimming in the ocean, riding a chair lift, and standing on a porch at midnight to watch the possums.

Later, we came to live with you. Excursions in my teens and twenties were closer to home: chasing you around on your mobility scooter on a myriad of adventures—museums, national parks, stately homes; eating lavender ice cream and trying to stop you from feeding all your lunch to the ducks; exploring anything and everything. Eventually, even these became hard, and we mostly stayed home.

Some of the best moments were evenings together, holding your hand, reading my favorite book to you. Those were the moments when we were closest, when the barriers of dementia vanished, and we were on a journey together. You, soaking in the words I already knew and loved, immersed in a story you wouldn't remember the next day. None of that mattered because we were traveling together, and in those moments, we were both whole.

You remain within that book, printed indelibly in invisible ink. I will never touch the spine without touching your hand, feeling the wrinkles and the strength in your fingers. You are pressed between the pages like a flower, the book preserving those moments where we curled together like cats, with the night falling around us, the book binding us together.

You remain in other things, too. In the light switches, in the brightness of the bulbs. In the banisters beneath our hands when we walk downstairs, in the way the sun comes through the windows. You thread through the conversations, sometimes quietly, sometimes in name. You exist between breaths, in the blinks of life, in the second where the sunset catches gold and throws it over the grass.

You aren't just in us, but in the ribs of our world, in the beating of our blood, in the DNA of life. You aren't just in our hearts but in our voices and our hands and in the way our left eyelids dip a little lower than the right. You exist in us and in the everyday—pouring cereal, making soup, tending to the garden. Some days, I miss you so much that it hurts, and I'd give almost anything for another hug, another glint of impish mischief in your eyes. Other days, I see you in everything around me and I know how deeply, fantastically lucky I was to share your home, share your blood, and share a little of your life with you.

Walking into adulthood, I wish we'd had more time, but I stand taller now because you stood beside me. And at night, when the house is dark, and I'm watching the shadows get deeper, I think of reading with you, walking with you, laughing with you, and it seems the past is so close I could reach out and touch it. I'm so glad you were my grandma and that we had each other for so many years. Thank you for the secrets, the smiles, and the privilege of knowing you.

Aba, My Angel

By Lyra Goga

In my hometown of Peja, Kosovo, almost everyone's dearest person is Aba. "Aba" is a common term for grandmother, and for twenty-two years, she was my grandma. Today, Aba is my angel. She passed away on January 28, 2017—a fact I know to be true, but my heart refuses to believe.

Aba was there from day one. I was born and lived in her house for my first years of childhood. In Albanian culture, it is common for families to live together. Aba was an essential part of my life. Even after we moved to a different house, my brother and I visited her every other day.

She was there for everything, even when she couldn't help. I remember both of us writing on the table in the living room. I was doing my primary school homework, yet her writing was much simpler. I was in second grade, yet I was academically ahead of her. By that age, I could read and write, but there was only one word she could read and write—her name.

I live in a patriarchal society, and it was even more so in her time. Aba was never allowed to go to school simply because she was a girl. So, I would copy from my textbook, and she would repeatedly write her name. She would proudly spell the letters one by one. As I grew up to excel at school, she was overjoyed. With a pang in her heart for not being allowed to study herself, she would always encourage me to focus on my studies.

Since her death, I have written to her often, although I fear my messages do not reach her. Not because she is dead but because she cannot read. Perhaps she can now. I hope she can.

Aba did not shy away from sharing her story. Well, she tried to dismiss her early marriage, but with everything else, she was genuine. I remember us sleeping in the same room while she talked about her life. As she spoke, tears rolled down my face. I was young, but I could read the pain behind her kind smile. Her mom had died during birth. Fortunately, her dad remarried, and she became friends with her stepmother.

Aba loved every single person she met, even the people who sold us goods or came to deliver bills. She insisted they come inside for a coffee and conversation. As a child, I would watch strangers follow her into the room. Aba was happiest when surrounded by people.

Her eyes were often wet—for a family member, a friend, or even a stranger. As a kid, it was hard to understand her profound compassion. Today, as I get teary about each sadness I witness, I recognize the same compassion in me. She had the most gentle and beautiful soul.

It was especially hard for her when I grew up and moved to a different city for college. She cried for weeks before I left. Though the new city was close and I came home every weekend, it seemed like an eternity to her. She told me so. During my college years, she called me every night. I would share pictures from my new life daily, and my aunt told me that she fell asleep every night looking at them. When I came home for the weekend, I would go straight to her home from the bus station before even going to my own home. I knew she missed me terribly. So did I. So do I.

I was studying for an exam when I received the most painful message I've received up to this day. It was early morning when I received a notification that read, "Aba died." I was alone in my dorm room, away from my family. It felt like the world had ended. I shattered into the ground. I kept looking at the words. I wanted to be at her home. I wanted her to be alive.

I cried hard and went to the bathroom to wash my face. As I opened the door, I heard a girl talking on the phone. With a lively voice, she said, "Grandmother." I turned around instantly. I could not bear to hear the word.

I had to wait a few more hours before taking the bus to my hometown for the funeral. My room was shrouded in darkness, and so was the world. It felt like the sun had abandoned the sky forever. I could see no purpose in the world going on. How could the sun dare shine after this? Yet, it did. Life goes on. However, I was mad at the entire world for almost a year. I was mad at the sun. I was mad at the people. "Why does the sun shine? Why do they smile? Aba is gone."

It was outside a shopping mall on a sunny day when I refused to return to Aba's house. "Aba is not there anymore!" I exploded.

"Lyra, everyone is grieving her death. We're all sad, not just you," my mom gently explained. I broke into tears.

For months, when I visited Aba's house, I almost expected to see her sitting in her usual spot. And when I didn't, it would hit me so hard that I'd have to rush to the bathroom and cry.

With time, I learned to accept that the sun continues to shine. Strangely, I have felt her presence all these years, even though she is physically gone. She is alive in me.

In my lowest times, when I am in total despair, she appears in my dreams. It is interesting that this is the only time she ever does. Aba meets me in dreams when my soul is most bruised—to heal it. She is my eternal angel.

Naani

By Shahana Arain

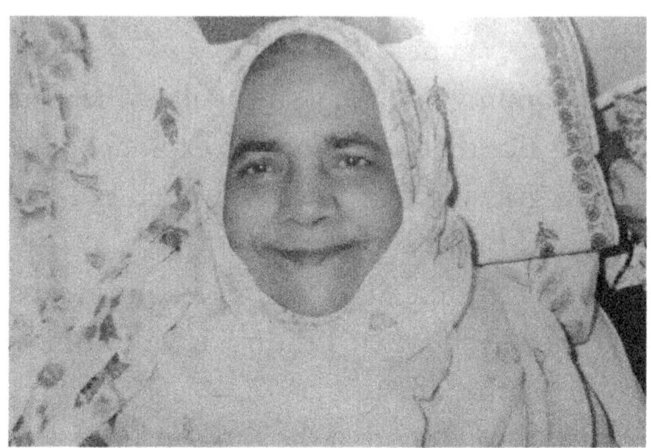

It's been twenty years.

"Marri Shuno, chipkali, tuum khan ho (My Shano, little lizard, where are you)?"

I loved hearing these words: it was my Naani's special nickname reserved only for me. Barging through the front door and down the narrow hallway of our small home, I could depend on these words being the first to greet me after school. Dashing into the tiny living room, I would find her sitting on her daybed, hunched over, peeling vegetables for our evening curry or rice, and I would launch right into her arms. With the smell of Rub A35 and almond oil from Naani's hair filling my nostrils, my mom could be heard from the kitchen warning me to be careful as Naani was bedridden and fragile.

In moments like this, Naani would draw me in closer and whisper in my ear, "Fiqur nye kurro (not to worry)," and then, her gummy smile shining with pride from ear to ear, practice her English: "How ... yoouur ... school?"

I would beam back, knowing she had been secretly studying her English by watching countless episodes of *All My Children*.

At 5'1", my Naani was a dynamo, never to be underestimated, and always to be respected. She was a deeply religious woman who had experienced many hardships in life, especially after marrying at the young age of eighteen. She was a mother of nine children, stepmother to six, and a Naani to countless grandchildren and, yet, she was so much more. Irresistibly youthful and humorous, like a child sneaking in a sweet treat before dinner, she was full of life and caught up in the curiosity of the new western culture she found herself in. On rare occasions you could witness her yelling in Urdu, fists clenched in the air, at WWE wrestlers smashing one another with steel chairs, her anger roused by the injustice Hulk Hogan was enduring. It was in these snapshots that my brothers and I clung to the small sliver of hope that, instead of being yelled at by our parents for watching gratuitous violence on tv, our Naani could be the one to bridge the two worlds together.

The magnitude of her presence extended well beyond our home. Naani frequently moved between the homes of her children. For Naani to stay at anyone's home was a great honour: she was the epicenter of our family. Naani defined what it meant to be a family.

Every weekend, regardless of whose house Naani stayed at, an open-door policy was in effect. Cousins, brothers, uncles, aunts, nieces, daughters, sons, grandchildren, and even in-laws, would clamor together in tiny apartments and houses to get a glimpse of Naani, and perhaps even be blessed by her—Naani's prayers were powerful. For years we all gathered, house to house, with afternoon visits turning into evening sleepovers, rooms filled with laughter, memories of the past, lively commentary on Pakistan's political state, and Naani always at the helm. Food was a must— the kitchen bustling with activity, fried onions in the air, and aunties blending spices to prepare dishes. Followed by calls for chai on the stove, rows of floor mats would be rolled out as the night sky became darker; Naani always loved having her family stay under one roof.

It was during these visits that Naani would ask me to braid the long wisps of her hair while she uncovered the treasures of her daybed; every trinket held a story, or a lesson learned. These were special moments shared between just us, with promises exchanged to always remember the strength of faith and the value of family, even in her absence. Watching her slowly pack each item away—an entire life neatly tied into bundles and bags lined along the cream-coloured railing of her bed—it was as though each one was waiting to be picked up, ready for the next journey ahead.

These are the most vivid memories of Naani from my youth. She died five days after my twenty-fifth birthday, and I never got to say goodbye. No one has ever made me feel as entirely loved as she did: Naani was magic.

Gone seems too simple a word for Naani. But her touch, her love, her embrace, were all gone. Gone too was our family. I'm not sure how to explain it, but the day she left this world was the day our family stopped being a family, each person lost in their own despair. I struggled to understand any of it. For Naani, faith and family were everything; it was her legacy, her life's focus. I spent a great deal of time struggling with the idea that our family was letting her down. I was angry, frustrated, and confused. I had to release the pain, so looking inward to locate years of advice, stories, and guidance, became my focus. In the interests of survival I let go of the lost familial relationships. With her passing, however, a desire to engage in daily prayers and build relationships with my faith community emerged. Being grounded in something bigger than myself felt healing. Through faith I felt connected to her, and the possibility of hope surfaced. It was through this opening that I started to have short visits with Naani in my dreams. This was an unexpected but appreciated reminder of her presence and love.

The birth of my first child also helped me cope with her loss. Humza's birth was a safety line I needed; it started a new chapter. He was raised for the first year of his life with my mom, his Naani, as well as his Naana, and two uncles. Similar to my experiences as a child, Humza was surrounded by family. Seventeen years later, Humza and his two younger siblings, Baily and Sofia, continue to be raised by their Naani, and see my family on a daily basis.

Raising my children with my family is how I honour Naani. When I see my mom interacting with my own children, I see so much of my Naani, her spirit, her faith, and her love of family. People say that over time, grief dissipates, becoming easier to deal with. I disagree; in grief is love, and my love for Naani continues, and may actually be stronger now. It's in myself that I aim to locate her, so that I too, one day, will be able to share parcels of myself with my children and grandchildren—parcels that they will carry on into the future.

Grandfather

By Harun Šehović

My grandfather was nothing but kind to me and everyone around him. He was rather emotional but always there to protect us whenever we needed it. He always put others first, sometimes forgetting himself completely. He often had a strong and stern look on his face, but he never let that fool anyone. Through all the trouble and misfortune of his life, he somehow managed to be a constant calm and forgiving support.

A little before the pandemic, he was diagnosed with a tumor, and his whole kidney had to be removed. The tumor was almost as large as his kidney by that time, and he hadn't told anyone that he'd been suffering from pain or discomfort. We found out, and surgery was scheduled. We could do nothing more but hope that the cancer had not spread.

During his recovery, he was always emotional. We were around him, and every word spoken was close and sincere, regardless of what was said. He could have died, and that thought made everyone more aware of our actions. I cannot imagine the pain that I would have felt had he died any sooner without that closeness we shared toward the end. I was an angsty and high-strung teen before my grandfather was diagnosed with cancer. I couldn't stand his constant sweet talk, inability to acknowledge that I was growing up, and tendency to treat everyone like he owed them something.

Whenever my brother and I visited him, he would stretch out his arms as far as he could and ecstatically scream: "There you are, kittens! Come to Grandpa!" Everyone heard that, of course, and I wanted to drop dead rather than hear it again. I was blind to that love and only understood it after the incident.

When his life began to waver, I somehow became the person who was always around him. I held his hand constantly, talked to him, and found nothing shameful about it—though it was short-lived. His cancer had spread, causing an edema to appear in his brain. First, his speech became simplistic; longer words were troublesome, and perhaps he did not want to complicate anything. He became more emotional and afraid, especially after we found out about his state. I slowly watched him become a child and held his hand more often. I loved holding his hand, and during the headaches of my own life, it seemed that was the only cure I needed.

I watched him pray silently many times in my life, but during those days, while he could still speak, I heard him call to God: "Please let the medicine come to me. Please, God, help me." The only prayer he ever uttered out loud was a prayer of desperation. He would say it until he could barely speak anymore. People in our house became simple nicknames called upon with the softest and calmest voice. Everything except us was unimportant. But there was immense love in his eyes. They were never bigger, never darker, and never filled with more tears than at that time.

I can only be thankful that my classes were online during that time, so I spent my time at his house. I helped Grandma between classes and did my best to stay around him as much as possible. He eventually had to be bedridden, and he lost the ability to do anything. His eyes became pale and seemed to move further back in his head. Only his chest moved slightly, so we knew he was still breathing. He blankly stared ahead, and that was it. That was the man. My hand was in his, but there was no grip; I felt like it had become the part with the least life. I was afraid of causing pain by even touching it, but I couldn't resist.

I stayed up late with him one night, holding his hand and chatting with his cousin, who had come to help us. My mom, grandma, and uncle were sleeping. Suddenly, my grandpa, who had made no sound for days, began to breathe heavily. I felt something was wrong and let go of his hand, hurrying to wake everyone up. He died by the time we all got to his bed. He died almost in my arms. Our goodbye was nothing but a light touch.

I feel I was not as good to him as I should have been, yet he loved me the most out of everyone in our family. Everyone knew that. My grandma even told me that once he had stopped talking almost completely, she heard him whisper my name and my mother's name in his sleep. That was the man whose arms are wider than the world whenever he comes to mind. I was devastated when he passed, grieving for not being good enough to him, yet he managed to teach me to put love first. For that, and for his teary, happy eyes and heavy smile, I am thankful.

GMD

By Steve Ladd

One of the few regrets I have in my life is that my sons did not have the opportunity to know my grandma. Grandmas are special; it's one of life's constants. But GMD (my nickname for my Grandma Dyer) broke the mold. I never knew her husband—my grandfather—because he sadly and suddenly passed away when my mum was just fifteen. My other grandparents showed little interest in us, so I effectively only had one grandparent, but it never felt like I missed out.

GMD lived halfway between my home and my primary school. I usually walked the mile trek with my friends, often popping in to see her. On Mondays and Fridays, when my mum worked longer hours, I would go straight to see GMD, welcomed by a cup of tea with some bread and homemade plum jam. On Fridays, she gave me some pocket money, which I would usually spend immediately at her local shop on either sweets or a comic. This time was precious, filled with vivid memories, and was just a natural part of my growing up. It's only now that I realize how lucky I was. My boys' grandparents live over an hour away, so they've never experienced the luxury of simply popping in to see them.

During school holidays, GMD would walk to our home to look after us. This allowed us to play with our usual friends on our street. It's only in writing this that I realize just how important that was for our happiness. Christmas wasn't Christmas unless GMD stayed.

After Christmas 1986, my dad drove her home. Fortunately, she struggled to put her key in the lock because she interrupted a break-in. Her struggle with the key gave the intruder time to escape, and GMD didn't come face-to-face with them—lucky for them! She never slept again in her home of forty-eight years.

In the interim, she stayed with us until we moved house … and she joined us! My parents bought a new house and created a granny flat. Bonus! From ages fourteen to eighteen, I was lucky enough to see her almost every day. Sometimes, it was for a quick chat; sometimes, I spent the evening with her. During the school holidays, I would eat my lunch with her just so I could enjoy the smell of her traditional cooking while I ate my cheese sandwiches. From ages eighteen to twenty-one, I enjoyed spending time with her when I visited from university, and she always gave me a £5 note when I returned—probably to make sure I went back.

GMD held legendary status with my friends. On New Year's Eve 1994, when I was twenty, I had a small party at my house with a group of friends. Throughout the evening, I popped upstairs to top up her favorite drink—a glass of sherry. At 11:55, just as we were about to sing "Auld Lang Syne," she appeared with a load of pots, pans, and wooden spoons so we could make some noise. She then promptly joined us for a conga at the age of seventy-nine!

When my parents split up in 1995, it was a difficult year for the whole of our family. GMD was my mum's mother, but it was mum who moved out of the family home. This could have been awkward, but such was the relationship between GMD and Dad; it wasn't. Ironically, it was on her advice that Dad took his future wife out for a meal. She heard him upset at home, so she gave him some money and suggested he take his new friend out. Such kindness and intuition were not unexpected from GMD.

The split and eventual selling of the house led to GMD moving into a smart warden-controlled flat. She spent just over a year there, but her health deteriorated both physically and mentally due to short-term memory loss that was becoming an increasing hazard to her welfare. Eventually, she had to move into a nursing home so she could receive appropriate care. I struggled with this because she appeared to still have all her mental capacities except for her short-term memory.

I proposed to my wife, Lizzy, in 1999. The ultimate test for her was the GMD evaluation, which she passed with flying colors. Getting married without GMD was not something I could contemplate, but this was no easy task. The home would have to agree, and she would need an ambulance to transport her from Bristol to the village of Ugborough in Devon. This was clearly going to be expensive, but despite being broke, we were determined to make it happen. There was some concern a couple of days before that the journey would be too much, but when GMD arrived thirty minutes before the ceremony, the mixture of relief and happiness was overwhelming.

In the weeks leading up to the birth of our first son, William, GMD was struggling with illness, and we all wondered how much longer she had. Soon after his birth, I was keen to drive to Bristol so she could meet her first great-grandchild. It was a special moment, but maybe it was also the beginning of me saying goodbye. We were so concerned before William's birth that I probably always made a point of saying a special goodbye every time after that. In typical fashion, she stubbornly carried on for another year, but in my conversations with her, she was at peace with the idea of dying.

GMD died on February 28, 2008. I knew before I was told because my sister never phoned me at work. As a teacher, it was one of the rare occasions when I could not hide my emotions, and my kind colleagues immediately sent me home.

Feelings about this divide opinion, but I didn't want to see her body. In my head were thirty-four years of memories, and that was how I wanted to remember her. Reading her eulogy at the funeral helped me say goodbye, but keeping her legacy alive for my boys has also helped. I always phone my mum on February 28 and October 24—GMD's birthday. Writing this piece has been a cathartic experience, but she was most definitely worth it.

Love, Lessons, and Lasting Memories

By Jelena Lukic

There are only so many people who really matter in our lives, who help us understand the world around us, give us unlimited support, and help us form as a person—preferably a good one. One of the people who played a huge role in my life was my grandmother Stamenka, or as I loved to call her from the moment I first spoke, Mena. She was more than just a family member—she was a guiding light in my life. Mena was a remarkable woman who possessed an endless well of kindness and wisdom.

Growing up, I spent countless hours listening to her stories about her childhood and how she overcame various challenges with grace and resilience. Her ability to find joy in the little things taught me to appreciate life's simple pleasures. Mena was more than just my grandmother; she was my confidante, mentor, and an endless source of love and wisdom during my life. Since she worked as a tailor while living abroad, I always had the most beautiful clothes, but because of her illness, tailoring and sewing were the only things she did not have enough time to teach me, and that always made me sad. Luckily, that is a skill she passed to my mother, so there is still enough time for me to learn and make my grandma proud.

Although Mena wasn't with me from the earliest days of my life due to living abroad and trying to earn more money so that she could provide a better life for her family, she had a strong impact on me. I learned to cherish the time we spent together during the summer. Summers hold some of my favorite memories with her as we would spend as much time together as we could. She taught me a lot of things and prepared me to handle life's challenges once she was not here with me.

One of my favorite things learned from her is making fresh bread with my own hands. As she was a great cook, we prepared various meals together, and one of the most important rules was to do it with your heart and not blindly follow the recipe. Preparing food for others was a special thing for her, and she adored making pancakes and other sweets in her kitchen. The air was always filled with the sweet aroma of fresh jam that she made by herself.

One of Mena's biggest passions was flowers, so she had a garden full of vibrant flowers that she used to spend a lot of time watering and admiring. Since hyacinths were her favorite flower, their fragrance always reminds me of her, and I love each spring because of that. She grew her own vegetables and taught me how to plant seeds, nurture them, and watch them grow. It wasn't only the gardening lesson, as it was much more—a true life lesson about patience and the importance of nurturing something with care and attention. As we worked side by side, she would share anecdotes about her own childhood, how she learned these skills from her parents, and the joy it brought her to pass them on to me.

My grandmother was full of stories. I can still vividly recall the warmth of her embrace and the soft, soothing tone of her voice as she shared stories of her youth. Her tales of adventure, resilience, and humor were not just entertaining; they were life lessons that shaped my understanding of the world. Her laughter was infectious, and her smile could light up any room. Even during challenging times, she remained optimistic and resilient, always reminding me that "this too shall pass."

Embracing Her Everlasting Spirit

She was waiting for me to leave her bedside before passing away; I believe that it was too difficult for her to leave me. In those final moments, I felt a mix of emotions—sorrow for losing her, yet immense gratitude for having had her in my life. I promised her that I would carry forward the lessons she had taught me and that I would strive to share her kindness and compassion. Saying goodbye was not easy; it was a moment of mixed emotions filled with love, gratitude, and a deep appreciation for the incredible woman she was. As I left her side, I took comfort in knowing that Mena's spirit would always be with me, guiding me through life's challenges and joys and keeping me grounded whenever necessary.

Although I was shattered after the phone call from my mother that came only ten minutes after I left my grandma's bedside, I quickly put it together. I felt grateful for the time we spent together and the special bond we shared from the very first moment, as I was her first grandchild and only granddaughter. One of our favorite things was drinking a glass or two of cherry brandy before lunch, which I still do, especially in special moments when I wish she was still here with me.

Mena's life is a true tale of the superhero: a grandmother, a guide, a shining example of kindness and resilience, and a true life coach before that even became a thing.

The Sweetest Person I've Ever Known

By Creshonda Smith

My grandmother was one of the most genuine and loving souls I've ever had the pleasure of knowing. Annie Ruth Seals from York, Alabama, was a warm and beautiful person, inside and out. My gram, as I always called her, would give you her last. And she frequently gave everyone her last, no matter how much it inconvenienced her. I will always remember her as a pillar of strength.

I always thought it was special that she and I had birthdays only one day apart. May 13 was my birthday, and May 14 was hers. Each year, I'd say, "Our birthdays are getting close, Gram!"

She'd cheerfully reply, "Yes, they are. You know, I tried to get your mom to wait so we could share the day."

We'd laugh about that and talk about how I was tickled pink to have this sort of bond with her over something so simple.

My gram was quiet, always pleasant, and valued family more than anything. She taught us that the family unit matters and that you should always go out of your way to help your family. Her belief in Jesus Christ kept her going most days, and she was always sitting and listening to gospel music and reading the Bible in her spare time. Ms. Seals (how friends referred to her) was resilient, resourceful, and really freaking amazing.

Whether she had a lot or a little, she told me to be content. Use whatever you have and make it work. I carry that with me to this day. I remember her showing me how to wash clothes in the sink if you didn't have a washing machine, bake with minimal ingredients, and be happy that you're alive, even if you don't feel the best. She was always in the role of a teacher and a supporter, no matter what decision you made in life. She wouldn't abandon you.

One day, it seemed like she started going to the hospital more and more often. I'd known that she had cancer at one point, but to my knowledge, she had overcome that obstacle. But then other body systems started to fail, and she was frequently in pain or taking a trip to the emergency room.

After a while, I started to see the writing on the wall, but I didn't want to accept that she wouldn't be around much longer. My gram had lived a long life—she was eighty-five years old and constantly suffering. I had moved to southern Italy with my family, so I didn't see her anymore. Part of me felt that was selfish and that I should be with her in her last moments.

At the same time, my Christian faith was extremely important to me, and Gram always told me to do what I felt was right. The support she showed me was unwavering. She never made me feel awkward or alone, ever.

I remember the day my mom called from the hospital to tell me that my grandma was at the end, and there was no more treatment available to her. Everyone had started to say their goodbyes. I made a video call and tried my absolute best to hold it together.

I didn't want her to think I was weak. I didn't want her to think I wouldn't be able to handle her passing. Internally, I felt like I wouldn't, but I needed her to know that I was okay, that I loved her, and that I appreciated her more than she could ever imagine. I tried to remember her warm hugs, beautiful smile, playing dominoes with her, staring out the window, people watching when I came over … everything.

At that moment, I was talking to her, she stared off into the distance. I panicked. So many thoughts ran through my head: "Is this really goodbye? Is she scared? Will I wake up tomorrow and feel differently? I'm scared! I don't want you to go." I was breaking down, starting to cry, and my tough exterior was melting away.

I wanted to hang up the phone and pretend like things weren't happening the way they were. I didn't want to say goodbye. I wanted to wake up the next day, call her, and ask what she had planned. I didn't want that to be the last time I heard her voice or saw her face. I was so emotional and trying not to make things about me.

Suddenly, she looked at me and said, "I'm not afraid to die. And you'll be okay without me; don't worry." It was such a brave thing to say, and I both admired her for it and didn't want her to be so sure I'd be okay. It was a very strange mix of emotions.

I told her I loved her so much, thanked her again for being the sweetest person I'd ever known, and said goodbye. It felt so final. A few hours later, she passed away, and I sat in the dark crying for hours. I wrote a note to her that read:

> Know that I appreciate you and always will. That you mean the world to me, and you always will. I love you, always and forever. Life won't be the same without you; oh, what I would give to hear your voice just one more time.
> See you later, Beautiful.

Goodbye for Now

Part IV

Other Relative

Swati's Story

By Sabrina Bachert

My aunt's namesake is the Hindu goddess *Saraswati*, the goddess of learning. When *Saraswati* blesses someone, she gifts them the power of speech, wisdom, music, and knowledge. This comes as no surprise to me, as I remember those summer afternoons singing in the car together, me the lyrics and my aunt the melody, filled with wonder and joy. My Swati *Masi* (meaning aunt in Gujarati), was my idol. She was a first-generation American, proud vegetarian, and had the talent of being able to make anyone laugh. Growing up, everyone told me I was a carbon copy of her. This was meant to be a taunt about how sensitive and silly of a child I was, but I held it like a badge of honor. Swati was the youngest of three daughters, charismatic, adored, and full of life. She loved to travel, and my childhood was painted with stories about the market in Morocco, the sweeping winds over the hills of Ireland, and the sound of the cicadas at sunset in Niger. Above all else, Swati was a storyteller.

I'd cherish the weekends when we'd take the train into New York City to visit her tiny shoebox apartment. My aunt was a social worker who started her career in the Bronx. She worked mostly with children and teens, and I'm certain that this influenced the care and understanding with which she treated my brother and me. One weekend, we sat outside in the spring-time with a pack of crayons and a stack of paper.

"What do you want to be when you grow up?" she asked.

"I think I'd like to swim in every ocean and see the whole world. Just like you," I replied.

"Then let's draw it!" she encouraged.

She helped me color a picture of myself adventuring the planet. Unbeknownst to me, she saved the doodle and had it framed for my birthday so I would never forget to dream big. This meant so much to a small girl who felt stuck in New Jersey, and I've always carried the sentiment with me. Today, the picture hangs in my office as a reminder of the person who inspired me to set my sights high.

Swati Masi was diagnosed with ALS while I was in college. By then, she was living in Texas with her husband and three little ones. Before she told me she was sick, I had flown down to spend my spring break with her. Looking back now, that week felt like the last full moment of sunshine before clouds would eternally move in. Before I left, we stayed up chatting over a late-night cup of tea. She talked about how she regretted never joining the Peace Corps, and how she wished she had told off those kids who had called her "fatti" instead of Swati in grade school. I didn't realize at the time that she was gifting me small pieces of herself; pieces that would soon fade in the enormity of battling a terminal illness. In my mind, I still see us at that countertop, laughing as we added a ridiculous amount of sugar cubes to our chai.

In the years to come, I would visit her a few more times. Each time was more painful than the last. She remained hopeful and positive through the changes that came faster than anyone expected. I helped her with her feeding tube and sat with her while she slept. Eventually, it became too hard for her to speak. This was the hardest for her—my aunt, the storyteller. On one of my final trips, she had been hospitalized for an infection. She was so exhausted, I could see that the positive front she had put on was starting to crack. When we finally had a moment alone together, I did my best to cheer her up. The oddest thing about these situations of utter despair is that sometimes, all you can do is laugh. For some reason, we both started giggling, which grew into a chuckle, which erupted into ridiculous belly

     Goodbye for Now

laughs. She got out her whiteboard and wrote, "I peed myself laughing." That set us into a further fit, until we were howling so loudly that the nurse came in and kicked me out. As I left, we exchanged a smile of what I swore was gratitude.

I left for the military soon after that. My visits became much less frequent, and even the news of her came slower once she could no longer text. In our last emails to each other, Swati Masi still encouraged me to dream. She selflessly championed me during a difficult time in my life, even as she was suffering immensely herself. When she passed, I was overseas. Suddenly, after all these years, this beloved person was gone forever and I hadn't been there to say goodbye. It is disorienting to watch someone deteriorate for years, only for them to slip away in a mere moment. It's like a bird that has sat by your window for your entire life but takes flight in the night, leaving only an empty branch behind. No big announcement, no grand song. Just a vacancy where there was once a life.

Even as the tides of grief ebb and flow, I prefer to focus on celebrating the woman that Swati was. The mark she left on my life was immeasurable. I am proud to say that I am like her in many ways: in humor, in empathy, in deference to a good cup of tea. Most of all, I am a storyteller, and I find solace in the fact that I have the honor of telling hers.

My Dearest Departed Aunt Norma Jean

By Brooke Gero

Growing up with narcissistic parents, I was often neglected. There weren't many adult figures in my life I could rely on. I am thankful to have had my aunt in my corner through important childhood milestones. Even as I sit here today and write this, I can feel my aunt with me, sending me a supportive and warm embrace. My Aunt Norma was my rock. Not only was she an amazing cook who taught me some of the best recipes I know, she was an amazing person.

My aunt was born and raised in the Azores in Portugal. It would be an understatement to say life was rough around the edges back then. However, despite all the adversity my aunt faced, she remained soft and kind. Before me, she had given birth to my older cousin, so perhaps it was her motherly instincts kicking in, but she never let me down.

Throughout my childhood, I was often at my aunt's house hanging out with my cousin as if she were my own sister. Norma was the event planner of the family. Every Thanksgiving, Christmas, and New Year's was hosted at her house. These weren't your average family gatherings, but rather a lavishly decorated fantasy world you would experience upon stepping inside the door. She went out of her way to decorate every corner of the house and, most importantly, make the experience a memory to cherish forever. Norma was great at keeping our family together and strong. Throughout my teenage years, she was always there for me—even supporting me after I had my first car accident by automatically lending me hers so I could get to work. This continued as I became increasingly defiant and found myself in more and more trouble. Eventually, I had gotten myself into enough predicaments that my aunt no longer wanted to enable me and we grew apart. I had also cut communications with my cousin, so I was out of the loop completely as far as family affairs went.

Fast forward five years later and her cancer diagnosis was the reason the door to our communication was once again opened. My cousin had reached out to me and let me know the heavy burden she had been carrying during my absence. I knew my next steps would be to sit and spend time with my aunt.

The very next day, I drove to her house—I can still remember the nervousness of walking up her front door steps. I didn't know what to expect. Would she be completely bald? Would she be crippled in bed? The first moment I sat on the couch with her, after not seeing her for five years, and seeing her struggling from the chemo, I felt ten years old again. I suddenly forgot everything I had been through in life and only remembered every moment we had laughed together. I was a child once again in the loving embrace of my aunt and mother figure.

After this, we became inseparable once again. We started hosting weekend bonfires to celebrate my aunt's life and welcomed all of her friends and family to join us around the fire and reminisce. During this stage, there were times that we were all sure the cancer was gone. However, a few months later, some bad wigs, and an endless amount of expensive medical bills …

The chemo didn't work but remission struck twice. False hope was more of a silent killer than I believe the cancer was. We spent hours and hours over many days making plans for a future that would not come. Finally accepting the truth, we stopped the chemo and my aunt was placed in hospice care. During these moments, I saw in her the ten-year-old I once was. My aunt was weak, she wasn't herself, and she was in pain. Yet she still reassured us everyday that we would be okay because *she* was going to be okay. My aunt Norma had always been religious, so she would often talk about her soon to be encounters with God and the other realm. I believe she also did this to inspire hope and a feeling of acceptance in everyone around her.

At the time of my aunt's death, I was overseas and could not attend her funeral. Instead, I called my sister right before the service and she brought her phone inside with her so I could listen and feel like I was there in spirit. I was okay with this because the last time I saw my aunt, we had made a toast to life, and I knew from then on that she would be with me forever in spirit. Looking back on it, I wish I had been there, supporting my cousin and sisters. However, I know my aunt would have understood.

Even today, my aunt is still with me, so it's never quite been a strict goodbye. I know we will meet again, in a different time and place.

Uncle Rog

By Anita Ellerington

My dear Uncle Roger was born a very sick baby in a refugee camp in Germany but moved to Western Australia when he was two years old.

Every second Christmas, my family would spend six glorious weeks in Narrogin where he lived. I will always remember those visits fondly: my uncle had a heart of gold, a smile that lit up a room, and a great sense of humor. Uncle Rog, as we often called him, loved to sing—especially after a few drinks at one of the many parties he hosted. He also loved to play pool, which he taught me as soon as I was tall enough to hit the ball with the cue stick. With a Victorian Bitter in a beer cooler and music blasting in the background, he beat me at every game.

During the hot summer days, Roger would come to Nana's and Poppa's and we would sit out on the lawn, eating watermelon and buttered corn—in all my years, those foods never tasted as good as they did while sitting in the garden with my Uncle Roger. When Uncle Rog eventually disappeared from the house, I always knew where he was: his shed. It was his favorite place and held all the tools he had gotten over the years. I would sit with Uncle Roger, chatting with him and watching as he tinkered away, sometimes for hours, listening to the stories he remembered from his childhood.

I was so intrigued by his life, I wanted to know every detail. Although I asked a lot of questions, he was always patient with me and willing to satisfy my insatiable curiosity.

It was a Christmas tradition that we played a game of cricket on the dusty road in front of his house. I remember the dry summer heat and Uncle Rog happily bantering as we played, trying to fuel the friendly feud between Australia and New Zealand (our two rival countries). I happily gave it straight back to him.

I always felt a sense of family with Uncle Roger. We loved to spend time in Poppa's garden, pulling out the carrots and eating peaches picked from the tree, with the juice running down our chins. He was a free spirit like me—we loved to be silly and have fun. It was natural when we were together to get into our own bubble, make each other laugh, and give each other cheek at every opportunity while sitting on the back porch in the shade eating the yummy fruits. He even taught me how to play chess. We would spend hours sitting across from each other while he patiently taught me the rules. Like me, I knew he cherished every moment we were together.

At least once during our visit, Uncle Roger would drive us to the nearby lake to fish for "guppies." He always wore a big hat with corks around it to keep the flies away. Afterwards, I would watch him prepare them to be ready to be barbequed for dinner. I remember sitting in the backyard with Uncle Rog with the smell of the barbeque and the sound of the cicadas serenading us in the background.

When my dad passed away in 2016, it was Uncle Rog I found the most comforting; he would call and would help me through the darkest days. It was as if he knew when I needed him and he was never too busy for me.

At the end of 2022, my dear Uncle Roger was diagnosed with dementia. Although he was deteriorating quickly, he wanted to come to New Zealand to see his sister, my mum, before he was unable to fly. During that visit, I recall all of us sitting around the table chatting when he spotted the guitar in the corner of the room; he pointed to it and looked at me. I only needed to look into his eyes to know what he wanted. I knew he played the guitar so I grabbed it and put it on his frail lap. With gusto, he started strumming it, but eventually he handed it to me. With my limited ability,

I started to play a tune that was easy for us to sing: "Over the Rainbow." It was like time stood still; emotions were high and I felt his happiness radiate throughout the room. I remember looking at my Uncle Rog and him looking back at me—both of us with tears in our eyes.

After this magical moment, he turned to me and stuttered, "My beautiful niece, I have something I want to show you." He walked out of the room.

He was away for a good fifteen minutes and when he came back, I asked, "What was it you were going to show me?"

He looked at me with confusion, but then quickly became the cheeky Roger I knew so well. "I forgot," he said and started laughing.

Although it was beautiful to spend those few days with him, it was deeply saddening to see him struggle with speaking and remembering, and seeing the fear in his eyes when he packed his bags and forgot why.

I brought Uncle Roger a pounamu, which is a Māori greenstone that symbolizes strength and protection—we had it traditionally blessed and I put it on Uncle Rog; he never took it off until the day he passed away. That pounamu was the symbol of the deep connection between me and my Uncle Roger. He passed away on December 15, 2023.

Even though I feel deep sadness over his loss, in my heart I will always carry Uncle Rog's wisdom, kindness, and love along with the beautiful memories we made together.

Echoes of an Encompassing Essence

By Charlize Venter

My aunt Amolinda—or Tannie Lindy, as I called her—was the eldest of my mother's two siblings. They grew up during, and very much in, the Namibian War of Independence. It's rare to come out of such a life, such a childhood, without some permanent scars—be they physiological, psychological, or both. For the most part, she grew up away from home, in fortified convents that kept the children safe. These convents didn't do much to break her fierce and fiery spirit—quite the opposite. Yet, however disciplined, stoic, and stubborn she could be, she was fun-loving, silly, empathetic, and had a prolific sense of justice at her core.

As a child, she often scared me—not in the sense that I feared her, but I knew not to test her or pick a fight with her. Still, I had the most brilliant adventures with her. She loved children and would go out of her way to teach us the most interesting thing no school could or would back then: balance.

She was a fairly tall woman who inherited my grandfather's dark features, while my uncle and mother resembled my grandmother's lighter ones. She had Opa's jet-black hair, deep brown eyes, and naturally tan skin. She looked exotic and foreign to me in more aspects than one; beauty is, after all, the sum of its parts. Perhaps she was precisely something precious and foreign, for her character and values stood out in a place filled with mundane and dogmatic personalities. She never stood back when something was unfair, never hesitated to lend aid when someone was hurt, never wavered in being exactly who and what she was.

She spoke her mind and held firm to her core values, whether it was a man twice her size or some tyrant of sorts. She never backed down from what she deemed unreasonable, cruel, or unfair. All the while, you could find her in her sun hat tending to her most beautiful and lively garden, a side effect (I suspect) of growing up in a desert country—just like my mother and grandmother, who grew life in places where it normally didn't even sprout.

A few years before she began slipping into an unrecognizable version of herself, I fell ill. I was misdiagnosed and subsequently mistreated. I lost the full use of my legs, and my strength withered nearly as fast as the color and life drain from a bouquet denied water. She was there in all the smallest of ways—the ways I needed most. I remember the December my family came to spend a last holiday season together; they all gathered from near and far to give me one last family Christmas … to bid me farewell.

Usually, there was always a stroll through some or other extensive public garden, an unspoken tradition of sorts. We did the same that year. My body had these ephemeral bursts of energy, and, of course, I shared the familial stubborn streak, so I gave it all my power. That day, on that stroll through the botanical gardens, she stepped in beside me and nonchalantly began telling me about this and that plant as we walked, things we both knew she had told me before. I recall her stopping at a cycad—a plant you need a permit to grow in our country due to its threatened status. I looked at her while she spoke of how dinosaurs were said to feed on it during prehistoric times.

I knew what she was doing. She gave me an indirect way to rest and regain my strength while the rest of the family thought she was just doing what she loved: teaching. She caught me staring, as she wasn't one to miss any detail, and smiled at me—knowing that I knew. She inconspicuously held my hand and continued to tell me about the cycad. She knew I didn't want the rest to see how direly I struggled to keep up.

She was one of the few people I have encountered who could understand and love me in a single breath. There were innumerable instances like these, these little moments where she saw me struggle in my stubbornness and showed up beside me, silently letting me know she was there in a language we both understood.

There wasn't a true goodbye, really. She had a premature degenerative brain disorder—a branching of Alzheimer's—that took both her body and her once fearlessly strong mind. In the end, she was a shell of herself, a body that had no traces of her other than her face and physical features. She had sparse and short, lucid moments, and we got to see her while she was with us every so often.

I remember the last time. We'd taken her up to bathe her, and suddenly she was there … for a few moments. We laughed, we joked, we smiled … we reminded her how much we loved her. My mother and I had tears in our eyes and smiles of gratitude on our faces as if we knew it would be the last time she would be present while she was with us. But we laughed because her silliest self had returned for a moment; she was with us for those brief moments. I picked up my phone and took a picture. Despite the pain, there is more joy in that single picture that captured that fraction of a second to negate the sorrow. *Auf Wiedersehen, meine liebste Tante.*

Amy's Story

By Sharon Wells

A my wasn't just my cousin: She was my sister, my friend, and my *Wizard of Oz* enthusiast.

Before I was born, Amy and her brother came to live with us after their mother passed away from pneumonia. Amy was already ten years old when I was born, so we didn't get to spend much time together. Even though there was an age difference between us, and we weren't particularly close when I was younger, we still ended up growing up as sisters.

During my late teens, I became pregnant with my son. Since Amy had also recently become a mother, our shared experience of motherhood brought us closer together, and we formed a strong bond. As our bond grew stronger, we did everything together, from concerts to craft shows, festivals, movies, beach vacations, amusement parks, and tea parties. We shared many good times together, making memories that I will always cherish.

The Wizard of Oz had always been our favorite movie. We watched it together so many times! So of course, when it came to theaters for the anniversary, we were ecstatic. As we sat in the front row and the music filled the air, we couldn't help but sing along to every song. Our shared excitement was palpable as we talked about our dream of one day visiting the Land of Oz together. It was a moment of pure joy and connection that we would always cherish.

After Amy discovered she had stage 4 cancer, it was a difficult time for everyone. We were all devastated by the news, struggling to come to terms with the harsh reality of the situation. I wasn't too familiar with the word cancer at the time, so it was difficult to fully comprehend until I witnessed it firsthand. Witnessing the various treatments, the physical changes, such as hair loss and weight fluctuations, and the daily struggles of sickness can be overwhelming.

Throughout her battle with cancer, Amy displayed incredible strength and determination. Despite facing setbacks, she remained resilient and never lost hope. She constantly sought out new treatments and refused to surrender to the disease. Her unwavering perseverance and positive attitude inspired me. I was truly amazed by her strength. Despite being in immense pain, she continued to be an exceptional mother to her children and a loving, supportive wife to her husband. Her resilience and determination made her a true superwoman in my eyes.

As time passed, she grew weaker and doctors informed us that she only had a few months left. We made sure to spend as much time with her as possible, cherishing every moment together. One day, she told me, "You're welcome here anytime," a sentiment that touched my heart deeply. Despite the difficult circumstances, her words brought comfort and a sense of peace. In her own way, she was letting me know that I would always be welcome in her home. It was a bittersweet realization, but it showed me how much she valued our friendship and wanted me to be there for her loved ones in her absence.

As we faced the unknown future, we avoided talking about what the end might entail or whether she was feeling afraid. Perhaps the silence was driven by fear of acknowledging the inevitable.

I vividly recall hearing the news that she wasn't doing well. My immediate reaction was to cry and express my fear of not being prepared for what might come next. Reflecting on it now, I realize how self-centered it was of me to think only about my own feelings of readiness.

During the week that hospice came to care for Amy, I visited her every day after work. I would make my way down the road to sit by her side, offering comfort and companionship. She would often be asleep, as the pain she was experiencing was overwhelming. It was a difficult time, but I was grateful to be able to provide support during her final days. I poignantly recall sitting by her bedside, softly playing the song "Somewhere Over the Rainbow" on my phone. Even though she may not have been fully conscious of her surroundings, there was a special connection between us as she reached out and placed her hand gently on my knee. It was a touching moment that will forever stay with me—a small gesture that spoke volumes without the need for words.

On July 11, 2020, Amy passed away. I felt so many emotions. I was in denial. I had experienced losing a loved one before, but this time it felt different. The pain was deeper, and the sadness was overwhelming. I couldn't believe that she was really gone. It took me a long time to come to terms with her death and accept the reality of the situation. I finally realized that life had led me to this point, and my responsibility was to assist her two youngest children during their time of need. It was a challenging task, but I knew it was important to support them in any way I could. As I took on this role, I felt a sense of purpose and fulfillment knowing that I was making a positive impact in their lives. Despite the difficult circumstances, I was determined to provide them with the love and guidance they needed to navigate through this tough time.

As time goes by, I take solace in the fact that I am here for her children. Whenever I spot a rainbow, I believe that it is Amy's way of showing us that she is watching over us from above. It brings me a sense of peace and reassurance knowing that she is still with us in spirit. The rainbow serves as a reminder of the love and connection we still share with her.

Until we meet again somewhere over the rainbow.

Gone but Never Forgotten

By Kevin Sawyer

Is there finality in death? The definition of "finality" according to the Oxford English Dictionary is, "the fact or impression of being an irreversible ending; a tone or manner which indicates that no further comment or argument is possible." I, however, would like to make a further comment on the life and death of my dear Aunt Ernestine.

My mother's younger sister was born with a rare medical condition, systemic lupus erythematosus, which is incurable. In the 1950's there was little medical intervention that showed promise of managing the disease. As my aunt entered her early years, doctors often stated that she would not live through her teenage years. She, however, did not hear any finality in their tone and lived well past her teenage years. Aunt Ernie, or Berstein, as I chose to call her, lived a productive life. She was a go-getter and confident woman, who stood proudly despite her constant hospitalizations and doctors' visits. As a baptized Christian, she received last rites numerous times as the notion of finality kept creeping back (last rites is a Christian practice where a person near death is given the last prayers and ministrations of the faith). She often volunteered for experimental treatments in the hope that she could help others with the disease. No sense of finality yet.

I recall her efforts in our community as she and her friend created a community project called DOES, an acronym from her name and her dear friend's name: **D**ale **O**wens **E**rnestine **S**awyer. The project was created to clean up our neighborhood in Hollis, Queens. She and Dale went about cleaning property lots, sidewalks, and backyards in the neighborhood, with my help of course.

Time passed and when I entered my teen years, Berstein began to groom me as a young Black man. She took me to restaurants and showed me how to conduct myself in those settings. She let me know ways to conduct myself with the opposite sex. She became teacher, mentor, and aunt for my formative years. Even after I completed my high school career and moved out of state to attend college, my aunt continued to provide me with insights, knowledge, and love. Her medical condition was being managed as best as it could be and it never got in the way of her living life to the fullest. She had a unique knack for staying employed despite having lost jobs due to her medical condition. Still no finality there. She maneuvered through her early twenties, but the disease steadily gained.

As a sophomore in college, I found the love of my life and decided to get a married. The family at large was ill at ease with my decision, but Berstein stood firm in support of my decision (I remain married to this day, some fifty years that she would be proud of).

As Berstein's health declined in the years that followed, the ritual of traveling to and from the hospital became habit. The doctors eventually exhausted their interventions and, as it was presented to the family, my aunt was receiving enough pain medicine to knock out an elephant, but to no avail. Despite the pain she must have been suffering, you never saw it written on her face or in her body language. She was peaceful and calm as if she felt no pain.

Even on that last day, she calmly called to me, asked me to sit by her side, and feel how cool the sheets were. She then began to vividly describe her death. She recounted seeing a body of water and wanting to know if the water was warm. She explained that when she puts her toes in, if the water is warm, she will cross it. I asked her if the water was warm and she replied, "*Yes.*" I then stood up, went to the doorway, and turned to face her, knowing it would be the last time I would see her alive.

The family gathered to return home and the trip from Manhattan to Queens that night seemed exceptionally long. Within minutes of arriving at the house, however, we received a call from the hospital informing us that my Aunt Ernestine, "Berstein," had passed.

So, this seemed like finality. Even so, as I sit recounting her story at the age of seventy, I realize that there is no finality in death in terms of what someone has imparted and left with you. I am grateful for what my aunt meant to me, and I have passed on her wisdom to my children and grand-children. We live as she lives in us: eternally.

Chaker

By Maryem Hmayed

mong all the family photos, I keep only yours in my drawer. It some-how has a way of reminding me of what it is like to live to only fifty-five years old and to leave not a single person untouched by your charming presence.

My uncle Chaker passed away in 2017. The morning was still, almost peaceful, until the phone rang at 7 a.m. My mother's face fell as she answered, her voice trembling with disbelief. The caller from Switzerland spoke words that shattered our world. In that moment, everything inside me collapsed. My heart raced, my body went numb, and a heavy silence filled the room as the reality of my uncle's passing sank in. I was devastated, unable to comprehend the loss that had just struck our family.

My uncle was a man who radiated warmth and joy—he was always cheerful, always full of life, and ever hopeful, even when life handed him more struggles than most could bear. With a brave face, he faced the pain of a fractured family, a failed marriage that left him shattered when his son was just fourteen. My uncle did everything he could to be there for his child. His son eventually grew up and drifted away, choosing the numbing escape of drugs over his father's outstretched hands. My uncle never abandoned him. He remained a constant presence, offering what little he

"

could. He was a lifeline in the dark, always hoping that one day his son might return to him.

Yet, despite the heavy burden of these personal sorrows, my uncle's kindness and generosity extended far beyond his immediate family. When my parents faced financial ruin and were struggling with the bank when I was just a child, it was my uncle who stepped in. He was our savior during those dark times, providing for us when we had little to nothing. I never felt the sting of poverty or need because my uncle was always there lifting us up and ensuring that we were cared for. He was more than an uncle—he was our guardian, our protector.

The last time I saw him was during my visit to Switzerland in early 2017, a trip that remains etched in my heart. We sat together on the couch, talking for hours. He looked at me with pride in his eyes, marveling at how quickly I had grown up. To him, I was still the little child he had once held in his arms, though now I was on the brink of adulthood. He spoke with a tenderness that brought tears to my eyes, promising me that once I finished high school, he would take care of everything—he would handle my papers and find me a job in Switzerland. For a girl from a third world country, this promise was more than just words—it was a beacon of hope, a chance at a better life that he was offering me. I know that if he had the time, he would have kept his promise. Destiny wanted otherwise, but I will remain forever grateful for his caring kindness.

I remember all the details of that day well, as if it were yesterday and wasn't just about promises and reminiscing. My uncle, in his usual spirited way, took me on a tour around the town, showing me the beauty of the country he had come to call home. As we wandered through streets steeped in history, he shared stories of Switzerland's past, stories that made the country come alive in my mind. He treated me to all my favorite foods, indulging me with a kindness that felt like a warm embrace. Every moment with him was filled with love, with a joy that seemed boundless.

To me, he was the very picture of happiness and vitality. However, as we walked through the picturesque streets, I knew there was a hidden pain beneath his cheerful facade. I knew how much he longed for his wife to return, and how deeply his son's troubled path wounded him. He had shared with me, in moments of quiet vulnerability, how the loneliness consumed him, how each night he would drink as he was trying to drown the pain that refused to leave him. He wished for a different life—he longed for a life where he wasn't so alone, where his family was whole, and where he didn't have to hide his heartache behind a smile.

My uncle's life was cut short by a heart attack, a consequence of the years he had spent trying to numb his pain with alcohol. The very thing he turned to for comfort ultimately took him away from us. It is a stark reminder of the dangers of how drinking can slowly destroy a life, robbing us of those we love.

Yet, despite all of this, he never let his pain define him. He was perfect to me—he was a man who gave everything he had, who loved without measure, and who stood by those he cared about no matter the cost. I wish I had told him how much he meant to me, how much his love and kindness had shaped my life. I wish I had been there to greet him at the airport the last time he came here; however, life, with all of its demands, got in the way, and I couldn't make it.

Chaker was a man who deserved so much more than the hand he was dealt. He was a man who made my world better, who filled my life with love and hope, who made me believe that, no matter what, everything would be okay. And now, with him gone, the world feels a little colder, a little emptier. But I will always carry his memory with me, a memory of a man who lived with a heart full of love and who gave everything he had, even when he had nothing left to give.

Rest in peace, dear uncle. I love you, and I'll miss you always.

With all my heart,

Maryem

Remembering Michelle's Spirit and Legacy

By Caitlyn McMorrough

Michelle was more than just my cousin; she was my confidante, my partner in crime, and my best friend. Growing up, we spent countless hours together, sharing secrets, dreams, and a bond that felt unbreakable. Her laughter was infectious, and her spirit, though troubled in later years, always had a way of lighting up a room.

As children, we were inseparable. Our summers were filled with adventures, from exploring the woods behind our grandparents' house to building elaborate forts in the living room. Michelle had an incredible imagination and a knack for turning the ordinary into something magical. We would spend hours pretending to be pirates, astronauts, or superheroes, with Michelle always taking the lead in our fantastic escapades.

Michelle struggled with addiction for many years. What started as a way to escape her pain soon became a relentless battle that she fought valiantly. Michelle was a vibrant and deeply caring person whose warmth and creativity left a lasting impression on everyone she met.

Her passion for painting was evident in the beautiful artwork she created, which adorned many of our homes. Michelle's love for animals was equally strong; she often volunteered at local shelters and had a knack for rescuing and caring for stray animals. Her tattoos were more than just ink; they were expressions of her personal journey and the values she held dear. Despite her ongoing struggle with addiction, her kindness and resilience shone brightly, making her a cherished family member and a source of inspiration for all who knew her.

I remember one Christmas when Michelle, fresh out of rehab, seemed more like her old self than she had in years. She helped decorate the tree with an enthusiasm that reminded me of our childhood days. We laughed as we hung ornaments, reminiscing about the times we had made them together. That night, Michelle confided in me her dreams of starting anew, of living a life free from the chains of addiction. It was a conversation filled with hope, and I clung to it as a sign that better days were ahead.

The last time I saw Michelle, we were sitting on my front porch, dreaming about the future. We were excitedly planning to get an apartment together in the fall. We imagined how we would decorate it, the late-night movie marathons we would have, and the endless adventures we would embark on. It was a conversation filled with hope and promise, a moment that I cling to even now.

As we parted ways that evening, I hugged her tightly and said, "I love you, Michelle. See you later, alligator."

With a smile that reached her eyes, she replied, "In a while, crocodile."

Those were the last words we exchanged. Little did I know that they would be the final words I would ever hear from her.

The news of her passing hit me extremely hard. I felt a mix of disbelief, anger, and overwhelming sadness. Michelle had overdosed. Despite all of her efforts and our support, her struggle had finally overtaken her. My heart shattered into a million pieces. The dreams we had built together, and the plans we had made, were all gone in an instant.

Saying goodbye to Michelle was one of the hardest things I have ever had to do. At her funeral, surrounded by family and friends, I felt a deep sense of loss and helplessness. I placed a small photo of us in her casket—a reminder of the happier times we had shared. As I stood there, I whispered, "Goodbye, Michelle. I hope you have found the peace you were always searching for."

In the months that followed, I found solace in volunteering. It was something Michelle and I had always talked about doing together. I threw myself into work at local animal shelters and hospitals, hoping to honor her memory by giving back to others. Through this, I discovered a strength within myself that I did not know I had. I also found a community of people who understood my pain and helped me navigate through the darkest times.

One of the most poignant moments came when I met a young woman at the shelter who was struggling with her own demons. Her story mirrored Michelle's in many ways, and I felt an immediate connection. We talked for hours, sharing our experiences, and offering support. In helping her, I felt like I was keeping a part of Michelle alive, honoring her fight by aiding someone else in their battle.

As time passes, the raw pain of losing Michelle has softened into a deep enduring ache. I have learned to carry her memory with me, finding ways to celebrate her life rather than dwell on her loss. I speak about her often, sharing stories of her kindness, her creativity, and her indomitable spirit. In this way, she remains a part of my life, guiding me and inspiring me to be the best version of myself.

Agape Love: A Tribute to Aunt Elizabeth

By Jemimah Silas

"Your beauty shines from within; never let anyone dim your light."

Those were the words my Aunt Elizabeth never failed to remind me of. She was a beautiful soul with nothing but love and kindness to offer the world. It always amazed me how resilient she was, even amidst all the trials and tribulations she endured throughout her life. One of the earliest memories I recall was when my mother and father took a business trip to Lagos, and she came to stay with us for a few days. As soon as she arrived, I immediately spotted her boho bag, and peeking out of the top corner was the holy grail of sweets … Tom Tom's.

I recognised the contrasting black, white, and orange packaging because they were my all-time favourites. She always brought them for me, and after she bellowed her usual catchphrase, "Jemi, baby girl, come here. Look what I've got for you," she would pick me up and proceed to smother me with a thousand kisses.

Because she was considerably younger than my parents, I viewed her as my cool and trendy aunt who travelled the world and sported a boatload of jewellery. Her sense of style was electric, and I wanted to be exactly like her when I grew up.

My parents would often go on business trips so this became part of our monthly routine and, over the years, we formed an unbreakable bond that was more than just blood. From a very early age, she became my best friend, confidant, and biggest supporter. She taught me how to piece together iconic looks, bought me my first bottle of wine, and helped me secure my first ever date with a charming boy who lived across the street. I loved my parents a lot, but Aunt Eli? I *adored* her.

Even when she had my cousins, she still maintained that carefree energy that she was known for. I think that's why we bonded so much; we were birds of the same feather—in other words, the "crazy" ones of our family. Growing up surrounded by so much love, I couldn't have asked for more; that was, until my parents' passing. It happened on the way back from one of their business trips; it was a tragic car accident that claimed the lives of not just my parents, but also the other passengers involved.

I remember the moment my Aunt Eli got the call. She let out a scream so loud it echoed into every single corner of the house. And when my siblings came rushing into the room, she began weeping uncontrollably. She was so distraught that, for a few moments, she became unresponsive. Not moving or speaking, she held the phone to her ear and cried in disbelief.

Not long after that, my aunt made plans for us to move in permanently and did everything she could to make sure we were as comfortable as possible. However, this caused a lot of problems in her marriage because my uncle never wanted the responsibility of taking care of four orphaned children. Eventually, he would leave and move to America with another woman, leaving his own children behind as well.

From then on, Aunt Eli became our sole provider and gave us a life that we will be forever grateful for. We never wanted for anything because she always made sure we had it all. She sacrificed her ambitions of becoming an actress to become a second mother, and even when things became financially tough, she still soldiered on with her signature smile. She lived a life full of adventure and humility, but most of all, integrity; she never failed to do what was right.

One of the hardest days of my life—with the exception of my parents' death—was the day Aunt Eli passed away. She had always been a woman of faith, so when she suddenly became ill with breast cancer in 2021, she didn't try to fight it—instead, she faced it.

Over the next few weeks, there were constant hospital visits. Many of them ended in family arguments because she adamantly refused treatment. No matter how hard both we and the doctors tried, she would not consider it. At first, I held a lot of anger because I thought she could have saved herself if she had say yes to chemo.

But on that last day, as we said our goodbyes in the hospital, her final words were, "I've done what I needed to do. You kids have all grown up and look at how amazing you are. Take care of each other. Mummy and daddy would be so proud."

At that moment, any ounce of anger I had felt completely vanished. Even though she had been suffering for a long time, she had stayed strong for us all, making sure we had a chance of becoming the people she knew my parents would have wanted us to be. For that, I can't thank her enough.

On November 6, 2021, we buried my Aunt Eli in her favourite crimson kaftan, adorned with her precious jewellery worn only for special occasions—that day was the most special of all. It was not just the day we laid her to rest, but the day we celebrated the life of the most extraordinary woman I have ever known, and the ultimate embodiment of agape love in its finest form.

One of a Kind

By Naomi G. Davis

My grandmother's youngest sister wasn't "Auntie" to me. She wasn't any form of her birth names inspired by flowers: Hyacinth or Condaisy. Of course not; a Caribbean child doesn't refer to any adult by their name. It didn't matter that I was American or raised in the Bronx, New York; my grand-aunt was always "Tante." I don't know what the word means, but that's who my grand-aunt was to me—my Tante. My Tante was born in St. John's, Antigua—the island's capital. When my grandmother immigrated to the States, my mom and aunt followed her. I don't know much about their childhood or early adulthood back on the island, but I knew that my Tante brought recipes with her.

Not recipes in a book or written on index cards; no, my Tante's recipes were in her head. As a child, I thought everyone had their recipes memorized. I didn't realize that the fact that they were all in her head meant that one day, I would not get another bite of her "peas rice." I should have known that her renaming something as normal as "rice and peas" meant that her dish was uniquely her own.

My Tante was like that. She was a secret wrapped in the interesting. She had more going on inside her head than anyone would ever know, and that was why she was a crack at Jeopardy, saying the answers before the contestants and knowing more than even the winners. Because her brain held so much information, some trivia was helpful, and some was just for fun. And if she fell asleep in front of the TV? It was best to leave the TV on because she would always jump up and declare, "I was watching that!" She was funny and smart, and while she was never a professional chef, I always dreamed of buying a restaurant for her to run.

It's my fault. I thought that my Tante would live forever. I thought I had time, but I didn't. The day I lost my Tante is written on my heart. It's a scar that will never heal. The year I graduated from college, 2011, was supposed to be the best year of my life. But it was only weeks later when I smelled something burning. I checked my house, but there was nothing amiss, so I went to my Tante's attached one-bedroom apartment to discover that the burning smell was coming from her fan. I remember thinking that she seemed a bit off. I remember wondering how the burning smell hadn't woken her up. I asked if she was okay; she swore she was, so I left. That was the last conversation I had with my Tante.

I didn't know she was having a stroke. I didn't know she was falling into a coma. I didn't know she would never be herself again. I didn't know that in just a few hours, I would lose her. I didn't know that my younger siblings would grow up without a presence I considered integral to my own life. When my Tante died, my family lost something special. Not just a one-of-a-kind taste in her food, but a one-of-a-kind person.

Growing up, I remember being in my older brother's shadow, but never with Tante! I was her favorite, and I relished her attention. Our relationship truly began when she noticed I wasn't getting the same attention as my beloved older brother. My Tante is the reason I have fun stories from my childhood. She was the first person to tell me that I could make it in Hollywood, and she was the only person in the family who didn't treat my intelligence as a given. Growing up, my aunt would come by my house every Friday to make my favorite dish of dumplings and saltfish. Many Caribbean people eat this meal for breakfast, but since my aunt made it the best, I had it for dinner.

I was twelve when my Tante was unemployed and struggling financially, so she made me a card. The card was blue, my favorite color, and she had drawn cameras and lights and told me to chase my dreams. It may seem obvious that an adult in a child's life would tell them to dream and plan. But I am from the Bronx—New York's forgotten borough. There I was with very little chance of success, but the most important adult in my life told me I could! So, I continued to dream and continued to plan. My Tante was there when I got into my dream school—New York University. She was there when I learned to write scripts, and she even cooked meals for my junior-year project. I remember my grand aunt as a silent strength in my life. When I decided to study screenwriting in Dublin, my Tante researched Ireland. In my sophomore year, when my mom fell sick with cancer, my Tante stepped in and cared for her so I could stay in school.

But my Tante missed the big things. She never saw my completed thesis film, and while she saw me walk in my graduation ceremony, she never held my bachelor's degree. My Tante didn't get to see my film projected on a movie theater screen. And more devastating, I live my dream. I have worked on six television shows. She doesn't know I took her words to heart and ran with them.

I do believe in the afterlife. I believe that my Tante is in Heaven and that she is looking down on me with pride. I like to believe that somewhere in our universe, she knows. She knows that I cook my rice and peas with a habanero pepper and make banana fritters the way she taught me. But what I hope she knows is that I will never quit. I hope my Tante knows that everything I have achieved is because of her.

Part V

Parent

Oma's Unconditional Love

By Sandre Griffiths

Oma. In German, this compact word means grandmother. For me, it is a word forever entwined with the memories of a woman I said my final goodbye to on April 1, 2017. This woman, however, was not my grandmother. She wasn't even related to me by blood, but over the course of thirty-one years, she became more of a mother to me than my own mother.

How do you say goodbye to someone like that?

Left behind at the age of three when my depressed mother's demons drove her back across the Atlantic to the familiarity of London, I had been raised alone by my father. Growing up, I had a few fleeting mother figures: kind and sympathetic teachers, a friend's mother, and a woman my father dated. But everything changed in 1986, after I began dating the man who would become my first husband, and I met his mother, whom everyone affectionately called "Oma." Eventually, I called her that, too.

It didn't take long for us to grow fond of each other. Our birthdays were both in July, and we shared an interest in crafts. Oma was an avid sewer, crocheter, and knitter, and I admired her skills. In no time, she was coaching me to crochet and sew. I still remember how my heart swelled with joy when Oma praised my first attempts at crochet and the first dress

I sewed under her guidance. I was young and lacked confidence. Her kind words and encouragement meant more than she would ever know.

Our bond grew over the years that followed and deepened after I had my son Ethan in 2001. My husband worked weekends and evenings, so I was often alone with our young son. Having been widowed in 1994, Oma was alone too, so I started inviting her to join us on day trips: the zoo, Niagara Falls, the beach … We also established some traditions, like our annual fall shopping trip to Buffalo and semi-annual visits to the Creative Sewing and Needlework Festival. Oma was a friend, mentor, and, more importantly, a mother figure. When other women complained about their mother-in-law, I couldn't empathize. I loved mine.

Then, in 2009, my husband and I made the difficult decision to separate. As I grieved the loss of my marriage, I assumed that I would lose my adopted family as well but, much to my surprise and joy, Oma remained steadfast in her decision to maintain our relationship. "I love you, and you will always be my daughter-in-law," she reassured me after we shared the news. She made it clear that I would always be welcome in her home, and she remained true to that.

In the years that followed, I was invited to every family gathering and we maintained the traditions we had established. We also remained travelling companions, exploring Ontario each summer with my son. Although I was no longer her daughter-in-law in the eyes of most people, Oma still introduced me as her daughter-in-law. And one day, when someone referred to me as her daughter, she didn't correct them—she just smiled at me. And I happily smiled back.

In the spring of 2016, Oma's health started to decline. By October, the doctors diagnosed her with kidney disease—she would need dialysis. Despite her age, eighty-seven years old, we remained hopeful. However, by March, her condition deteriorated, and she was admitted to a palliative care home. Sadly, after less than a week in the home, Oma returned to the hospital. The next day, I got a call from my ex-husband: Oma wasn't doing well.

My gut reaction was to rush to the hospital but my ex-husband suggested otherwise as his whole family was there. I wasn't welcome. I remember sitting at my kitchen table, feeling heartbroken, restless, and full of dread.

A few hours later, I got another call. My ex-husband and his family were going home. If we wanted to see Oma, now would be the time.

Even as my son and I walked into Oma's hospital room for the last time, I was in a state of disbelief. Her illness had left her a shell of her former self, but I still couldn't believe that Oma—*my Oma*—was going to die.

That night, as we sat with her, told her we loved her and held her fragile hand, Oma told us not to be sad. Instead, she spoke of the adventures we had shared, and urged us to continue exploring so that my son would see and experience new places. She asked about our plans for that summer, and I spoke of the trip we were planning: Disney World. And then I listened, eyes brimming with suppressed tears, as Ethan sang softly to her.

When we left her later that night, Oma was sleeping. And I was still in denial that the end was near. Within a mere few hours after our visit, however, Oma passed away peacefully in her sleep. Later on, one of my former sisters-in-law told me, "She was waiting for you and Ethan."

They say that there are five stages of grief: denial, anger, bargaining, depression, and acceptance. After Oma died, when denial was no longer possible, I became engulfed by anger. I felt wronged. How could my Oma—my only source of true parental love—be gone?

Although many years have passed, this feeling has never completely gone away. But now, a profound sense of gratitude has emerged. I feel grateful for the privilege of having known Oma. And I'm grateful that we had the chance to say goodbye to her that night—grateful that Oma waited for us.

Today, I find solace in the memories we shared and the love she showed me. Sometimes, angels do come down to earth, and Oma was one of them.

Cut Short

By Jim Landwehr

My father was murdered when I was five. Wait, did I say that out loud? I guess it doesn't matter because it's true—though that's not how the legal system refers to his death at the hands of multiple assailants. Manslaughter is the technical term—the legal term—for what happened in the bar that night in 1967. Manslaughter is a milquetoast synonym for murder and cheapens it, in my opinion, but it is what it is. Everyone is entitled to their opinion. Mine is likely skewed by blood.

But I think it's the circumstances surrounding the loss of my father that make the story more tragic than just another case of manslaughter. The fact that it resulted from a racially charged fight between Dad and five youths, most half his age, makes it a story that epitomizes the turbulent times of our country in the late 1960s. Adding to this, his death left my mother with six kids to raise on her own, and, well, the story morphs from tragic to impossibly sad.

I've spent the last fifty-seven years trying to digest not only what happened that night but who I am as a man who grew up without a dad. How did that reality shape me? For example, one thing I've struggled with my whole life is low self-esteem. One way it manifests is through my self-deprecating sense of humor. Somehow, I rationalize that if I add a laugh to a jab at my own weaknesses, it's all okay. Only recently have I realized that using humor to put myself down is a mask for my insecurities. It begs the question: Would this lack of self-esteem be an issue had my father been around and part of my life? I guess I'll never have an answer to that.

I know that my story is not much different from those of kids whose parents got divorced or who lost a parent at a young age to some health issue. Like many of those people, I often pause and think about how his absence may have affected my life and the lives of my siblings as well. He was not there for my football games, high school and college graduations, weddings, and countless birthdays. His absence required my mother to act as the sole disciplinarian, caregiver, homeowner, handyperson, and bread-winner. Dad's death at the young age of forty-two changed the trajectory of everyone in our family.

While our mother tells us that Dad loved his kids and was a victim in the wrong place at the wrong time, I choose to extend him a bit of grace. After my sister died at age five of a Wilms tumor, Dad was devastated, and his chosen balm was drinking. He was unhappy at his job, and the stress and sorrow he carried led to a drinking problem. My mother had no choice but to separate from him so she could focus on the remaining six kids she had to care for.

By God's grace, I've never had to deal with the grief of losing a child or dissatisfaction with my career. Dad was in a state of depression at the time of his murder, and I know enough about all that comes with a depressive state to forgive him. Forgiveness is all I have left. Forgiveness will have to do.

I have a handful of memories of my father that I hold precious. Without question, my favorite, ironically enough, was sitting with him at a bar where I sipped root beer and ate peanuts while he drank a beer. It was a special treat to have time alone with my dad, even if it was in a bar in broad daylight. Little did I know that the habit I was helping to foster would lead to his demise. All I knew was that I was with my dad, feeling all grown up. I guess there are worse memories for someone you miss as much as I miss my father.

I'm now sixty-two years old and the father of two adult children. If my dad were alive, he'd be ninety-nine, and though I don't think of him every day, key events in my life as a father trigger thoughts of what I missed out on. Fishing, canoeing, and camping with my kids remind me that I never had the chance to do those things with my dad, an avid outdoorsman.

Encouraging my son in sports and praising my daughter for her grades was a privilege he never got to experience. Even something as mundane as eating around the table as a family, which we did religiously with our kids, was just not there—or was there, but without Dad.

In some respects, my dad's story, the way it was cut short, and the resulting fallout challenged me to do better for my own kids. I was determined to be there for them, showing my love and pride at every opportunity because of what I was denied. I am a firm believer that this is his legacy to me. His absence and poor decisions caused me to increase my presence and make better choices in the lives of my own kids. And that's not a terrible legacy to leave.

A Thief in the Night Has Stolen Her Away

By Timothy Law

She was the life of every family gathering, the favorite aunt of all my cousins, and the smartest woman I have ever known. She encouraged me to think big, dream strange, and embrace who I truly am. She was Anna Maria who emigrated from Holland at a very young age to Australia. She was a teacher, a friend, and my mother whom I loved. Too early in life, both mine and hers, she was taken from us—stolen, never to be returned.

As the eldest of three boys, I was the shy one who had no knack for sports or social scenes, and yet my mom encouraged me to be myself, and to not change into something else to suit the crowd. When Dad wanted me to continue playing basketball like my younger brother, something for which I had no skill or passion, Mom told him I should stay home with her and read instead. We were kindred spirits, she and I. Mom would always tell tales to us, my brother and me, as we settled down to sleep. Sometimes it was stories from a children's book, or something from her past; more often than not, it was something she made up on the spot, and this taught me the joys of creating new and exciting adventures, and gave me the building blocks to become an author.

With Mom, chores like cooking and cleaning became such fascinating fun as we debated and discussed the important and the ridiculous in equal measure. One time, while she was washing the dishes and I was drying them, we talked about time, and how fast it seems to fly.

"Time flies, blowflies," my mother laughed.

"Perhaps we could find a time swatter?" I suggested with a wink.

She taught me about being brave, standing up for what you believe in, and how to be kind.

I remember at every family gathering, Mom would spend more time at the beach, rolling down the sand dunes with us kids, than getting involved with the adult conversations of my dad, uncles, and aunts. Mom knew all of the great games, practical jokes, and how to have fun. She was a child at heart, someone who never wanted to grow up, and I guess that her wish came true.

I was so inspired by her that I decided I wanted to become a primary school teacher, just like she had been. However, my love of reading, gifted by this brilliant, beautiful woman, caused me to change my plan slightly. As my studies went on, I found that teaching was not my calling. Instead, I would be a librarian in a school somewhere, encouraging kids to learn to love reading just like I did. As Mom celebrated her sixtieth year, I returned home from my studies and noticed a change. Mom was different; her mind stumbled and struggled with some simple things. My father suggested that the change in Mom was related to recent events. Her father, the man she adored in the same way I idolized her, had passed away. More members of her family and some of her friends had also shockingly passed away. Each time I returned home, I noticed Mom fading from us; she was wandering the streets aimlessly, and forgetting faces and important dates. The doctor told us it was early onset dementia, a diagnosis that we did not want to accept, but sadly could not deny. By the time I finished university and was living back at home, Mom had stopped reading and doing crosswords and logic puzzles—she did not talk much, but wandered often.

It was difficult to watch the woman we knew, who was so much fun, so intelligent, and so caring, simply disappear from our lives. Our poor father witnessed it all, whereas we boys merely caught glimpses. Mom ended up in a home where we visited her when we could. It was local so we did not have the excuse of distance for why we did not see her more frequently; when I did visit, it was heartbreaking to see who she had become.

Even family gatherings were not the same. Mom's absence sucked the joy from each occasion. It felt like she was dead months before she was. Our mourning had begun the moment the horrible disease took root. On

Christmas Day of 2009, Dad took the call we were all dreading. Christmas dinner was set aside as Dad and I drove to the home and packed up Mom's things. I witnessed her lying there—she was all clammy, silent, and still. I brushed her forehead with my lips and whispered to her that I loved her.

Now I visit her grave whenever I find the time, but time seems to be a commodity of which I have less and less. Life gets in the way and I do not go as often as I feel I should. I try to forget the sounds of her harsh breaths in those final dying days. More often, I recall her sparkling eyes, melodic laugh, and innocent spirit.

I wish I could have made that time swatter, or found some way to turn back the clock. If I had known we would lose her so early on, maybe I would have pursued teaching or taken her traveling. To see the world through her eyes, and witness that wonder and true delight. We have all been robbed—not just me and my brothers, but everyone whose lives were touched by my mom—to have lost such a soul. It is my vow to follow her example: to be kind and caring, to do what I can for my community, and to maintain that childish spirit … all in memory of someone truly special, and gone too soon but never to be forgotten.

Harmony in Redemption

By Selena Mell

The engraved wooden sign declaring, "Top of the morning, Charlie. It feels just great to be Irish," along with the hand-carved Shillelagh, held profound sentimental value for my father. Passed down from his own father, Charles Sr., the cherished artifacts found a place of honor in our home, adorning the space next to a photograph capturing the festive spirit of my grandfather in a floppy hat during a St. Patrick's Day parade.

Despite never setting foot in Ireland, my father embraced his Irish heritage with unwavering pride, immersing our family in the joyous celebrations related to the Irish. Raised in the Montreal suburb of Point St. Charles, my father navigated the eastern region of Quebec and the Maritimes as a skilled bilingual salesman, excelling in his role as a regional manager. His professional success brought recognition but also demanded sacrifices, often leaving him on the road for extended periods, creating a distance that weighed heavily on our family.

His three children, myself and my two brothers, eagerly anticipated his return from business travels, cherishing the moments of play and laughter that defined our moments together. The hallway became our playground, the top of his shoulders our launching pad, and Saturday nights were reserved for burgers and fries and laughter-filled moments watching Disney movies.

At times the kitchen, filled with cigarette smoke and camaraderie, echoed with the passionate voices of his friends sipping Labatt's 50 beers from stubby brown bottles and conversing simultaneously in both French and broken English. During my pre-teen years, the routine grocery trips to town were more than just a necessity; they were opportunities for me to delve into my dad's gift of new books about the mysteries of Nancy Drew or the Hardy Boys, escaping into their worlds while waiting in the car as my father spent hours visiting at the local Legion.

The shared memories from this time are scarce, marked by the toll life's choices took on our family. The divorce of our parents became a harbinger of change, thrusting my father into a lifestyle dominated by socializing at bars, house parties, and leisure trips. Slowly but surely, he evolved into an absentee figure, his presence diminishing as he succumbed to the clutches of alcohol, encasing himself in a self-imposed glass cage. In periodic moments he sought connection with his children, although often in ways that seemed elusive.

As the years flowed by, the initial waves of disappointment, anger, and resentment gradually subsided, making way for a second chance at reconnection. As a young adult, visits to my father's home became an annual platform for renewed contact, accompanied by the comforting aroma of large plates of homemade spaghetti or lasagna, followed by spirited games of cards.

A subtle transformation unfolded, imperceptible at first but steadily growing more pronounced with time. My father's demeanor underwent a shift as he began to express pride in our achievements and a genuine interest in our professional endeavors. Once elusive, he found a new voice, attempting to forge connections by referencing moments from our shared past, such as the Shannon community performance he attended where he witnessed my primary-aged brother and me sing "Daisy a Day," and shed tears during my younger brother's group of toddlers singing their rendition of the "Toora Loora Loora" lullaby.

A profound connection through music emerged, with my father often sitting back quietly, contemplating the Irish melodies, jigs, and heavenly

Celtic representations. This shift marked a subtle yet significant step towards redemption, a melody of reconnection harmonizing with the echoes of a troubled past marred by his own hidden melancholy and maternal abandonment issues.

Despite his continued involvement in a circle of friends, admired for his quick wit and comedic relief, a transformation occurred within him after the birth of my daughter, his first grandchild. A newfound interest in family blossomed as he navigated the internet to connect online, engaging in lengthy Skype calls and immersing himself in stories and photos on Facebook. My daughter's delights, be they songs or academic and artistic triumphs, became shared moments of joy, revealing a renewed side of my father dormant since the time of the divorce.

The complexity of our relationship evolved and transformed with time, fostered by the connection created by the next generation of five grandchildren. As my daughter began singing in festivals and musicals, my father praised her efforts and made a poignant request: "When I pass, I want you to sing 'Danny Boy' at my wake."

Despite his ongoing struggle with alcohol, the years unfolded, and my father and I were able to move past old wounds. The rekindling which had taken root after the birth of my daughter fostered laughter, song, and a shared connection to an unknown homeland that echoed on both maternal and paternal sides of my family. Soon after though, wheelchair-bound and with his health rapidly declining, my father passed away in the hospital on June 4, 2016.

Upon learning of his passing, my daughter dedicated a heartfelt rendition of "Danny Boy," which she shared on social media and later performed again at his "celebration of life" held in a neighborhood Legion in Montreal on June 11.

As my own tribute, I embarked on a trip to Ireland for the first time, symbolically leaving a part of my father in a country he had never visited, but that had brought him solace and peace throughout his life. This excursion with my husband served as a means to ground my father's memories and soothe the haunting echoes that persisted throughout his lifetime. It was a place where both he and I could find peace—a final healing to our journey.

Living Life's Lessons

By Kay Keiser

Miss Margie was born in 1925 and began teaching in rural Nebraska in 1943. At age seventeen, she drove her Model A to the one-room school, where she started her day by stoking the furnace with corn cobs and ended it by sweeping the floor. In between, she positively changed the lives of kindergarteners through eighth graders. She was known for her students' high academic achievements, and yet her students stayed in contact with her for over seventy years because, along with teaching them content, she taught them how to live—respectful, creative, and trustworthy.

Miss Margie revered education. To her, all experiences were teachable moments. Beyond teaching elementary school, every encounter was an opportunity to learn about someone and help them grow. She even taught strangers how to use subway passes, figure out sales prices, buy a car, or whatever helped them. When meeting someone she liked and admired, her highest compliment was, "You'd make a great teacher!" She said that often to me, her daughter, so I have been an educator for over forty years.

As a mother, Miss Margie taught my brother and me to love learning not by drill and instruction but by making every task, from setting the table to deciphering roadside signs, into playful learning opportunities. We knew our letters by eighteen months and read fluently before age three because we were surrounded by books and her love of reading and, of course, her love of us. She taught us to challenge ourselves and reach for our potential. As children and adults, she and my father (also a teacher) protected us when needed but fostered our self-reliance.

Miss Margie never did anything halfway. She won a set of salt and pepper shakers in ninth grade in a Bingo game. The lady beside her whispered, "Why don't you start a collection?" Over her life, she amassed over 10,000 pairs of shakers. She was interviewed on national ABC, NBC, and CBS news and television shows and many collectors' journals over the years. Anyone who came to tour the collection heard the story of why she started collecting, and she would look each person in the eye and say, "All this started because of one comment. If she hadn't said that, I would never have started, and look at what it has become. Watch what you say because one comment can change a person's life." People came for the novelty but left with a lesson.

For decades, Miss Margie taught me how to live through coaching, praise, and her example. To live is to learn, love, laugh, and lead so that life is full and rich for yourself and everyone else.

Then, when Miss Margie reached her eighties, I gradually took over the care of my parents. Mom was diagnosed with colon cancer at age eighty-four, and her reaction was typical. She did not cry or wonder, "Why me?" She stuck out her chin, and with fire in her eyes, her response was immediate—"I'm going to beat this thing." Mustering determination and pushing herself to follow doctors' orders, she beat it. Twice. Even though it is rare, she conquered the second round of treatments. She was frail but just as spunky as ever. She was still teaching me. This past winter, when I was diagnosed with breast cancer, I did cry but then thought of my mother's example. I work every day to be healthy. In many ways, I am better than before the diagnosis, and her model has always guided me through tough decisions.

When she turned ninety-five, my mom was sent home from the hospital for hospice care, but as her physical strength dwindled, her emotional will survived. She made sure every visitor was thanked and gave them a smile, no matter how she felt. One day, when she became bedridden, she asked me for paper and a pen. She carefully composed and copied a letter to me detailing what a wonderful job I was doing and how thankful she was that I was caring for her. She was getting me ready to move on when she was gone.

It became my twenty-four-hour job, sleeping on a couch in her room and working online when she slept. I asked her what she would like each day, and she always said, "Tell me stories." So, for over two hours every day, I held her hand and told her the stories she told me growing up: her childhood, marriage, motherhood, jobs, travels, pets, and so much more. She asked me how I could remember all that, and I realized that she had always used her stories to build character and share memories. She continued planning for my happiness, leaving me notes in her Bible, reminders to care for all her family, and discussions of what I should do in retirement. So, in the final days, we never actually said goodbye. She had made sure we were ready, and on her last day, I held her and prayed for her heavenly peace, thanked her, and promised to fulfill her wishes.

She squeezed my hand and whispered, "Thank you."

I was watching her sleep when suddenly she looked different. She was gone, and yet she still wore a little smile. Miss Margie had taught her last lesson—how to leave a legacy with grace.

How Do I Weep?

By Darian Jones

Within three months of my mom finally leaving you, they found you dead—cardiac ischemia because of drinking way too much for way too long.

It was in November of 1996, just after midnight, when Mom called. It was odd for her to be up so late. I was five miles away, sitting at my computer, when I answered. I don't recall any pleasantries or emotion, but Mom said simply, "They found Tom. He died today." I don't remember much of the remaining conversation after asking if she was okay and hanging up, but I remember, as emotional as I typically am—never too dry for a tear—none came. I sat there and typed a question to myself: *How do I weep?*

How do I weep for a man, a Black man, an African American king who let the world drag him down? How do I weep? How do I weep for a man I watched destroy the promise of not only our greats but of his own famous civil rights lineage from the hallowed halls of Howard and North Carolina Central? How do I weep? I weep when Wild Irish Rose and Thunderbird became hobby and habit replacing books and debate, argument became aggression, and your heroic physical size became laughable and pathetic drunken stumbling. How do I weep? How do I weep when I saw the deep respect you had for my grandmother, yet you would be called to intoxication in her presence and spew absolute trash and contempt at my mother in front of us? How do I weep? How do I weep for the man who, by the time I was summoned to give up my spring break for the wedding, filled me with such contempt as I stood in solidarity with my mother?

The first time we met, when I was seven or eight, you were a Black God to me. The first college-educated, law school graduate, Omega Psi Phi fraternity Black man this young Black boy had ever met. You had the lingo, you spoke the language, and you exposed me to places my mind had not yet gone, dreams not yet formed, paths my feet had not yet set—them damn seeds you planted in that kid. How do I weep?

But TMBIII, how do I not weep for the man who, despite his addictions and flaws, despite a lifetime battling demons, I only later would understand or even know? How do I not weep? How do I not weep for a Black man who handed an eleven-year-old his first novel and said, "Read and let's discuss." *The Spook Who Sat by the Door* by Sam Greenlee set my world on fire. Our conversation following it was like the Morpheus and Neo, red pill-blue pill. Then, you handed me *Behold a Pale Horse* by William Cooper and set flame to my consternation with what the pastor was preaching, what my people were living, and our secrets.

How do I not weep? How do I not weep when the third book was *The Autobiography of Malcolm X* by Alex Haley, and I found the prince I had been seeking? How do I not weep? How do I not weep when you exposed me to the pool hall of your fraternity brothers and these strong, loud, proud, educated Black men who spoke in audacious liberatory theology and Black man voice? How do I not weep when you taught me to love not just who I was inside my skin but the hue and texture of that skin itself? How do I not weep? How do I not weep for a man who gave me Tulane the day you said you were proudest of me because it was where your mom had become the first Black female professor? How do I not weep?

I weep because after repeated blackballed bar failures, your life's dreams were not simply deferred but dead, like raisins in the sun, and you fought to hydrate them with cheap wine. I weep because I wasn't aware nor strong enough to pour into you the hellified strength and resiliency that became your legacy in me. I weep because of the travails of systemic and institutional racism on a man whose last name no longer worked for him but became the cancer that ate him from the inside out. I weep because this country assassinated yet another strong Black man, not with bullets or a Bible, but through exhaustion from fighting barriers and brick walls without doors. I weep because you could not find the solace and self-compassion to reconcile your childhood dreams with your adult realities—the very stuff all Black boys who make it to manhood must reconcile when the façade and promises of childhood turn to bitter microaggressions and racial battle fatigue. How do I not weep?

TMBIII, I carry you in my sadness and my pride, in my hope and my defiance, not me, not like him, not this one world, not my boy's world, not my male students' America. I weep for you so that others may one day not have to weep for Black boys who never grow up to realize their potential and their promise. I weep because you never got to see me fall in love with James Baldwin and become not just a scholar but an activist and revolutionary. I weep because you never got to see the tree that grew from the many seeds you planted. Until we meet again, I weep in sadness and solidarity. Light up the darkness; I weep.

The Final Symphony

By Lesli C. Myers-Small

The birth of a child is often described as a harmonious beginning, a new chapter that promises the crescendo of a lifetime of experiences. For me, that chapter began on May 15, 1969, at 3:30 p.m., when my mother and I formally met. But before that moment, the months preceding our introduction were marked by a different kind of rhythm.

I had chosen to be a bit of a troublemaker even before I saw the world. In the womb, I had decided that my sport was kickboxing, and my mother, bless her heart, had to cope with my energetic antics. To soothe me, she placed a portable radio on her belly, filling our shared space with classical and jazz music. It was as if those genres were a gentle lullaby that pacified my restless kicks. To this day, the soothing strains of Bach and the lively beats of Ellington remain my favorite melodies—a lasting gift from my mother's early efforts to find peace amidst my prenatal chaos.

As I grew, it became clear that my mother was not my friend in the conventional sense. She was something more profound: my guide, my mentor, my enforcer. Experts often debate the fine line between being a parent and being a friend, but my mother understood that boundaries, rules, and guidance were essential. Her role was not merely to be liked but to shape and mold. And oh, how I needed that shaping.

One vivid memory stands out from my childhood, etched into my mind with startling clarity. I had an accident that involved falling headfirst through a storm door, leaving me with a serious injury that required 36 stitches. As I bled and panicked, my mother's composure was a steadying force. Her calm demeanor was a stark contrast to the chaos surrounding us, allowing me to find solace in her presence. Even as I watched the doctor work, with her gentle encouragement, I was able to transform my fear into a lesson in resilience.

Years later, as a freshman at college, I made a mistake that many young adults make: I left without paying for car repairs. I was certain I had done everything right, but my mother's investigation revealed otherwise. She showed up at my work-study job at the University of Rochester, and her confrontation was stern with a touch of theatricality. In a scene that could only be described as a blend of embarrassment and discipline, she made it clear that family matters were to be handled with seriousness. Her ability to combine reprimand with a kind of fierce affection was a lesson I will never forget.

As my mother grew older and moved into assisted living, life continued to present unexpected turns. One day, I received a call informing me that she was involved in a new relationship. The awkwardness of having a "birds and the bees" conversation with my elderly mother was a reminder that even as we age, life remains full of surprises. The experience was a blend of humor and discomfort, a final frontier in the evolving nature of our relationship.

Throughout my life, my mother was my constant cheerleader. She attended every concert, graduation, and event with a pride that was palpable. Her support was unwavering and unconditional, a constant source of encouragement that pushed me to achieve and excel. Despite my many attempts, I could never quite thank her enough for her steadfast love and belief in me.

Even as age began to slow her down, it did not diminish our shared adventures. Our escapades, from shopping sprees to spontaneous road trips, were highlights of our bond. We sang real and made-up songs, and our joyous connection was a testament to the strength of our relationship.

Strangers often commented on the bond we shared, a bond that was both powerful and inspiring.

Although I knew my mom was gravely ill, I didn't expect her to leave so suddenly. When the news came, I rushed to the hospital, hoping for just a few more moments with my mama. There she was, lying still with her beautiful face serene and mouth slightly ajar, a final quiet reminder of the vibrant spirit she had always been.

In that moment, amidst the sterile hospital lights and the muffled sounds of the busy corridors, I took a deep breath and let my memories flood in. I thought about all the beautiful times we had shared—the laughter, the lessons, the unconditional love. Each memory was a testament to the incredible person she was and the profound impact she had on my life.

I spoke softly to her and shared that I would miss her deeply, but would carry forward the legacy of service, excellence, and compassion that she embodied so fully. I promised to honor my mom's memory by continuing the path she had paved, and embracing the values she had taught me.

As I stood there, feeling the weight of goodbye, the last words I whispered were, "Tell Dad, Nana, and Pop Pop hello from me." It was a simple request, but it was filled with love. As my husband drove me home from the hospital, I sat quiet and numb, trying to figure out how I was going to do this thing called life without her.

Molecules

By Debbie Donsky

Everything that you love, you will eventually lose, but in the end, love will return in a different form.
—Jordi Sierra i Fabra, *Franz Kafka and the Traveling Doll*

As I have experienced loss in my life, I have tried to find meaning in it—because what is the alternative? I smile to myself as my grandmother flows through me, reminding me of her saying, "I have no shame in getting older because you know what the alternative is ..." Sometimes, we have to walk through it and let it happen.

When people kindly ask, "How is your father?" I have struggled to find the right response. Is it a question people just ask when they already know the answer? Is it hope that moves them to ask? The hope that maybe, by some miracle, he got better? Is it President Obama's *Audacity of Hope* or President Snow's warning in *The Hunger Games,* "Hope. It is the only thing stronger than fear. A little hope is effective. A lot of hope is dangerous?"

Like Pandora's box, once all the evil, hurt, and pain is released, what is left, at the bottom, if only a glimmer, is hope.

After a series of infections, which ultimately exacerbated his dementia, my mother brought my father to the hospital. February 2020 would be the last time he slept at home—a home we moved into as a family two weeks before I was born. The world shifted on its axis and my father was isolated in rehab for four months, his dementia reaching a tipping point where the slow decline was certain. It was through this process that I began to develop the awareness that time is morphable. It can stretch, fold, overlap, and shrink. We do not control time; however, we can develop our ability to understand it in a different way.

Before the vaccinations started, but the antibody tests were available, the only way to see my father was to get swabbed, wait fifteen minutes, determine if I was cleared for entry, and then visit in full personal protective equipment, and attempt to have a conversation with a man losing his language. I was complaining to a friend who did the proverbial Cher slapping Nick Cage in the face in *Moonstruck* by telling me, "Snap out of it!" Having lost her father in his early sixties, she told me she would give anything to see her father for only five more minutes.

Rather than spiralling in my own self-pity, I have become more present, and am able to bear witness to and care for my father as he moves towards the end of life, knowing it can, like time itself, expand and contract at will. There are stages of loss: changes to personality, fear, depression. There are social expectations of communication and behaviour, and there are bodily realities, including incontinence, that exacerbate isolation from friends and other social situations. As the disease progresses the process of loss speeds up. Then comes the loss of autonomy: no more driving, being on your own, dressing yourself, cleaning yourself, feeding yourself. Mobility. Communication. Understanding. Engagement. Consciousness. Muscular. Organs. Each has its own morbid details.

In an effort to map this path, we looked back to consider when his dementia started. But, like the poisonous vines of bittersweet nightshade, dementia creeps slowly in all directions so that, even if you try to recognize it or dare to try to change the trajectory of the disease, it will surface in another way. The roots of dementia are rhizomatic and will multiply in different places until the disease overwhelms and takes over, wrapping itself around everything you knew of that loved one.

We work to engage my father's brain with the music he loves, my mother on piano: Bob Marley; Neil Diamond; Elvis; Leonard Cohen; "Moon River," their wedding song; Billy Joel; Boney M; the Beatles—we even got him a "Yellow Submarine" blanket as we sing the anthem, "All You Need is Love" to "Nowhere Man." As the disease progresses, we try to access different memories—the deeper and older ones—and together we sing prayers in Hebrew; gratefully, right in that moment, we get another piece back, if only fleeting. There is no holding on, only presence.

And yet, like a molecular gastronomy chef, we can slice these moments like my mother slices his food, refusing to accept *this* loss–the loss of swallowing. This loss will be another tipping point and the pot has only a few drops left. My mother has engaged us in every aspect of this loss: her anger, fear, shame, mourning, agony, frustration, ache. Though she never says it, my mother's love is about action. We have discussions about care, what works and what doesn't, the bad days, the disappointing friends, the new friends, the friends that stand by you no matter what, and all the struggles with him in care. Her deep love for him is the fuel that keeps my eighty-something mother as his primary caregiver each day. The one piece that is non-negotiable is the use of a feeding tube. If he needs a feeding tube, that will be the end. A nurse by trade and heart, my mother warns us of why this is non-negotiable. That will be the last slice. The molecules will have to be split into atoms and if we go any further than that, well that never ends well, does it?

With dementia, every moment is a goodbye and a stark reminder to be present and open our eyes to the layers of love, light, beauty and connection—even in the midst of loss.

So we stand by, bear witness, tell stories, sing, whistle, play piano, care for him, laugh together, and cry together, while we gently live life around him so he will know, even if it is his last thought, that he was loved deeply.

Toolbox

By Charlotte Bennardo

The battered metal box was stuffed with an odd assortment of tools, some rusted, others part of a set with siblings long since lost, and some so old, I think they were my grandfather's. All were a testament to my father's life as a vacuum salesman, builder of the lunar module during the Apollo years, carpenter, commercial artist, one-time race car driver and mechanic, and "I'll fix that later" handyman. In a sweltering Florida August, my father reverently touched the lid with its broken lock. It too was caught in the vagaries and degradations that came with age. Years, journeys, and tasks took their measure on both man and box. Dad's final act, as the cancer slowly feasted on his body, was to give the box, his last earthly possession of any value, to my brother.

A NASCAR mechanic at the time, my brother didn't want the clunkers cluttering his pristine, organized garage. He had perfectly matched sets of shiny, top-of-the-line, pampered tools, all lovingly assigned their own space in lined drawers in professional-grade toolboxes. But tamping down the tears that my sister and I let freely flow, he thanked my father, put them in the back of his truck, and promised them a good home. I hugged my father's frail body gently, my words of goodbye sticking in my throat.

After the funeral, my brother drove the toolbox from the RV park that our dad managed to my New Jersey home. His voice choked and hoarse, he told me he didn't want the tools or the box. "Give it to one of your boys."

When he left, I explored the box. Faded NASCAR stickers of the teams my brother worked for adorned the outside, a silent homage of pride. A dried layer of old grease and dirt covered the faded and gouged paint. The top drawer stuck, refusing to reveal its contents. Wrenches and other tools had tangled on the journey—the same route my father used when he traveled between a dirt-water town in Upstate New York to Florida. His *Easy Rider* lifestyle on the road with his RV steered him away from the suburbs where his children and grandchildren lived, making him a stranger.

I had to wiggle my fingers in to push aside one askew wrench to unjam the drawer. The glide pinched my finger, but I won the contest, unlike too many arguments with my father. These wrenches fixed everything from overworked washing machines to well more than second-hand cars, our bikes, and sleds. Most were dotted with rust and sported worn grips but still worked. There were two brand new ones he must have recently purchased or been gifted. Did he ever have the chance to use them?

His battered ballpeen hammer in the second drawer reminded me of when it smoothed out dents in Dad's number 32 stockcar back when my brother and I were tots. We sat on the fender and quickly learned the difference between flathead and Phillips screwdrivers, box and open-ended wrenches, and pliers and needle noses.

The third drawer contained hexagon screwdrivers, a tire pressure gauge, rusted clamps, odd drill bits, and other things I had no clue what purpose they served. The final drawer held bent screwdrivers, good for prying off can lids and stirring paint, and odd nails and screws.

My hand slid down the side, almost caressing it. Over the years, I'd borrow a tool, thinking fondly of the rare moments I spent watching my father fix cars, or tighten door handles, or replace a flat tire on the wheelbarrow. Many times, my brother and I borrowed, then misplaced, a number of Dad's tools, so every Christmas he got more. When I bought my first car, I used them; they testified about a girl learning to do minor repairs on her '65 Mustang because all the mechanics in her family were too busy. Now they sat, ignored, in my cold garage, serving no purpose other than to house memories, pleasant and painful—once silent companions of Dad's youthful potential, slivers of achievement, and shards of unrealized dreams.

I like to think my dad passed on his passion for cars and mechanics to my eldest son; it's a small piece of him, like the tools, still present. When my son became a mechanic, we gifted him a complete set of professional tools. He didn't want my father's few relics.

So the toolbox remained, forgotten. As my youngest approached driving age, I cleaned off the thickened grease and dirt, then tossed out the insect carcasses and broken tools. I oiled the recalcitrant drawer till it glided smoothly. I wire-brushed the rusted tools and sprayed them with WD-40 to prevent further corrosion. The pliers and wrenches now moved smoothly. The tools were then organized: screwdrivers in one drawer, pliers in another, wrenches and assorted sockets in the third, lined up like proper soldiers. I offered the box to my youngest, but like his brothers, he scorned it. Once again, time, dust, and bug bodies settled in.

Like my father, the box represented a life separate, alone. When I am gone, what if no one wants it? A promise was made to give the tools a home; the burden of that promise and the inability to keep it weigh on me.

My father's ashes lie in a faraway cemetery, an ironic reflection of his chosen isolation. His home was ever the road that ran past ours. The tools have come home to family, but I am the last rest stop.

The Passing of Betty

By Carol Kay

Her hand slipped out of mine just as her last breath slipped from her lungs. Her pale face was ashen, and her eyes had lost what little luster had remained. I inhaled a painful gasp of air to commemorate the moment. It was one of the most gripping of my life.

Death had come knocking for Betty Donnell just when the door of hope had suddenly opened. Mom had rallied for a short time a few days before, at the age of eighty-six—something not uncommon during the last moments of hospice. It is a gift from God, allowing loved ones to arrive in person and share last words … allegedly those of comfort but actually of grief.

"Mom, you can go now," I sighed, wiping the lone tear from my cheek. There would undoubtedly be thousands more. Her death, though expected, rattled me. Losing a parent is a terrible blow, even in old age. Everyone says, "Their time has come." A book like *A Death in the Family* by James Agee captures the depth of despair caused by such a passing. The novel's emotional depth now explained what was happening to me. My own experience was beyond words.

The memories came flooding back, creating a great river of remembrance within me. I wanted to savor each one, but that would have to wait.

I dabbled my toe in the water instead. For now, it was time to make preparations. God had taken an angel from this earth—my mother. I accepted the dusk of life as any mature soul would … but it didn't make it any easier.

Mom was a terrible loss, and the pain would stab my heart repeatedly in the days that followed. I had multiple visions, both asleep and awake. She was a real beauty throughout her life. Everyone said how lucky I was. Seeing her cook dinner to please a kid at fifteen was one knife wound. Teaching me to swim at five was another. Coming to my college graduation, witnessing my endless dance recitals, and making my prom dress generated acute heart attacks. More were to follow.

She excelled in many things that others might consider mundane: needlework, knitting, singing hymns, baking pies, and sketching the family dog. She wrote no great novels nor made her mark in history. It was a simple life, yet it was filled with love, compassion, empathy, and sorrow for those experiencing loss. Betty was loved by many and cherished by all.

How do you think of someone who brushed your long hair and set it in tight pin curls every night so you would shine at school the next day? How do you forget a Girl Scout leader who wore her own sash full of badges to prove her special heritage? And how do you dismiss those moments of terror when you come home late after falling asleep on the beach in Santa Monica?

Her patience was strong but wore thin in time. There were times of punishment and forgiveness so that, in the end, the family unit remained solid and intact. Mom was the heart of the matter, with Dad waiting in the wings for his moment of glory. Clearly, Betty ruled the roost, and no one objected.

Most of the time, it was all about Betty: the stories of her youth and parents' divorce, how she met my father and married him in a week, and the day she broke her nose surfing in Long Beach, her hometown. She rolled bandages during World War II alongside her mother and became President of the USC medical faculty wives. Her life had been ordinary but full … just like everyone else's. But she was unique and one of a kind.

A mother's tasks are endless. She drove me everywhere, even when she was tired or sick. She had a strong sense of duty and understood the needs of a growing child, waddling from my preschool days into my edgy teen years. We stayed close after I left home, married, and moved away. Of course, she came to visit and suffered the grueling Arizona heat. Her loyalty was unmatched.

As I matured, I was by her side to make sure she was cared for and well-fed. She was my responsibility now! I made sure that she could find pretty nightgowns, her trademark for sixty years of her married life. They were lacy and came in pastel colors—old-fashioned and extreme but required until her dying day.

That was the day I broke. I had remained stoic for months while she deteriorated after a stroke. Watching her last breath was a privilege—even a joy. I was happy to be there to see her fly to heaven. With a heavy heart, I sat by her bedside, waiting …

The emotions that coursed through me switched from happy memories to current dread. The day had finally come—the one I had anticipated and expected but wanted to deny with every fiber of my being. Death is so cruel. Most people experience it from a distance—a phone call or text tells the tale.

I had to be present in mind and spirit, if not body. I felt numb to my core. My nervous system had ceased to work, mercifully sparing me the full impact of Mom's death. The tears would spill in due time, of course. But for the moment, I wanted her to feel my calm demeanor and quiet heart. It was all about her now.

Saying Goodbye When You Just Met

By Terra Sanders

How do you let go of the exact thing you wanted your whole life when you finally get it? That's a question I never knew I'd have to answer.

I was raised by a single mother of three girls, with me in the middle. In our neighborhood, fatherlessness was common, and the community helped each other out. I never felt like anything was missing in my life. But my sisters and I were different in personality, outlook, and physical looks. This isn't something I noticed, but children in the neighborhood did. They always asked if I and my sisters had different dads, to which we replied, arrogantly, "No." But deep inside me, I had this strange desire to be adopted. Not because I didn't like my family, but because I thought it would be cool to have a secret family somewhere looking for you. I always wanted a really large family with lots of people.

When I went off to college in Milwaukee, I finally let go of the notion that I was adopted. There was no secret family looking for me. Then, about six months later, when my mother was taking me home from spring break, she dropped a bomb on me: I had a different father than my sisters. Her friends had told her to stop being afraid and to finally tell me. She was so scared of how I would react, but I was so happy. I can't emphasize my excitement enough. I wanted to know anything and everything about him.

I plied her with questions, and by the time we got to the dorm, we were determined to find him. My mom knew he was still in Chicago because he loved it and would never leave. Using some research and the last known addresses and phone numbers from database searches, we ended up finding a few phone numbers to try. I got through to my oldest sister.

When she answered, I said, "Hi, is this ______? I'm looking for ______. I'm your sister."

My sister immediately burst into tears and said they had been looking for me. She gave me the phone number for my dad, who was living with my second youngest sister of the four in Iowa (he had left Chicago after all), and I immediately called. I don't remember anything that was said.

I remember the first time I saw my dad (Zyah, as I called him), what he was wearing, how he looked, and my impression of him. He looked exactly like me, had taught my mom everything she knew about our religious beliefs, and was a reggae musician. Most of all, I remember seeing my sisters; I saw myself in them!

I kept in contact with my dad, and during the next few months he and my mom reconnected. Not long after came the wedding! My mom and dad actually got married. For the first time in my life, I not only had two parents but both of my parents. As my dad moved in with us, I got to see up close just how much nature plays a role in all we do. We were the same in almost every way: walked the same; were strangely goofy in the same ways; had the same hair, skin, and positive outlook on life; the same strong religious commitments; and had even sucked our thumbs as children. I was surprised, though, that he was left-handed and I wasn't.

Having a dad for the first time isn't easy. You aren't used to another person telling you what to do. Overall, bossiness wasn't in his nature; he would suggest, not force. He never got mad, and the one time he did, he apologized to me. He told my oldest sister that he had to give me all the same things that they, his other children, had had.

My dad was the leader of his seven younger siblings, a guide and rock for his children, a father to other children in his neighborhood, a mentor to his daughters' boyfriends and husbands, and way more than a grandpa to his many grandchildren. He would always meet and talk to strangers, and he loved to cook and teach you what he knew. He practiced his reggae

   Goodbye for Now

music in the basement and had taught himself to play everything, including the drums, piano, and harmonica. This man was the most loving man I have ever met in my life.

But on July 4, 2012, that was all cut short. After a short phone call with my parents, my father had a stroke, closed his eyes, and never opened his mouth again. My mom fasted and prayed in the hospital for three days, hoping for a miracle. His whole family came to see him and surrounded him on the day we decided to take him off life support. I wasn't there. I ran out, crying. I wanted to hear his voice, pay more attention to the things he had told me, and have more time to see all of the ways we were alike.

So, how do you let go of the exact thing you wanted your whole life when you finally get it? The answer is that sometimes you have no choice. We only control a small piece of our short lives and none of other people's lives. Every day, we get things we want and lose things we worked for. We always face highs and lows, disappointments and triumphs, and life keeps being lived. Time forces you to let go.

And time is the gift that took the grief of the loss of my father, Zyah, and turned my story of a fatherless child, who wanted a large family and didn't seem to fit anywhere, into the beautiful story of a woman with six sisters, over thirty nieces and nephews, eleven uncles and aunts, and way more cousins who look, talk, and act like me.

Emily LaVonne

By Linc Johnson

We think we *always* have time. The last time I saw my dear mother, I told her that I would be back to spend more time with her. That day never came.

I have to preface this with the admission that I am a mama's boy. I mean, literal, in real life, still to this day, mama's boy. If you look up mama's boy in the dictionary, there would be a picture of me smiling ear to ear. If I could, I would still be sitting up under my dear mother, talking her ear off about any- and every- thing. Now, when I say mama's boy, I need to give you some context. I mean a mama's boy who listened when my mother admonished, "If someone messes with you at school, go tell the teacher." Then coming home, proud to have done so with *two* black eyes: one received before I told the teacher, and the other after! Snitches do get stitches, as it were. My mother could tell me to jump off of a two-story building and I would do it: what Mommy wants, Mommy gets.

My mother was the most loving and caring person. She supported and cared for six generations of our family, from her grandmother's generation all the way down to her great-grandchildren until her death in 2015. This included allowing other children to live with us, helping her friends out financially, and providing end of life care for countless uncles and aunts, her mother, and my paternal grandmother. She was a pillar in the community, going from teacher's assistant to assistant superintendent, changing lives, and benefitting families and our community during her forty-one years with the Compton Unified School District. My mother was everything to me, and losing her still stings with a pain I have not felt since.

When I was told my mother was diagnosed with stage four cervical cancer, I did what I am sure most people do in that situation: I embraced *hope*. My mother would pull through. She had done too much for too many to go out like that. I was in the sort of denial where I could not even fathom a day without my mother here with me. "She'll live to a hundred and twenty," I joked. "She will outlive all of us." The first round of chemotherapy went by without a hitch. My mother looked good, claimed to feel good, and the prognosis seemed to be positive. They gave her a radiation implant, and she trudged on. For four years, she was still ever-present in our lives: loaning gas money to children that were far too grown and far too educated to be borrowing gas money from their mother, having fish fry Fridays every week—it just felt *normal*. I took it for granted. I did not savor the moments, or commit those times to memory because I was in mama's boy denial. I should have taken note every time she would say to me, "Whatever happens, I lived a good life." Or when I would be worried, stressed, or upset that others would want her stuff if something happened to her, she would respond, "There's nothing to get." Those phrases haunt me today, because she was telling me that the time was nigh in her own way.

The last time I saw my mother, I had just finished teaching an English 101 class. One of my former students, who had recently been released from prison, was coming to visit me and I was taking him to get a cheap, pre-paid cellular phone and taking him to dinner with my daughters—something so similar, so *simpatico,* with something my mother would do for her former students. I was rushing because I was excited that this former student had completed his education inside the correctional facility, learned stock market trading, and was really doing well for himself.

She did not feel well that day, so they did not meet. A second round of chemo was debilitating to her system. Instead, I lay next to her on the bed and we talked. She showed me the swelling all over her body, which I now consider the sign of the end for people who have cancer. She was trying to tell me, yet again, I was not paying attention. The denial was so thick, so stubborn, and hardheaded that I could not see until it was too late. Her cancer had metastasized into her lymphatic system and was attacking her organs. Oblivious, I told her, "I won't be in a rush next week, so I will come by after class and sit with you all day!" I do not remember if she responded, but if I could go back, I am sure she gave me the hardest side eye and eye-roll she could.

"I love you!" I exclaimed.

"I love you, too," she responded.

I thought we had time. We *always* think we have time. My mother was gone within forty-eight hours. The pain in the many voicemails I received from my three sisters still rings in my ears and pierces my heart. Say the things you need to say, spend the time, be late, be patient, and be *present*. Because once the time is gone, all you ever want is that time back. I love you, Mommy.

An Unintentional Farewell

By Glenda Braganza

Dad was truly the apple of my eye; to me, he was a superhero hiding in plain sight. An unassuming civil servant, his huge heart and outgoing personality fueled a lust for life. So, when he passed away in July 2015 after a week unconscious in the ICU, there were literally no words.

Shattered, I felt I had been robbed of our goodbye.

A marine engineer, Viv—as most knew him—was a fixer, a traveler, a helper, and social butterfly. I have no clue how he juggled being a family man, serving in the church, and supporting our immigrant community. As the first member of his family to come to Canada, Dad was intent on paying it forward.

From day one, we had a connection. Cut from the same cloth, I shared his constant curiosity and "doer" energy. As much as I enjoyed Mom putting me in dresses and playing with dolls, most times I could be found in the garage or garden assisting Dad. Being invited to join him on runs to Canadian Tire was a thrill. There was nothing like walking in, hand in hand, as that familiar scent hit me.

Growing up as a first-generation kid, his support and patience proved invaluable. Dad did his best to instill traditional values while accepting how different things were for my brother and me. Suburban Ottawa was a world away from India. Dad walked the challenging line of protecting and demonstrating, knowing we would have to spread our wings.

My rebellious teenage years resulted in a desire to go away to university. Despite my parents' fears, I needed space to find out who I was and take ownership of my life. Dad encouraged me to go for it. A phone call away, he often said: "Do your best and have faith in the rest." He inspired me to trust myself, find my own path and carve out a life I loved.

Getting my degree and having Dad walk me down the aisle a few years later were treasured moments—gifts we gave each other. As adult life in Montreal took over, trips home for the holidays were anticipated. In our traditional household, Mom did the cooking, but Dad's love of food couldn't keep him out of the kitchen. He'd tandoori a whole turkey and specially make caramel custard—my favorite. After dinner, we'd play cards for hours while sipping on scotch he'd bought for the occasion.

Then came the blindside: Just after retiring, Dad was diagnosed with an incurable, rapidly progressing lung disease. Rather than relaxing and traveling the world, he faced waiting for—and hopefully surviving—a lung transplant. Our family was in shock and instead of turning to our fearless leader, it was Dad who needed support. I immediately knew I wanted and needed to do everything I could to help save his life. He was only sixty-six and I wasn't about to lose him.

At twenty-nine, I put my career on hold and left my understanding husband to hold down the fort while Dad and I moved into a small apartment in downtown Toronto. For ten months we waited for the call. Dad, constantly hooked up to oxygen, tried to stay as healthy as possible. My days consisted of getting him to appointments, cooking and cleaning, filling portable oxygen tanks, and falling into my futon each night, praying that God would send us an organ donor in time.

It was a difficult period. Dad was doing his best, keeping his trademark positive attitude while struggling to get through the day. I didn't realize that while he wrestled with his mortality, I was experiencing anticipatory grief—something very common amongst caregivers that I'd learn about later. I was too busy to process the fact that he might die so soon. The silver lining? As an adult, I got to know Dad even better; we went to the movies,

   Goodbye for Now

played cards, and explored nearby restaurants. This gave me the precious opportunity to show and tell him how much he meant to me.

Then, in January 2009, we were blessed with a donor and Dad received a new lung. A full recovery allowed him to relish this gift of extended life. Finally getting to his bucket list, he and mom visited Egypt, China, Greece, and Turkey, to name a few. Now, everyone knew he was Superman. Except he was on borrowed time.

The doctors said five years, but he made it last six and a half. Dad caught pneumonia which unexpectedly turned to sepsis. Due to his weakened immune system, he had to be ventilated immediately. By the time I got to the ICU Dad was already unconscious. All I could do was hold his hand, watching helplessly as his body shut down. We made the painful decision to turn off the machines. With my hand over his heart, he peacefully took his last breath, and for the first time ever, my rock was gone.

Even though we didn't get to say our goodbyes, I've come to realize that Dad already knew how much he meant to me, how grateful I was to be his daughter. I got the chance to show him while he was alive, a reflection of his unconditional love and service to those he cared about. Our farewell wasn't a tearful goodbye, it was a living embodiment of our connection and life together.

Flotsam and Jetsam

by Angélique Davies

Flotsam

In October 2000, my mother died in her sleep. The doctors said it was a heart attack. I believe her mind and body were exhausted from the power she gave her personal demons, and the effort required to battle them. At fifty-nine, she was finally free from her troubles. *Would I be free too?*

The previous evening, we'd argued on the phone. Again. *I'm hanging up now.* I'd begun saying this to avoid getting lured in. What I didn't say this time was, *goodbye.*

When my father told me Mom was gone, debris from the past came pounding on my shore. Growing up, I couldn't feel her love. She was mercurial, as dark and changeable as a river. I built a protective breakwall against her unpredictable moods. Each day, I didn't know who she'd be, how she'd feel, or what she'd want. I feared her. But she was my mother, and I loved her.

Mom was adventurous. She rode a motorcycle. She scoured yard sales and antique fairs for treasures. When hosting parties, she cooked excellent coq au vin. With a style like Grace Kelly, Mom adored sequined dresses and feathered mules. She was a photographer. A perfectionist, she stitched miniature Oriental rugs in petit point. She was my father's first mate during the many summers we spent on our boat. Mom loved Edith Piaf, and "La Vie en Rose" was played at her funeral. Listening to this song, his eyes closed,

Dad wept. But I didn't cry. Instead, I apologized for being none of the things that Mom was. For disappointing her.

Dad was soon diagnosed with terminal cancer and became too sick to answer any questions about Mom: *Why couldn't she accept me? What made her so controlling? Did she always have to be so critical?* Unlike Mom, Dad had not been overinvolved in my life and had let me know I was loved. But I had left home anyway to save myself. *Jump the sinking ship and swim, or stay aboard and drown.*

After Dad died, memories resurfaced like flotsam. Letters. Photos. Her voice in my head. Moving away hadn't freed me from my mother's grasp, but diving in and making sense of the wreckage might help me let her go.

Jetsam

I think Mom didn't enjoy being a mother. She always seemed so unhappy with her life. It took time for me to consider her perspective. What had happened to her?

Mom's childhood had been difficult. At convent school, she was called "a dirty Indian." Was marrying a British man at the age of nineteen a way to escape her French-Canadian family and Indigenous heritage? She often expressed profound guilt—about who she was, how she felt, and what she wanted. Having children so young gave her no escape. Mom was raised with 1950s values, influenced by society's expectation that she be an ideal wife, a good housekeeper, and a nurturing mother. An allowance from my father and "Baby Bonus" cheques were what gave her financial freedom. Perhaps realizing that her daughter could live independently, study, work, have different relationships, and enjoy self-discovery, left Mom feeling robbed of such choices. In response, she scuppered my efforts to sail forward and explore my own horizons.

As a child, I never questioned my mother's authority—even when it confused me. In adolescence, when friends opened up the world beyond my family, Mom asserted increasing control: *Your friends are unacceptable. You can't wear that. Who said you could go out?* As the conflicts escalated, I began lying about my activities, and would feel guilty for wanting to do normal things my friends could do freely. But I was terrified of getting caught. *As long as you live under my roof, you'll follow my rules.*

Living this way became intolerable for me. Dad knew I was sinking, but he could offer no lifeline. My parents seemed astonished when I actually left home. Moving away, however, felt more like an act of betrayal than a proud achievement. Mom never acknowledged the significance of my departure. She never visited my apartment.

And we never said *goodbye.*

I know now that Mom struggled with mental illness, and that she did her best. I mourn our lost opportunity to talk, to understand each other, and to have a normal relationship. But I've learned that even broken love can be repaired and become something new. Perhaps it is no accident that my career has involved teaching young children, writing parenting resources, and developing a trauma-informed curriculum for educators. Hopefully, this will help others. Since Mom's death, I've viewed these memories through different eyes. They will never leave me. They just can't hurt me anymore.

Mom and I did experience some happy times—mostly during those summers on the boat, when I was very young and our relationship seemed less complicated. In my favourite photograph, we sit holding only each other. The water is peaceful, our turbulent emotional cargo tossed overboard. I watch as our sorrow disappears with the undertow. It is jetsam now.

I love you, Mom.

I love you too.

Dad

By Cynthia Thompson

I lost my father to Parkinson's in July 2019, on a night that should have been the happiest of my life. The love of my life had proposed hours before, and we were on our way home from celebrating when the phone rang with the call I had been dreading. Dad was gone. I didn't want to believe it. How could a man who meant so much to so many be taken by such a vicious disease? How was I supposed to say goodbye?

It had been a long, arduous journey home, but as I sat in the car crying while my fiancé drove, I realized that I said goodbye to him long before he was gone. Years before the disease took away my father, it had already stolen my Superman. Watching his slow decline was like witnessing the disintegration of a hero I thought would always be invincible.

My dad was raised primarily by his mother and grandmother after his father passed away from a heart attack when he was only fourteen. This loss shaped my father in ways I still don't fully understand. Though he loved baseball, hunting, and all things manly, he wasn't above sitting in my room and having a tea party with me. All these years later, I can still see him sitting there sipping his "tea" like it was the best thing on earth.

That memory is etched in my mind now that I'm a parent. I know he was exhausted, but he took the time to sit and have a tea party with me while also making sure to spend time playing soccer with my twin brother. I can only now appreciate the selflessness of the man I call Superman.

Throughout my childhood, I watched my dad struggle, especially through the oil crisis of the 1980s. The industry downturn hit hard, and I could see the weight of the world on his shoulders. But he never gave up. He fought through the adversity and came out stronger, eventually becoming a top salesman for a medical company. His resilience and determination were awe-inspiring. He was my role model, my pillar of strength, and my Superman.

As Parkinson's began to take hold, I noticed subtle changes at first. His hands trembled slightly, his movements became less fluid, his feet shuffled across the floor, and his once-booming voice became hoarse and raspy. These small signs were easy to overlook initially, but they gradually grew more pronounced. The disease crept into our lives, insidious and unrelenting. It wasn't just his physical abilities that deteriorated; it was his spirit, too. The man who had once seemed unbreakable was now fighting a battle he couldn't win, and he knew it.

I remember the day the doctor told us it was no longer safe for him to drive. For a man who spent his life on the road, this was a tough pill to swallow. As a family, we sat in our living room and did our best to make him understand. It broke my heart to see the light go out of his eyes. I could tell that driving was the last thing he had left, the last symbol of the man he once was. It was a devastating blow to his independence and a stark reminder of his vulnerability. The car keys, once a symbol of freedom, now lay locked inside a drawer. He tried to maintain his dignity, but I could see the frustration and sadness in his eyes. Every small loss chipped away at him, and I found myself mourning those pieces of him even as he still lived.

The hardest part was watching the light fade from his eyes. My father, who had always been so full of life and humor, became a shadow of his former self. The man who always made everyone feel like they were the most important person in the room was gone. Conversations became shorter, his laughter rarer. He was trapped in a body and mind that no longer worked, and it broke my heart. I missed our long talks and his stories about his childhood. I missed the way his eyes would light up when he talked about his dad, whom he had lost so young.

When I got the phone call after midnight the night I got engaged, I cried tears of sadness, anger, and relief. The sadness was for the finality of his passing, the undeniable truth that he was gone. The anger was for the years Parkinson's had stolen from him and from us. But the relief, that was for him. My father was no longer trapped in a body that betrayed him, no longer confined to a mind that couldn't keep up with his spirit. He was free, and I found solace in the thought that he was reunited with his father, whom he had missed terribly for so many years.

I will always love my Pops. He taught me more about strength, resilience, and love than anyone else ever could. His struggle with Parkinson's was a testament to his enduring spirit, even as the disease tried to take everything from him. Saying goodbye is never easy, but sometimes, when we truly love someone, it is the best thing we can do. Letting go was an act of love, a way to release him from the suffering he had endured for so long. As I move forward with my life, I carry his memory with me. His legacy lives on in the lessons he taught me, in the strength he instilled in me, and in the love he gave me. Losing him was one of the hardest things I've ever faced, but it also taught me the depth of my own resilience and the power of unconditional love.

Fred Gurnham: A Man of Modest Courage

By Brian Gurnham

"You can never have too many friends." Most young teenagers, and I was no exception, would not always heed a parent's advice. However, those words, spoken by my father, Fred Gurnham, have remained with me to this day.

My dad was born on March 27, 1926, in Montreal, Quebec. He was a miracle baby, having arrived three months prematurely. At that time, he was one of the first babies to be cared for in an incubator.

Fred attended school in Valleyfield, Quebec, where his father was employed at The Montreal Cottons Textile Company. Academics took second place to his love of sports, especially football and hockey. Although favouring physical pursuits over studies, Dad did receive third place over-all marks in his grade seven class. I discovered this in a book awarded to him when I was at my grandparents' home one day. When I had asked Dad about this, he told me, in humour typical of his personality, that his seventh-grade teacher had boarded with his family, thereby ensuring that homework was an accomplished feat.

After his public schooling, World War II was a stark reality. Eager to enlist, Dad joined The Royal Canadian Navy at the age of seventeen. Soon after his basic training camp, he was engaged in combat as a gunner aboard ships in the Atlantic. Like many veterans, who had experienced war, Dad rarely mentioned his military experience.

What he often did recall was his time in the first few years immediately after the war. This was when Dad served in The Canadian Merchant Marine. During this period in his life, he sailed to many exotic and faraway places, enjoying great experiences for a young man while being employed. Dad had survived the war years unscathed, but he did sustain a serious injury during his merchant marine years when a cargo hold became loose and fell onto his foot, thus abruptly ending his career upon the seas.

Upon his medical release from The Merchant Marine, Dad went to his sister's farm in Waterloo, Quebec, to convalesce. Waterloo was where, in 1948, he met my mother, Nancy Robinson. Three years later, they were married. Into the family eventually arrived me and my two brothers. Dad enjoyed spending time with the three of us whenever his work as a sales manager would permit. During our formative years he was greatly involved in the Boy Scouts movement, first as a leader and, eventually, in the role of district commissioner.

In time, I became married to my lovely wife, Diane. Later we welcomed our two beautiful daughters, Alison and Heather. Even though geographic distance separated my family and my parents, the times we would spend together were precious. Dad was a loving and fun grandparent to my two girls.

In retirement, my parents moved from Montreal to Victoria, British Columbia. For several years, Dad volunteered at the Maritime Museum of British Columbia. His past experience in the navy made Dad a natural fit for guiding tours, which he could conduct in French as well as in English. For him, his time spent at the museum was a labour of love.

My father passed away on November 21, 2001, at the age of seventy-five, after a valiant battle with cancer. During his illness, I was often amazed at how he never complained. After he died, I expressed to my mother that he must have been stoic in order to shield both his children and his grandchildren. To my surprise, Mom said that he had never complained to her either. He was brave to the end. Sadly, I had lost my father, but because of his famous words, years ago, I have acquired many friends over the ensuing times of my life.

He Knew Me

By Ronda Williams

By the time I arrived at his bedside, he could no longer speak. Shocked at his condition, I wept in anguish. I had never seen my dad so helpless. When he finally opened his tired, hazel eyes, a peaceful gaze of familiarity met mine. He knew me. I had prayed it for years: *Please, God, let him always know me.*

Talking about nearly anything had come naturally between us all my life, but now, like the wind, that was gone, replaced by a silent, wrenching chasm. I held his hand and stroked his head as reflections of the life we shared began to surface.

When I was young, he carried me on his shoulders to the lake, where we fed the ducks. Later, he steadied my two-wheeler during lessons in the grass. Rainy weekends held board games on the kitchen table, while fishing, swimming, picnics, and vacations brightened summer days.

He was a manufacturing engineer and knew I loved to draw, so he brought home discarded work paper for me to sketch on. When I volunteered to create a donkey for the Christmas play, he carefully sawed the wood along the lines of my drawing and then helped me paper mâché and paint it.

As I grew older, we played countless games of tennis, ping pong, and pool. He taught me how to drive a riding lawn mower, a minibike, the family station wagon, and a stick shift pre-owned car that he brought home as a surprise. It was yellow, my favorite color. He also taught me how to drive on an interstate. Each time I approached an exit, he nervously waved his hand to the left just in case my teenage mind thought my lane veered to the right and up a ramp.

He was an army veteran—a paratrooper—and a jack of all trades. He fixed our cars, and he remodeled our house. When I was ten years old, he knew I wanted to be a teacher, so he crafted a full-sized desk with four drawers so I could play school. One spring day, he brought home a Bridgestone 175 motorcycle in a box from a garage sale. When he finally finished putting it together, he gave me the first ride to town.

He believed in women's rights, so he pushed me to stand up for myself, but sometimes he chose to intervene. After a shift of bussing tables, I complained to him that my boss had been picking on me for weeks. After hearing the details, he grabbed his keys, drove to the restaurant, called my boss a "pipsqueak," and informed him that his daughter would no longer be working there.

Throughout my adult years, we remained close, but not in location. I moved out of state after finishing college and getting married, and then he moved even farther away to play golf nearly year-round. The decades took their toll when he began losing his memory and his bearings. For the first time on one of my visits, I drove him to what he called "my place," which was adult daycare. There, I was cruelly introduced to what he had become: one of many who sat and stared, repeated the same questions, recited the same answers, and possessed no point of reference. For too long, I had pretended that he wasn't so ill. That day, the harsh truth pierced my heart like an awl: I had forever lost the intelligent, witty dad whom I had always known. Grief overwhelmed me.

Now, I stood facing a different kind of grief, fumbling to find a voice and the words to say goodbye to this shell of a remarkable man whom I had and always would call "Dad." After dwelling on the serene garden through the French doors beyond his bed, I used my phone to begin recording:

This is my sweet dad—been the best dad ever to me; always there for me, standing up for me … taking us on vacations, helping us with school projects—wonderful man. He got himself a college degree out of the army and then another college degree. We graduated the same year—1984. Funny guy—everybody likes him.

I've been told that you might have just two days left, and I don't want to miss this opportunity, Dad, to read to you. "The Lord is my shepherd …"

Thank you, God, for giving me this man for my dad. It was a wonderful gift. I love you, Dad. I'll always love you, and I'll miss you so much. The angels will be here to take you, and you'll see God's glory, and you'll be well. You'll be able to think and talk. You'll be like a young man. You'll be whole, and you'll behold the face of the living God.

Three days later, on Sunday, after I sang several songs to him, I whispered in his ear, "It's okay to go, Dad. Look to the light. Look to Jesus."

He turned his head toward me, our eyes met, and he clearly spoke, "Jesus."

The sorrow of letting Dad go is now a fading memory compared to happier ones from the more distant past. I can still hear his voice, but it resonates with the lively tone I memorized as a child. I can still see his face, but it mirrors the younger, vibrant version of him I knew best. I can still see his hazel eyes each time I look in the mirror. He is a part of me and always will be. Most precious of all, though, he knew me. From my first breath of life to his last, he knew me.

Remembering Margaret

By Susan Hartzler

Margaret Agnes McGill Hartzler, affectionately known as Mom to me, had her own unique way of enjoying life to the fullest and imparting that wisdom to me. With her knack for uncovering the humanity in everything, she made friends wherever she went. The clerks at the grocery store, the mailman, employees at Macy's, and even my friends from high school were all captivated by this unconventional woman.

Standing at a petite five foot two, Mom had the appearance of a cupcake, with her frosted brown hair cut short and teased high—ironic, considering she was anything but sweet. Tenacious? Yes. Opinionated? Yes. Witty? Yes. Clever? Yes. But sweetness? That was not her forte.

Hailing from the quaint town of St. Johnsbury, Vermont, Mom embodied the values of rural simplicity and boundless kindness. Her career as a first-grade teacher stood as a testament to her strength and resilience, creating an environment where young minds felt safe and inspired to learn.

I was her youngest daughter, the black sheep of the family. Unlike my sister and brother, who followed Mom's strict rules and seemed perfect—or so she proudly proclaimed—our relationship was strained. Her high expectations and demand for perfection fueled my teenage rebellion. As a result, Mom and I clashed, our stubbornness creating deep divides that often felt

"

impossible to bridge. My rebellion against her started when I hit puberty. Fueled by raging hormones and a burgeoning sense of independence, I resisted her overbearing attitude. Well into my twenties, our relationship remained tumultuous, further straining our bond. It wasn't until my late thirties that a shift occurred. Perhaps it was maturity or a newfound appreciation for life's fleeting nature, but from then on, we both worked diligently to mend our relationship. Her passion for shopping became a trait I inherited from her. She particularly relished sales and would enthusiastically share stories about her latest bargain finds with anyone who would listen. Additionally, she had a habit of returning items she second-guessed. From her, I learned the wisdom of keeping the price tag on until I actually wore something.

She also instilled in me a deep love for animals, particularly dogs. When the veterinarian suggested putting down our family mutt, Siesta, Mom couldn't do it. Instead, she brought Siesta home and treated her to a donut. That dog lived six more years to the ripe old age of twenty. Later, just six months before she passed away, Mom surprised me with a rescue dog—a living testament to the bond we fought so hard to build.

One thing that always fascinated me was Mom's family history. From a young age, whenever I showed interest, she eagerly shared stories of her past while we pored over old photographs retrieved from the bottom drawer of her dresser. I would spend hours sitting beside her, enthralled by her childhood memories and surrounded by sepia-toned images of grandparents and distant relatives, each picture a portal to a bygone era.

Mom died suddenly in her sleep the morning after her eightieth birthday. After her passing, I found myself drawn to that dresser drawer, a treasure trove of memories. But the old images were gone. Envelopes, papers, and photos from my childhood replaced them. I found a plain white envelope on the top of the stack. Mom's perfect handwriting spelled out my name, the capital S-curved, so it looked like a work of art. "Susan's first tooth," I read aloud, peeking inside to find a single tiny white baby tooth.

I found another envelope labeled "Susan's first haircut." A lock of my white-blond hair tied with a pink ribbon had been carefully placed inside. I pulled out my baby announcement and remembered how Mom told me she taped bows to my bald head so everyone would know I was a girl. I

     Goodbye for Now

found a picture of me on grad night in 1976. My Farrah Fawcett hair was perfectly in place, and my white pantsuit with low rider bell bottoms complemented a tight, button-down plaid blouse. Mom took me shopping for that outfit.

I fanned a stack of report cards—all mine. I found pictures of me as a toddler, pictures of me in grade school, high school, and at the prom. I uncovered announcements sent to Mom when I made the dean's list in junior high and again in college.

"It's all me. Everything in this drawer is me. She did this; she moved the old photos and replaced them with all this stuff about me. She knew I'd come here." At that moment, all the painful memories of the tension between me and Mom faded away. The resentments I'd carried for so long disappeared. The proof of Mom's true feelings for her youngest daughter was right before me. She loved me.

I imagined Mom reaching out to do something I'd wanted her to do my entire life. In my imagination, she cradled me in her arms, rocked me back and forth, and let me cry. I saw myself as a child, sitting at her side, my arms wrapped around her leg, my head in her lap. She stroked my hair and leaned as close as possible to whisper in my ear like mothers do: "There, there, baby girl, I'm here for you. I love you no matter what, and everything will be all right."

Though I didn't have the chance to say goodbye, I honor Mom's memory in a way that reflects her quirky spirit. In her memory, I visit her favorite store, Macy's, each year on her birthday. I select something special for her, buy it, and then return it the following day, on the anniversary of her passing. Afterward, I indulge in a cupcake—chocolate with white frosting. It may seem unconventional to some, but I believe Mom would appreciate the sentiment—a lighthearted yet heartfelt way to commemorate an unforgettable mom and her love for life's simple pleasures. Rest in peace, little cupcake, rest in peace.

Life Lessons From Dad

By Lisa Muldoon

My father, Keith Muldoon, spent forty-five years in education as both a teacher and a principal. He devoted his career and his life to educating others. Teaching was never a job for him; it was truly a calling. He wanted to make a difference. His sudden death at sixty-five, just six short months after his retirement, came as a huge surprise to all of us. He left a "dad-sized" hole in our lives, but his passing has given me the opportunity to reflect upon his life, and the things he taught me during the time we had together.

My dad taught me the importance of loving and prioritizing family. He married my mom, and I was born a few years later. Our family was complete when my parents adopted my little sister from an orphanage in China when I was twenty-three years old. Family was everything to him, as evidenced by the way he fiercely loved and cared for my mother, my sister, and myself. We were his three girls, and he never hesitated to consistently put our needs before his. Together with my mom, he helped create memories that made our time spent together very special. Christmas holidays, family meals, trips, birthday parties—he made sure that all of these experiences were documented with the family camcorder and commemorated on VHS forever. He also had a special place in his heart for his parents,

Goodbye for Now

parents-in-law, his five siblings, and their families, always willing to visit, support, and be there for them.

My dad taught me about his faith and having a personal relationship with God. Being a part of a church community was important to our family. He modelled the importance of taking time for prayer and devotions. He loved Christian music, and sang in choirs. He enjoyed teachings and messages on Christian radio because he said it helped to focus his heart and mind on the right things. Volunteering at church, and serving at events and camps, were priorities in our family.

My dad taught me to have a sense of humor. He loved to have fun and he loved to laugh. Through the jokes, pranks, and light-heartedness, we would laugh together, at times making somewhat difficult situations better. As I got older, we would still talk on the phone or email almost every day. We enjoyed many laughs, sharing stories from funny and ridiculous events that had happened at school and things we had encountered throughout the day.

My dad taught me the value of time and showing up. He was always there. He did not miss a graduation, sporting event, game, concert, musical, or play that he could reasonably get to. He spent copious amounts of time driving and shuttling me all over the province: delivering things, attending events, and taking me out to eat. He also helped me mark and figure out the best way to explain math to my students. He spent so much time—all hours of the night—editing my assignments, papers, and, eventually, my master's thesis. When I purchased my first house, he was there to help me take care of the endless fixing and maintenance that goes along with home ownership. Even when I was an adult, he came to my hockey games and cheered for me from the sidelines. He was always there for me.

My dad taught me to be positive and to focus on the good in people. He would always find something positive to say or share at the start of a meeting, conversation, or in an email. He made sure I knew how much he loved me and how proud he was of me. He knew that those little things mattered and he never passed up an opportunity to say something nice to someone or write them a positive card or note. Particularly, when talking to the parents of my students, he would remind me to slip in something positive, some praise, into the conversation—even something small. He said that one of the greatest things parents love to hear is something good about their child.

My dad taught me that relationships matter. He taught me to learn and use the names of people you interact and work with; find a way to connect and learn more about them. From the school custodian to the superintendent of education—make every person feel valued and important. After his passing, I remember one of his colleagues saying that she will never forget how much my father cared. She said he was a remarkable individual who counselled staff in distress, helped teachers and educational assistants with their students, and was attentive to parents who needed a listening ear. He always listened to others, gave suggestions, and cared about everyone. She said my dad demonstrated to others what a good person does and says every day.

My dad taught me to be even-keeled, quick to listen, and slow to speak. He talked about listening to the whole story. He admitted to having a temper, and I know at times that there were things that angered and upset him, particularly if he felt someone had unfairly treated one of his family members. He would deal with it immediately, when necessary; more often, he would take some time to think about it, hear the whole story, and follow up with a lengthy but well-thought-out letter or email to help address the situation.

My dad is gone, but he is not forgotten. He was my mentor, and my friend. That "dad-sized" hole will never be filled, but reminders of him are with me always; things he wrote and things he said. He would be the first to admit that he wasn't perfect and that he made mistakes, but I know I'm challenged to be a better person and to make a difference through the lessons he taught me throughout his life.

The Unspoken Loss

By Gigi Smith

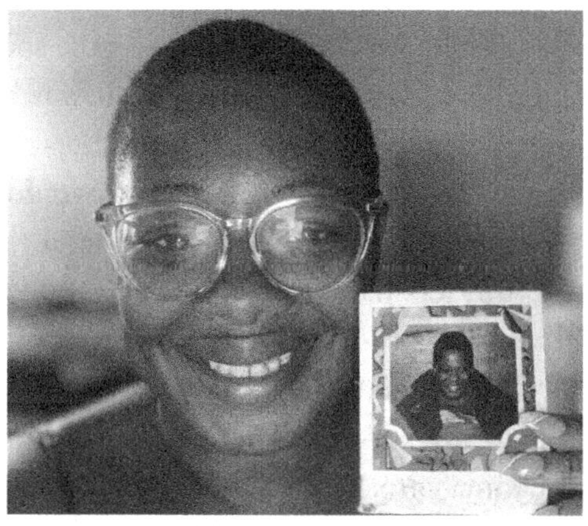

"You're one of the lucky ones," they say. It is an unforgiving, sharp cut to the heart of adoptees—especially those brave enough to share their HORRIFYING experiences with their adoptive families. The unspoken truth is that, no matter what, adoption is a big loss, and few understand how it feels or how to talk about it. So, the grief and loss many adoptees feel go unaddressed and unspoken.

I was three years old when I last saw my biological mother, Toni. It took me twenty-four years and several therapists to fully grieve that loss in all its complexity—and obtaining a few degrees in mental health myself. This loss is unspoken, and uttering even a whisper of it drudges up feelings on both sides. For adoptive parents, it's "Am I good enough?" For adoptees, it's "Where are the people who look like me?" In many cases like mine, it goes unspoken out of guilt or fear—though it is a healthy feeling to explore, as I learned through my studies. Children often feel guilty about things beyond their control, like parental actions. This is something the woman who adopted me never understood, but the mother I was taken from did.

My greatest loss was my mother, Toni. Most people would think of a woman who had her child taken away as a failure. Not me! My mother was my hero, my savior, my one true north in a world plagued by the uncertainty of poverty. She sang to me when I was sad or afraid, she named me, and all she could see when she looked at me was someone simply "precious." She taught me to pray, hope, and be great by being myself!

I lost her when I was three because the mother who adopted me was the opposite. To ensure I thought nothing of myself, my adoptive mother cursed the day I was born. I was not allowed to talk about my biological mother. As a young child with so much trauma, it was hard to remember Toni the way we were. My adoptive mother would teach me by saying *my mother* (her words) gave me up because she knew I would be worthless and ugly! She said this so many times that I tried to forget the mother I knew because I believed all mothers hated me.

It wasn't until I was twenty-seven that I received old letters from my former foster parent. These letters stay close to my heart but also burn scars into my soul. Thanks to my adoptive mother, I could only remember my birth mother as someone who hated me. However, in these letters, my mother begged my adoptive parents to take care of me and to remember that I was destined for greatness. At that moment, I felt the unspoken loss. I felt profound sadness and heart-lifting joy. My mother loved me and wanted what was best for me! She had tried everything she could to provide for herself and me. Reading her words was like being torn in two. I was overjoyed to reconnect with her through these letters but also heart-broken. I had grown to hate this woman for what I thought she had done or said. The pain never left, but I grew around my grief. I grew enough to understand that even though I lost physical time with my mom, I didn't lose who I was to her. We were taken from each other, a loss that pains me to this day. One thing about grief that is so painful is remembering that, at one point, it was the last time—especially since we won't meet again in this life. So, the words remain unheard, and the loss stays forever unspoken.

The grief faced by many adoptees is unique. It's not about creating new grief but giving voice to the existing unspoken grief. As a collective, we share in certain griefs—the loss of a pet or loved one. However, a category of grief remains unspoken, encased forever in silence. This grief takes many forms, from never having a chance to say goodbye to wishing it was good-bye. Silent grief makes invisible mourners. I know because I have been one. I never got to say goodbye to my mother, Toni, and it haunted me until I

   Goodbye for Now

realized she wrote to me for a reason. That's how I grew bigger around my grief. I took everything she believed about me and turned it into an incredible life filled with everything she had hoped for me. I may never be able to say goodbye to her, but every day, I say thank you.

Charles Roy Reid:
Much More Than a Security Guard

By Chuck Reid

It is a common cliché, but it rings painfully true: we often fail to appreciate what we have until it's gone. Such was the relationship I had with my father. He was defined not by his occupation but by how he lived his life. My mistake was taking a man who held a wealth of life's wisdom and loved me unconditionally for granted.

Standing just under six feet tall, with a muscular build and dark wavy hair, my father was a striking presence in any crowd. He was a security guard at the International Harvester plant in Hamilton, Ontario, for thirty years. After retiring, he spent another ten years working part-time at Canadian Tire, selling tools.

A staunchly conservative man, my father's actions were framed by strong convictions about right and wrong, with little room for gray areas. What set him apart from many of his generation was his deep belief in human rights. He did not measure a person's worth by race, creed, or religious beliefs but by how they acted out their principles. This was evident in the diversity of his circle of friends. Their common bond was a shared set of values, not appearance or faith. For him, principled individual choices were to be respected. When it came time for me to be confirmed in the Church, for example, instead of assuming I would follow our family's tradition, Dad advised me to make an informed personal decision. He supported my attendance at several different religious denominations in our area, allowing me to choose my own path.

Countless vignettes could be used to paint a fuller picture of my father's life and character. There is the memory of four-year-old Patti, my best friend's little sister, knocking on the back door, asking if Mr. Reid was "coming out to play." It was not unusual to return home and find my father sharing company with one of my friends. This even extended to my former girlfriends, more than one of whom would visit my parents with their new partners. Dad became a trusted confidant and father figure to everyone who crossed his path.

Dad had a strong commitment to community service. He actively participated in United Way campaigns, blood drives, and Christmas food drives. Scouting was one of his greatest passions, and over two years, he successfully built a small pack of twenty boys into three troops, numbering over three hundred. Within three years, he had become one of the regional commissioners for scouting in Hamilton. Although he did not own a business, he was invited to join and serve on the Stoney Creek Business Men's Club, where he dedicated himself to community service. He was a man defined by his actions, with an unwavering commitment to his fellow neighbors and the community.

Like most young people in our working-class neighborhood, my summers were devoted to summer jobs. With Dad's shift work and community service and my school and work schedule, my father and I lead parallel lives with limited opportunities to connect. It was my father who ensured we maintained a quality bond—a bond I have duplicated with my own children.

When I was sixteen, on Christmas Eve, he asked me to join him in the recreation room, where he poured us each a shot of Canadian Club despite my being under the legal drinking age.

He smiled and said, "Don't tell your mother." After downing the toast, he declared we would have one drink together every Christmas Eve. We continued this tradition until his death, sometimes meeting and sharing a toast at the front gate of the International Harvester as he completed his shift.

On my twenty-first birthday, my father asked me to meet him at Van Wagner's beach. There, on the shores of Lake Ontario, he gave me a long gold chain with a Saint Christopher medal attached. He stressed that the chain was not a piece of jewelry but a reminder that he would always be with me, like Saint Christopher, guiding me through life's journey. I have worn the chain every day since and have passed on an identical one to each of my children.

When cancer struck, it struck hard. My father was given three months to live, but his will was strong, and he fought for six more months. His once 190-lb. muscular frame was reduced to just 85 lb. I was in Edmonton attending meetings when I received the call that he might pass away in the next forty-eight hours. I caught the next available flight to Toronto but missed him by just one hour. At the age of seventy-two, he died peacefully in his bed in Simcoe, Ontario, thanking his nurse for her care before slipping into an eternal sleep.

Over three days, a stream of people came to pay their respects to my father—men he had supported in their youth as their scout leader, colleagues, and neighbors. Even the young ladies I had once dated came with their families to say goodbye.

Sadly, I know my story will be repeated. We all become so consumed by the daily demands of our immediate family and work that we often take those who laid the foundation for our success for granted. I greatly miss the security guard, my father, who demonstrated that a person's worth is not measured by their position in life but by how they live it for others. The gold chain I wear is a constant reminder of him, and the Christmas Eve toasts continue, knowing his spirit is there, raising his glass with me.

Only Yesterday

By Rochelle Lazarte

The day I moved out of our family home and into my new apartment for the first time, all I could think about was *Nanay*—the Tagalog word for *Mom.*

And all I could think of since I moved to my apartment was that if *she* were there, she would've fixed it up much more nicely and made it homier. She would've brought her warmth with her. She would've decorated every corner with plants and tacky curtains that would eventually grow on me, and the house would smell like fried garlic at 5 a.m. because that's how early she used to make breakfast.

I'm sure I'm not alone when I say that I never really imagined a life without my mother. She was a constant commanding presence in my life, even into adulthood. And Filipino moms are very hands-on. She loved taking care of everything and everyone. I'm the youngest of three kids, and my mom was a full-time mom until I turned eighteen. And even after that, after she no longer *had to* take care of her adult kids, she needed to take someone into her care. She needed to nurture something. And so we ended up with ten dogs. And her plant collection grew, with our small garden looking more like a mini forest of colorful orchids and crawling pothos circling the front window and the door frame of our house. The house was full of life and warmth because of my mom—but that still wasn't enough for her.

She had more space in her full hands to take care of people. She had space for a whole town. So she ran for councilor in our small town or *barangay,* where she was in charge of allotting the budget for the town

"

projects, ensuring everything checked out and everyone on payroll was paid on time. She was a fifty-something former full-time mom with no background in finance or politics whatsoever, but she did the job with so much passion and dedication that even years after she retired, those who knew her still affectionately called her *konsi*—short for konsehal, the Tagalog word for councilor.

Eventually, everyone in the family grew older and moved out. Only my mom and I were left in our family home. But she still found ways to be busy and to do something for someone. She entertained neighbors who came by our house to ask for help with local town matters, even when she was no longer councilor. When my dad died and my brother married, she never wavered in her routine: wake up early to make breakfast, water the plants, feed the dogs, clean the house, and finally settle in her favorite chair to watch videos on Facebook from her phone. She was the most selfless person I knew, content in her little life and always wanting to care for others however she could.

Shortly after COVID hit, my mom began to lose weight. She also began to look more tired and frail—her favorite sundresses were wearing her. With all the checkpoints and restrictions, we finally found a way for her to get some tests done, but by then her condition had worsened. After a preliminary ultrasound and CT scan, the doctors were sure it was colon cancer.

I wanted to do everything for my mom. I had never felt so useless and helpless for the woman who had done everything for me and cared for me my entire life. We didn't have enough money as it was, but because of COVID, the options the doctors gave us meant we would face instant bankruptcy. My mother, who always said she never wanted to be a burden, declined. She said she would stay at home and manage the pain.

The last two months before my mom died were a blur. The constant pain she felt didn't allow her to sleep anymore, so we all tried to be there for her at her constant beck and call. It was the least we could do. All those months before and until now, years after she died, the guilt still weighs on me. Some days, it weighs heavier than grief.

The last time she was rushed to the emergency room, the doctor told us they would need to operate on her, but the risk was higher, and she might

 Goodbye for Now

not make it. Before the nurses wheeled her away to admit her, I whispered "*Mahal kita*" (I love you) to my mother for the first and last time. I stayed with her that night, holding her hand. I thought she was sleeping soundly, and she was visibly breathing, but when the nurse checked the urine bag and saw that it was empty that morning, she immediately called the doctor to revive my mom.

I thought I had felt helpless before, but there is nothing worse than seeing a bunch of doctors and nurses trying to resuscitate your mother while you stand alone in the corner crying. I don't know how long it was, but it felt like forever. Even after the doctor told me she was gone, even after the nurse cleaned her up and covered her with her blanket, I just sat with her, crying uncontrollably.

It is one thing to know someone has died. It was another to watch your mother—the one who gave birth to you, the first face you saw and recognized, the one constant person in your life—die right in front of you.

I'm writing this years later, long after I settled in the apartment. But I'm not sure I've learned how to say goodbye yet, even though I've let go of our house and all the memories in it. On most days, it feels like it happened only yesterday. But I also get some quiet days when I get to miss *Nanay* and remember her vibrant energy, off-key singing, and the warmth she brought into many lives. I know I have a long way to go until acceptance, but I'm taking it one step at a time, writing about *Nanay* one story at a time.

A Stepfather's Affection

By Abriana Gardley

Bold and stern. That was my stepfather. But he could effortlessly make you laugh. Unfortunately, our close-knit family has been doing quite the opposite since his passing.

My stepfather would give away his very last coin—even his very last item of furniture—but not his very last piece of steak. As much as he loved to eat meat and avoid veggies, he loved his children and his wife, who is my mother. My stepfather always knew he had a duty to serve as a father figure for me, even though I was in my thirties. He taught me how to stand up for myself and how to be who I am. He was never afraid to say what was on his mind, even when it rubbed folks the wrong way. He never lied, and his heart was always in the right place.

A funny memory I have of him is when he sat me down and asked a million questions about a guy I was dating. Of course, he was mocking my date and mentioning different ways he wasn't good enough for me. While he was standing at the door watching me get into the guy's car, he did the "I'm watching you" hand gesture with two fingers at his eyes and then on us. I couldn't help but bust out laughing.

There's also the time when he gave me a mini jujitsu lesson, trying to make sure I stayed on my toes if anyone ever tried to attack me. He snuck up behind me and put me in a light headlock (playfully, of course) and said, "Whatcha gonna do? You know your next move?"

Three years ago, he sat me down on a more serious note. My mother had talked to him about my strained relationship with my biological father and gone into detail about it. He let me know how sorry he was about the things that had transpired and reassured me that he would always make me feel welcomed and loved. He told me he loved me and gave me a hug for the first time. (I was still getting to know him at the time since he and my mother had just gotten together.)

Two days after New Year's Eve in 2023, he was diagnosed with stage four throat and bone cancer. My mother and he had just come home from the doctor's office; they had gone after noticing a lump on his neck. Hearing him state his diagnosis in such a calm and unusually content manner shook me. I actually thought he was joking until I saw the look on my mother's face.

As the months went by and they both spent hours attending his chemo treatments, he remained in good spirits. One funny memory that lives in my head rent free is the time he needed to go to one of his appointments but my mother had an injury and wasn't able to drive. My mom said to him, "Let Bee (my nickname) drive you."

He immediately exclaimed, "HECK NO! THERE'S NO WAY I'M GOING THROUGH THAT TOO!"

Him making fun of my driving left me a little hurt but more bent over from laughter at his resistance.

On May 30, 2024, we had to say goodbye for now. He had been admitted to the hospital two weeks prior as his health was declining, but we kept our faith and hope. The night before his passing, he wasn't vocal at all. The tumor had grown so big that he couldn't speak very well. Instead, he communicated with his eyes. That was his way of saying goodbye to everyone. My mother mentioned that that morning his soul had already left his body as he wasn't responding to anything. They moved him to the hospice room.

I was getting off work at around 5 p.m. when my mother called me and my stepbrother. We raced to the hospital where we found my mother distraught and him unresponsive—but his heart was still beating. We called the girls, my stepsisters, to come to the hospital as well. They showed up about twenty minutes later. His heart was still beating. The amazing nurse kept checking his heartbeat for us as we let more of the family know what was occurring. My aunt-in-law spoke to him. His best friends stopped by. Everybody who needed to be there was able to see him and say their last words to him. At six o'clock on the dot, after he had spoken with my other stepsister on the phone, his heart finally rested still. We had all said our peace and loved on him before and after he fully transitioned, and in our hearts, we knew that he saw us.

Everything shattered as the reality of him being officially gone set in. Seeing his obituary was the most surreal pain I ever felt. I was so torn that day and in the days that followed. But despite the pain, I often still feel his energetic humor within me. As I tear up now, I can hear him saying, "Alright, now, stop all that crying and boss up. Don't be a punk." Even though it stings knowing that he's not here with us anymore, I can't help but giggle. He had such a huge impact on so many people. People I didn't know he had impacted had wonderful memories to share at his funeral.

I thank God for allowing me the time I had with him. I thank God for putting him in both my mother's life and mine. I thank him for loving me as a daughter of his own. I thank him for genuinely getting to know me and allowing me to be myself around him without judgment. There are so many things we have to be grateful for, even as we grieve.

Goodbye and Hello

By Jennifer Holmes-Dziuba

I've said goodbye to my mother more than once in my lifetime.

One time was when she died in January 2010. It wasn't a surprise that she was ill enough to pass away. My mother was admitted to the hospital on December 26, 2009. On Christmas Day, she hadn't been well enough to attend church or spend time with her grandchildren at my home, though Christmas was very important to her.

Earlier that December, I did her Christmas shopping for her, wrapped her gifts for the family, and offered to decorate her Christmas tree. She wanted nothing except white Christmas lights and the angel topper on the tree. This was unusual and significant. On Christmas Day, she refused to go to the hospital when I went to see her, and with a conflicted heart, I went home. There certainly was a tentative goodbye in my mind that day.

In early January 2010, I visited my mother in hospital. I was impatient with her because she told me she was getting well and asked her doctor to let her go home later in the week. I had no idea how I would navigate her care once again. I didn't think a successful release from the hospital was possible, and it frustrated me that false hope was being offered up by the doctors. I left the hospital with less than a charitable state of mind, and I regret that I wasn't supportive of my mother's dream of being at home where she desperately wanted to be.

She died the next day, on my first day back at work after the holidays. On my drive to the hospital after receiving the call that resuscitation was being attempted, I asked God, "How much more?" When I arrived at her hospital room, I was greeted by a closed door with a sign telling me not to enter. Instead, I was to ask for the social worker at the nurses' station. Afterward, I was taken to a quiet room and told that my mother had passed away. They didn't want me to enter her room to say goodbye until they removed the medical equipment used in the effort to resuscitate her because I had to decline an autopsy first. I told them that my mother's body had been through enough in her lifetime and that she needed to be left in peace. I felt guilty and selfish for having cried out to God on that drive to the hospital.

I mentioned that I said goodbye to my mother more than once in my lifetime. To be clear, my mother's mental and physical health was in decline for about thirty years before her death. The decline began in 1980 after we returned from Australia, her homeland, where she had taken me and my sister to live when my sister was starting high school and I had recently graduated Grade 12. She moved her Canadian children to Australia because, long ago, she had said her goodbyes to her family and personal history when she met my Canadian father, to whom she was married for less than five years. She was seeking reconnection, but it was a failed attempt because what she dreamed wasn't reality.

Throughout the thirty years after that unsuccessful attempt to reconnect with her heritage, there were many goodbyes to the mother who had raised me and my sister as a single mother. We had lived a life of situational poverty, and my mother attempted suicide just as I was entering my first year of university. She had taken me aside and told me, "Now that you're on your way, I'll be going." I didn't want to hear her goodbye and adamantly refused it. However, I didn't have that option, and that was the turning point when I became the caregiver.

When my mother died, everyone in our church community told me that she was like the "energizer bunny" and that she had relentlessly fought against her ill health. I now recognize the truth of that, but when I was her caregiver, I was exhausted by the role reversal. I regret not seeing caring for her as a gift rather than a burden. I know I resented the circumstances that made her so tired. There were so many small goodbyes as I watched her health decline.

Then, of course, there were the goodbyes during the days that followed her death. I said goodbye when I placed white roses, one from each of her grandchildren, with her body. I said goodbye when I put her cherished grandmother's brooch on her clothing in the funeral home before her cremation. I said goodbye when I sent her cremated remains to Australia to be scattered on her parents' grave.

Finally, I said another goodbye when I returned to Australia after forty-three years. During this visit, I focused on understanding where my mother came from and our family roots. I have confirmed that my mother was resilient, hopeful, and brave and that having her as my mother was an honor. I visited the graveyard where her ashes were scattered by members of our Australian family, and I took yet another white rose with me. I wanted this to be a final goodbye.

Then I came home and re-read this quote, in my mother's handwriting, that I have saved on my refrigerator, where I can read it regularly, since 2010: "To live in the hearts of others is not to die or be forgotten." This, to me, felt more like a hello than a goodbye. To acknowledge her value as a complex, vibrant person who, sadly, happened to be unwell, I need to keep saying hello to my mother.

Memories of a Memory

By Johanna Douglas

My father was an enigma to me. Not in the way most fathers are—in their aloof and mysterious masculinity. Doug Jameson, my biological father, was a man I never met in person. I recently lost him in February 2024—if it's even possible to lose a person you had no claim to. Doug passed from a stroke caused by medicine meant to mitigate his poor health. When we think of loss and grief, we think of people we loved and knew dearly. But grief tastes bitter and acrid when you lose someone who, by technicality, was supposed to be in your life.

From what I gathered over the years from my mother, his family, and his wife, Doug was a complicated man. He lived his life in the shadow of his Type 1 diabetes. It haunted him from the time that he was diagnosed until the day he collapsed in the driveway of his home. This, coupled with his issues with his family, turned my father into someone who was, in essence, a runner. He ran away from responsibility and family with a fervor that drove him for years. Doug had a difficult life. His family, though they are kind people, were not often kind to him. Doug's father was a military man, and Doug was sensitive. His mother supported his father in everything. As an adult, Doug was often homeless and could not find steady work, traveling all over the western United States. He looked for comfort in the arms of many women, something to soothe his vulnerability and hurt.

Many events in my father's life carved out his soft pine heart. His father didn't believe in his illness, and his sisters treated him with disdain. But I believe that one of the events that shattered Doug was how my oldest brother was taken from him. In the early 1990s, my father divorced his first wife and became the sole provider for a young child. He reached out to his family for help and received it in-kind from his sister. She offered to look after my brother while my father established himself in Alaska to have a stable home for his son. While my father was away, my aunt went to the courts and, somehow—the details are fuzzy on all accounts—convinced the courts to allow a petition for adoption. When Doug received those papers, the fight went out of him. He gave up on his firstborn and all subsequent children—another brother and me. He began his wandering in earnest after that.

His rambling ways brought him to Bozeman, Montana, and a janitorial job where he eventually met my mother. They shared a love for the outdoors and mountains. My mother described him as gentle and intelligent. They eventually moved to Worden, into an old farmhouse that was embraced on three sides by lilacs. Everything was at peace. But even if you run from hurt, it follows. Doug grew restless. Then, my mother hit him with something he feared above all else. She was pregnant. In his fear, he accused her of trying to entrap him. My mother is a woman who is independent to the core, and she told him she wasn't going to stop him from leaving. And so, he left.

This is where I come into the story. I grew up playing in the lilacs surrounding the old farmhouse and cavorting in the alfalfa fields. My mom was always honest about my father, never speaking ill of him. Even as a child, I understood he was someone who had endured a lot of pain. I was also convinced that he was not aware of my existence. I clung to that as a child. That hope that if he knew, he would love me enough to come home.

This dream dissipated when I was sixteen and I finally found the courage to call Doug. I had received his phone number from my oldest brother, with whom I had been in contact off and on for a few years. When I called, my father thought I was a seller off Craigslist from whom he was buying barstools. I informed him of our shared genetics, which he took in stride. He told me about how he had spotted my mother with a baby stroller one day and pieced the story together. I honestly don't remember the rest of the phone call—only brief promises of future emails. I was devastated. The fact that he knew and never did anything hurt more than I could have imagined. It clung to me like anxious sweat. We only emailed once after that, as he was exceptionally vulnerable with me, and as a sixteen-year-old, I had no idea how to respond. He took my silence as rejection, and by the time I could handle it, he no longer answered my emails.

I tell you these stories not to speak ill of the dead but to understand. If I piece together the story, it'd bring him back, make him real. Maybe I could relate the parts of me I don't understand to a person. The cruelest joke of all is that my father never lived more than two hundred miles from where I grew up.

In losing Doug, I lost a life I could have had, a person I could have known and loved. I lost a part of myself. He has always been an ambiguous figure, but I assumed I had time. Now, he's more of a figment—a man stories are told about without having his own voice. While it may not be a sharp, ripping grief that ebbs with time, it is a grief that I have always carried like a sore tooth. Only now, there is a finality to it that promises never to leave.

Goodbye for Now

Momma's Light

By Charles A. Taylor, PhD

I was only five years old when my mother died, and the fabric of our family was torn apart. I still remember her love—the warmth that wrapped around me like a soft quilt on a chilly night. Momma had a way of making everything feel safe, even when the world outside our small shack in Smelterville, on the poor side of Cape Girardeau, MO, seemed so vast and uncertain. She wanted the best for her children, and her love was the light that guided us through our darkest times.

She died in childbirth at the age of thirty-nine, on the day my younger twin siblings were born. It was a day that brought new life—but cruelly took away the anchor of our existing one. So instead of three people coming home, none of them did. In those difficult days, my grandmother, a caring and godly woman, took my newborn siblings under her wing. Her home became their home, away from the dysfunction of our new family life.

The image of Momma, peaceful in her casket, is etched in my mind. I remember, with the innocence of a child, shaking her gently in her casket, naively trying to awaken her from her sleep. My older siblings, tears streaming down their faces, gently pulled me away and shared an irreversible truth that my five-year-old mind couldn't quite grasp: Momma was never coming home again.

Nights in our household were filled with sorrow and uncertainty. My older brothers and sisters cried themselves to sleep, and I knew they missed Momma as much as I did. My twin sister and I clung to each other, our grief a silent bond that only we understood. We whispered secrets in the dark, promising to be strong for each other.

Our once brimming family home, echoing with the laughter and cries of eight children, even though we didn't have running water or an indoor toilet, soon turned into a house of silent yearning. Our father, heartbroken yet resilient, remarried quickly. It was a practical choice, born out of necessity, to help raise us while he worked from "can't see in the morning until can't see at night" as a construction laborer. I forgave Daddy long ago for his choice to marry my stepmother because the burdens he had to bear as a Black man trying to raise a large family in the Boot Hill of Missouri in the 1950s and 1960s would have broken anyone.

Our stepmother, who brought two children of her own into our blended family, was a stark contrast to the warmth we lost. Unyielding and distant, she lacked the affection and understanding we desperately needed, and soon, one by one, my older siblings left home and sought refuge elsewhere. Left behind were just three of us, under the stern rule of a woman who believed discipline was best instilled through the harsh lash of a switch or belt. We tried our best to tiptoe around her volatile moods.

Grandma was the silver lining in my anguished childhood. Her words became my guiding star, instilling in me the belief to never relinquish my dreams. Through her unwavering support and encouragement, I learned to embrace my inner light. She saw the flicker of hope in my eyes and would say to me, "A light will shine anywhere, Charles. So let your light shine." I would sing back to her, my voice trembling with hope, "This little light of mine, I'm going to let it shine."

It was Grandma and my aunts who kept the memory of my mother alive. They told me things about her, such as how she cherished and believed in her kids, which only made me love her more.

As the years wore on, the sharpness of my childhood memories dulled, but the essence of my mother's love and her dreams for us remained a guiding force. I left home at eighteen, with nothing but the clothes on my back and faith that I would make it somehow. Her spirit, like a silent guardian, watched over me as I journeyed through life, leading me to the esteemed halls of UW-Madison, where I earned my doctorate, a testament to her unwavering confidence in her children.

In hindsight my mother's passing became the catalyst for a life I doubt I would have pursued otherwise. Her absence shaped my path, her love a constant compass guiding me through life's myriad challenges.

One day, when time has run its course, I imagine I will meet her again. There are so many things I'd like to tell her—and then just hold her for a little while and let her know that her expectations for us were not in vain. I am certain that Momma's light continues to guide me because it has shone brightly through my life's work. And in that luminous glow, I find the enduring promise of a mother's love that transcends even the darkest of times.

She may have left this world too soon, but her spirit lives on in me reminding me to let my light shine, just as she'd wanted.

Momma, wherever you are, know that your son kept his promise. Your love carried me through the darkest nights, and I'll carry it with me always.

Journey to the Lake

By T. J. Hoogsteen

It was late September 2022. I was making breakfast when I received a text from my cousin asking if she could call me. I knew something was wrong. The last time she had texted to ask if she could call was when our grandmother had died thirteen years before. My intuition was right. I picked up my phone, and my cousin told me that my father had died. She had no other details but promised to stay in contact and tell me if she found out anything else.

As I got ready for work and went about my day, I considered whether to make the 2,200 km journey to my hometown to say goodbye. Would I even be welcome? I hadn't seen my father since my grandmother's funeral, and even then, we didn't speak. This wasn't unusual, though. Throughout my life, I had sporadic, if any, contact with him.

I was six or seven years old the first time I met him. It was also the first time I met his wife and my younger half-sister. We went fishing. I had never been fishing before, and I had never been on a boat. I must have had a stroke of beginner's luck because I caught my first fish, and from what I remember, it was a fair-sized pike. My father took the hook out and released it, and the boat started to rock from all the movement. I was unnerved, to say the least. My half-sister stood up and began jumping back and forth to show me it was no big deal. I have few memories of my father and what he was like, but looking back on that moment, I see he had the same laid-back attitude and humour as his mother and siblings. I wouldn't get to know him much more than this as it turned out that this would be the last time I would see my father for several years.

Flash forward thirty-five or so years—two days after I received the news and school had just finished—and I was still waiting for information and grappling with the decision of whether to make the trip. I was doing typical end of the day things when my neighbour, the retired principal of the school where I was now principal, came and asked me if I wanted to help him set a net on the lake. It was out of the ordinary, although I considered him a mentor and friend. It hadn't happened before, and didn't happen again. Having never set a net before, I was excited for the opportunity to learn. We drove down to the lake, put the boat in the water, and set out.

As we travelled across the lake, my neighbour pointed out spots, told me moose hunting stories, and showed me where eagles nest. I couldn't help but take everything in. This was the type of experience I was looking for when I decided to work in the north, and it was the perfect opportunity for some deep reflection. We got everything ready as we arrived at the spot where we would set the net. My job was to make sure the net wasn't tangled as it went into the water. As I was standing and watching the net sink below the surface, I couldn't help but recognize the full-circle moment. I thought to myself, my father had the chance to do things like this with me for all these years and didn't. It was just another milestone or moment that he missed. It was seemingly a moment of closure, and I made the decision to forego travelling home.

I held on to that idea until recently. On a whim, I decided to reach out to be a contributor for *Goodbye for Now,* and I knew this was the story I wanted to write. Only I didn't know how it would end until after I sent the email. All of a sudden, it came to me. That out of the ordinary event on the lake in late September 2022 wasn't just a chance for me to get some closure. Even if I didn't recognize it then, it was a chance for my father to say goodbye. Now, this story is mine.

Infant Mother

By Tom Seaton

She always used to tell us we had to become like little children to enter the kingdom of heaven. Little did she know that the biblical passage to which she referred, Matthew 18:3, would become her truth and test of faith. A heart valve replacement, which led to two strokes, transformed my mom from a vibrant, youthful eighty-three-year-old to the child of the scriptures.

Her second stroke left her paralyzed on the right side. She needed to be fed, toileted, bathed, dressed, reassured, and hugged. She needed everything her five children needed when they were infants. We *expect* little children to need us, and we revel in their care. Even changing dirty diapers can be joyful! However, we *never expect* to change roles with the one who brought us into the world.

When the benchmarks had been met, indicating that transition was imminent, hospice was contacted. I admired and respected her hospice team but would have been fine with fewer clinical explanations and predictions of when time would run out. Mom's process already taught me that real people don't die like actors do in the movies. Leave-taking is messy and unpredictable. Demonstrating the stubbornness and determination of a child, Mom was not ready to throw in the towel. Did you know that the stronger one grips the oral hydration swab, the greater their determination to survive? She surpassed all predictions of longevity. Many times, the child gets her way.

We were asked to "help her let go." I left work and began the forty-mile drive to the nursing home, knowing that I was going to encourage my mother to let herself die. I will never be able to capture into words how that felt. Intellectually, I believed I was being responsible, helpful, even loving. Emotionally, I felt like a traitor. I was on my way to encourage my mom, a stoic, first-generation Irish-American who loved life, to leap into the unknown. A devout Catholic, she was at the intersection of theory and practice. Given my moniker of family "crybaby," how would I get through this without tears? I cry at commercials!

Her shared room at the nursing home made me claustrophobic, and my mouth was a desert. Standing over her, I stroked her now gray hair, my other hand holding her good hand. Trust me when I say that the presence of gray hair was the greatest indignity of all. Mom looked forward to her weekly trips to the neighborhood beauty salon. Thanks to the magic of a good dye job, I always teased her about her authentically artificial hair color. How we joked with her about her "lacquered look" and the promise of neighborhood gossip that was part of the ritual of going to the beauty shop.

The highest compliment one could pay my mom was to compare her to her mother. An Irish immigrant, widowed at thirty, six weeks later, she gave birth to my mom. With only a second-grade education, she raised two kids, working as a cook. Adding insult to injury, Gramma died young, leaving my mom permanently bereft.

Mom's generation fared better, but her life wasn't easy. She lost her firstborn when he was seventeen, experienced another child come out as gay, saw her kids leave the Church, celebrated their weddings, stood by them through divorce, and witnessed a grandson's diagnosis of the disease that claimed her firstborn son. Her marriage was not without incident, but she endeavored to enjoy, endure, forgive, and rediscover Dad cyclically for sixty years.

I kissed my mom on the forehead, on the nose, on her chin. I sat back down, our hands interwoven, and said, "Thank you for having me and for loving me. I will miss you the way you miss your mom. I will remember you the way you remember Gramma. I will always keep you alive in the family, and I'll be sure the grandkids know you. Dad, Pat, and Gramma are waiting for you, and so is your father, whom you've never met. It's okay to go be with them."

As I spoke those words, she studied my face intensely, just as I had studied her face hundreds of times when I was the infant. At one point, I leaned in because she was trying to tell me something, but I wasn't able to decipher her message. Please don't let it end this way.

With the passage of time, I am comfortable knowing that sometimes the best messages are those spoken through a look, a touch, a loud, word-less love that exists between people in those grace-filled moments. I have a good idea of all that was held in her heart as we traded places. Her mission accomplished; my infancy yet to come.

Unspoken Lessons

By Justo Quiroz Chilcumpa

In the small town of Ovalle, nestled in the heart of Chile, my father's life unfolded against a backdrop of hardship, resilience, and unspoken lessons. Born on August 26, 1927, Justo Santiago Quiros's early years were marred by the untimely demise of his parents, leaving him an orphan at the tender age of eight. His father, Phillipe, had died following a physical assault, while his mother, Lastenia, succumbed to a grave illness. As was common at the time, his extended family sent him to a boarding school, where he embraced engineering and found solace in independent contracts after graduation.

Returning to Ovalle to reconnect with his maternal roots, my father sought to establish his life path. In the winding course of life, he crossed paths with my mother, Myriam Chilcumpa, a local Ovalle woman who would soon become his devoted wife. Their union brought forth eight children, each a testament to their shared journey through the challenges of twentieth-century Chile. I was the firstborn and carried my father's name, although a clerical error changed my legal family name from Quiros to Quiroz.

Despite the tight-knit community and bustling family life, an underlying sense of isolation lingered. My father, a dreamer with a mind full of ideas, faced the harsh reality of financial constraints. The desire to start a business, whether in car services or groceries, remained unfulfilled due to a lack of financial acumen and the pervasive poverty that spread throughout the country. This time of depression during the Allende and Pinochet era left deep scars on Chilean society, increasing political polarization and societal divisions that affected families and livelihoods for a long period. Despite becoming a more economically stable country, it also contributed to great upheaval and social inequality, which our family certainly felt.

When my father befriended a German man, it influenced his perspective and shaped his beliefs. Through this friendship, he envisioned a future for his offspring that involved navigating foreign languages and immersing them in cultures beyond their own. This vision led to a decision which impacted me as his eldest son—he enrolled me in the German school system. The rigidity of the learning structure and a focus on harsh discipline starkly contrasted my desires, leading to a persistent resentment toward my attendance at this institution. Despite never thriving in this system, ironically, in life, I would be led to reside in Germany for four years alongside my wife and stepdaughter.

Our relocation from Ovalle to Santiago meant building the walls and framing the home once the foundation had been laid. As the eldest, my father relied on me to assist. As a fourteen-year-old, I resented my engagement in manual labor. However, I now recognize that the lessons I learned about helping during those formative years would echo through my future actions.

Although he was a smoker for most of his life, one of the unspoken lessons my father imparted was a stance against smoking and drinking due to the potential for addiction, as he understood the difficulties of breaking free from their grip. He advocated for moderate drinking, emphasizing that a glass of wine was acceptable with a meal but that alcohol should not be abused. These words resonated with me and persuaded me to develop lifelong health goals related to eating and exercise.

My father also demonstrated great affection for my mother, and this has influenced how I treat my wife.

In the final days of my father's life, I was left without closure. As the eldest, I found myself blindly navigating the responsibilities of payments and funeral arrangements, grappling with emotions left unexpressed. I hadn't realized back then that I never took the time to say goodbye, so I recently penned a message to my departed father, which I have shared below to express my gratitude for the unspoken lessons. I seek solace in the hope that, in some ethereal realm, these sentiments may finally reach the man who shaped my life. The relationship between a father and son can be complex, so through this gesture, I bridge the gaps of silence with a final farewell:

Hello Dad,

It's been over twelve years since you left. I never said goodbye; everything happened suddenly, and at the funeral, I was responsible for making sure your grave was ready when they brought your coffin. You were sick for a long time toward the end of your days. I knew you were going to die, but when it happened, it was a difficult moment for me and my siblings. I thought I was prepared, but no, it was painful.

We never talked much; I don't think I'm very good at this. I've always been one for short messages. Well, now I want to say goodbye and thank you. I know you're okay because you've told me so in a couple of dreams. You're probably back there already.

I hope you're in a good family, with a father and mother, since you lost them at a very young age and grew up independent and without anyone who truly loved you.

We went through tough times together as a family, and you were always there. I was very critical, but time showed me that you were a better father than I could be. As a father, you surpass me by far.

Well, old man, thanks again, and I believe I'll see you soon.

Your son,

Justo

My Mom. My Rock.

By Jarvis Ottum

My mom, Patricia Sanchez Ottum, was born July 8, 1944, in Second Ward, Houston. Everyone called her Pat. She and her brother, Florencio, grew up in a two-bedroom home her father had built. At one point, my mom's uncle, aunt, and their two children came to live with them. That's eight people in a modest two-bedroom house. The second bedroom was about the size of a guest restroom.

Mom paid her way through college by working sixty hours a week and attending school part-time. Avoiding distraction was a goal of hers. She would tell the boys, "If you want your $20 worth, go out with Betty Sue." Whoever that was. Pat was determined to graduate college. Seven years later, she earned and paid for her teaching degree. Pat was the first in her family to graduate college.

My mom would say, "I went to the University of Houston to get my MRS. Degree." That was her way of saying she went to college to find a husband. In her last semester of college, she met my dad, Joe, and married him shortly after graduating in 1976. She wanted to get to know him first, but my dad had enlisted with the Navy, and he was shipping out. He told her, "There will be time for us to get to know each other later." So, she married him and moved out of Houston. Dad was an officer in the Navy, making Mom an officer's wife, which is a full-time job. An officer's spouse has to arrange for housing when moving and scrub out the old one so it can pass inspection.

When I was born, Mom told Dad, "I'm not going to work. I'm going to stay home and take care of Jay." When I graduated college, Dad said, "Your son graduated. You can work now." So, at fifty years old, she got her first teaching job—a kindergarten position at St. Louis Elementary School in Castroville, Texas. She taught there for ten years.

Pat was one of the smartest and warmest women I ever knew. Before she got Alzheimer's, she had a photographic memory. Mom often recounted stories of her grandparents and reminded Dad of mistakes he made years ago.

I had a great childhood. In elementary school, my mom would take me to McDonald's after school most days. I would get a Happy Meal, and she would get a quarter pounder. She loved their coffee. In her older age, I repaid the favor. It was my turn to take her out. She loved the Chinese buffet in town. That is where I took her every week. After eating, I would take her shopping. Walmart and HEB were her favorite stores. When I dropped her off at her home, she had to have a kiss on her cheek.

Mom was an angel, and now she is my guardian angel. Her nickname for me was Jay. "My Jay," she would say. Dad named me Jarvis, but my mom always called me Jay. They both called me Jay. That was my parent's agreement. I didn't find out my legal name was Jarvis until the sixth grade. I had thought that Jarvis was my middle name.

I carry a picture of my mother behind my work badge so she can always be with me. In 2000, I was assaulted. She told me, "Don't stop working. Put one foot in front of the other and go to work every day. You have a child; you can't afford not to work." It was the truth, and it's what I did. Over the years, I turned to my mother for advice. She was my concierge. My counsel. If my mom said something, it was always sound advice.

My mom's life began in Houston—H-Town! Her life ended in a different H-Town. Pat died on December 28, 2021, in the suburbs of Hondo, Texas. Her last home was a five-bedroom house with a pool—not bad for a Chicana activist from Second Ward, Houston.

There is a beautiful wooden urn sitting in my living room. I will keep it until my dad dies. Then, per her wishes, she will be buried with my father at the San Antonio National Cemetery. Until then, I hold my love for her in my heart and her words in my brain.

I think of my momma every day. She always said, "I'll always be with you," while touching my forehead. "I'll always be right here in your head. You can talk to me whenever you want." Mom was right. I'm grateful that she shared this wisdom with me. Not a day goes by that I don't think of my mom and talk to her in my brain.

My Father–A Pioneer Who Built Community

By Kumanan Kunaratnam

Karunakararajah. This Tamil name, meaning the compassionate king, encapsulates the essence of my father—a man whose life was a testament to self-lessness, resilience, and unwavering compassion. To many, he was not just a patriarch but a pioneer: a refugee who forged a path of hope and opportunity for his family and community in a foreign land.

In 1983, amidst the turmoil of the Sri Lankan civil war, my father made the courageous decision to seek refuge in Canada. At that time, the Tamil community in Canada numbered barely two thousand. He was among the first Tamil pioneers, driven by a relentless determination to provide a better future for his loved ones. Little did he know then that his journey would not only transform his own life, but also lay the foundation for countless others to follow.

Upon arriving in Canada, my father faced the daunting challenge of starting anew in a foreign country with unfamiliar customs and language barriers. Undeterred, he tirelessly worked to sponsor all of his family members, ensuring they too found refuge and opportunity in this new land. His efforts were not confined to his immediate family; he extended his support to friends and relatives who sought asylum in Canada, helping them secure jobs, housing, and navigate the complex refugee claim process.

His days were long and arduous, often beginning before dawn and ending late into the night. By day, he laboured to provide for his family, and by evening, he assumed the role of a volunteer social worker: driving people to employment offices, aiding them with paperwork, and offering comfort and guidance during times of uncertainty. His evenings were spent not in leisure, but in service to his community, a testament to his boundless generosity and deep-rooted sense of duty.

I remember the deep sorrow of saying goodbye to him during his final days in the hospital. For those two weeks, visiting him was heart-wrenching. Watching him endure pain was almost unbearable. In his final moments, I held his hand, feeling an overwhelming despair as he passed away. The process of mourning and grieving was long and challenging, but his memories remain vividly with me, a source of both solace and strength.

Among the many cherished memories I hold dear, I remember how my dad showered my sister and me with unconditional love. Every weekend, he would take us out for family outings—visits to the movie theatre became a special tradition, where he would spoil us with popcorn and candy, making us feel like we were part of something magical. He also prioritised family visits, teaching us the importance of connections with our cousins and showing us the warmth of being surrounded by loved ones. I fondly recall him picking us up after school, often taking us out for an after-school meal, even when my mother insisted we should eat at home. These little acts of rebellion revealed his zest for life and his desire to create joyful memories for us. His ability to live in the moment, filled with love and laughter, has profoundly shaped who I am today, instilling in me the values of compassion and family that I carry with me.

At his funeral, attended by thousands whose lives he had touched, a common refrain echoed through the crowd as they embraced me: "It is because of your father that I am here in Canada today." These words, whispered with gratitude and reverence, illustrated the profound impact he had on the lives of so many. His legacy transcended familial ties; it resonated across generations of Tamils who found hope and opportunity in Canada, inspired by his example of resilience and compassion.

In the tapestry of his life, my father's compassion was interwoven with strength forged in adversity. His journey from refugee to community leader mirrored the struggles and triumphs of an entire community striving to rebuild lives shattered by conflict. Through his unwavering dedication and selflessness, he embodied the spirit of resilience that defines the Tamil

Goodbye for Now

diaspora—a community bound together by shared history and a collective determination to thrive in new lands.

Reflecting on his life, I am reminded of his quiet dignity and humility, traits that endeared him to all who crossed his path. He did not seek recognition or accolades; his greatest reward was seeing others succeed, knowing he had played a part in their journey. His compassion knew no bounds, extending beyond borders and cultures to embrace all who sought refuge and opportunity.

As one of the first Tamil pioneers to settle in Canada, my father's impact reverberates far beyond his immediate circle. He was a beacon of hope for a community finding its place in a new homeland, a guiding light whose legacy continues to inspire future generations. The exponential growth of the Tamil community in Canada—from two thousand to over three hundred thousand—is a testament to the seeds of hope and opportunity he planted decades ago.

In his final moments in 2017, surrounded by the love and gratitude of those whose lives he had touched, my father's legacy was affirmed. His life was not measured by material wealth or personal accolades, but by the lives he transformed and the hearts he touched. His compassion, his resilience, and his unwavering commitment to others define a legacy that will endure for generations to come.

In honouring my father's memory, I am reminded of the profound impact one individual can have on the lives of many. His journey from refugee to community pillar reflects the transformative power of compassion and the enduring spirit of hope. Karunakararajah Kunaratnam, my father, was, and will forever remain, the Moses of my family—a compassionate king whose legacy of selflessness continues to inspire and guide us all.

Part VI

Pet

Lacy: The Mole-Catching Bird Dog

By Kevin Roberts

My best friend passed away on the night of December 31, 2023. The profound loss I felt after discovering her body at the foot of my bed has only slightly faded since. Lacy was a stray English Pointer mix pup who turned up at our home in East Tennessee one spring morning in 2007. After a day or two of seeing her around, I called her over and, on inspection, decided to help her, noticing that her body was covered in ticks and fleas and in an overall poor condition.

Believing she was only seven-to-ten-months old, I attempted to locate the pup's owner, with no success. Over time, Lacy quietly became the family dog. She was a special girl, and our bond grew quickly and completely. She was a bird dog at heart, so she was full of life and eagerness to train, and the bond we shared was tightened as we worked together in training sessions.

One unusual skill Lacy developed on her own was catching moles—you know, those little destructive critters that reside in the ground. I never understood how or why this developed, but it became her obsession. I had an ongoing and continuous issue with moles on the property, and they would cause havoc in the yard. On more than one occasion, I would open the door to find a mole's body lying on the doorstep, which I initially suspected was the work of a local cat.

Then, one evening in the twilight hours, through the kitchen window I noticed Lacy standing pointedly over a fresh mole mound. As I stood quietly watching, I observed her standing motionless except for her head moving as she raised one ear after the other from one side to the other. I was fascinated because I had never seen this before. Suddenly, she pounced. So fast, she raised her front quarters in the air, and as her legs came down and her paws met the ground, she furiously dug at the ground with a large mole in her jaws. I was momentarily stunned and riveted by this, and I stood amazed when she immediately dispatched the writhing and squealing mole. Once she was sure it was dead—dropping it on the floor and nudging it with her nose—she casually picked it back up and carried it to the doorstep.

Mole-catching became Lacy's signature. Sometimes, when we had a particularly bad infestation, the yard resembled a miniature war zone with holes, large and small, scattered all over. Sometimes, I wondered if the dog was doing more harm than good, but it was "her thing," and I don't think I could have stopped her even if I wanted to.

Lacy aged well into her sixteenth year. Although I had noticed the decline in her stamina and longer naps, I never noticed many visible signs of aging: some graying around the face, clouding of her eyes, and a change in her gait and posture. She developed arthritis over the last few years, and it was this that affected her most. Even with medication, it pained me to watch her inevitable decline.

I sob as I write here because her death was a shock to me, even though I know now it really shouldn't have been. I have since accepted that I had been in denial leading up to her passing, and the guilt I feel for that is often unbearable.

Lacy had stopped eating during the week between Christmas and New Year's. She struggled to stand and would only go outside for short periods to pee. As the week progressed, she became less and less active; I finally accepted that she needed a vet's help and resigned myself to take her in. It was New Year's Eve, and it would be a couple of days before I could take her to my local vet, so I selfishly thought I didn't have to deal with what I knew this was leading to, at least for a day or two.

That evening, Lacy refused to even take a drink, and she lay at the foot of the bed that night. I could and should have taken the poor dog to an emergency vet days before, and I'll always regret that I chose not to.

On New Year's Day, I got out of bed and noticed Lacy immediately. I stood staring at her lifeless form, and I groaned deeply under my breath. I eventually kneeled beside Lacy and stroked her head gently, tears streaming from my eyes as I whispered, "I'm sorry, old girl," repeatedly. I was devastated.

Loss is amplified tenfold when guilt is present. I felt a lot of guilt and anguish because I fully understood she didn't have to go the way she did. I let her down so badly it was eating me from the inside out. How could I have allowed her this suffering? My lack of action meant she needlessly suffered in her final days when I owed her the right to a peaceful passing.

That day, I wrapped Lacy in her favorite bedding and took her outside to a spot close to the kitchen window, where she had spent so many happy times hunting moles. As I sobbed uncontrollably, I dug her grave and laid her to rest. After, I sat beside the mound of earth and cried my eyes out.

The pain of the loss of my best friend lingers on, and here now, sixteen months later, I sob again.

A Friend for Life

By Toshi Allan Alibudbud

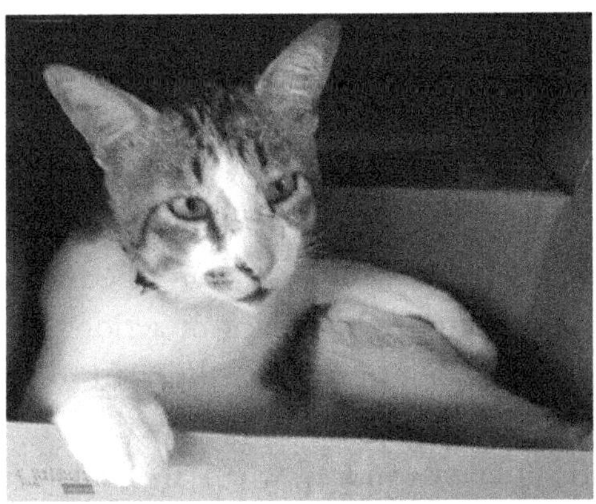

From a very young age, I've always been a dog lover. Through the years, I've had different pets accompany me at every stage of my life. Each dog was fiercely loyal and had a gentle disposition that made me love them even more. I believed that cats, however, were different.

I would often argue with my friends whenever they shared the opinion that cats made great pets as well. Cats frightened me with their sharp claws and unmoving stares, barely blinking as they watched you walk away—as if they were peering straight into your soul. Those common cat characteristics made me doubt I would ever own one.

Some years back, though, a stray kitten made its way to our house. It was small and furry, covered in shades of gray splattered over a creamy-white body. My dad instantly felt sorry for the lost animal and decided to adopt it. As he was a Star Wars fan, he named the kitten "Jedi." He would feed Jedi in the morning while I took over at night. I have to admit that I slightly resented the chore. Initially, I was afraid that our family dog, Kirby, might end up fighting with Jedi (or maybe even devouring the kitten), but in those early days, they kept their distance from each other.

Little by little, Jedi wormed his way into my life. He would follow me around, rubbing his body against my leg whenever I saw him. It annoyed me at first, but I soon understood that it was his way of expressing his love. The first time he fell sick, I rushed him to a vet several cities away. I hate driving long distances, but I wanted Jedi to feel better, and hearing the doctor's reassurance that he would be okay was definitely worth the drive. When I'd go out with my friends, I'd make up an excuse to leave early because Jedi needed his dinner. As soon as I'd get home, I'd see Jedi eagerly waiting for me, his tail slowly swishing from left to right before meowing his soft hello.

Jedi had won me over. I knew then I had met my friend for life. I was willing to adjust my routines and make exceptions for this adorable, helpless furball. From patiently administering his medicines to carrying him on my shoulder whenever he asked, I gradually opened up and let him in.

As Jedi grew in size and maturity, he became even sweeter, destroying all my previous misconceptions about cats and how, unlike dogs, they seemed aloof and uncaring. Whenever I would arrive home, Jedi would rush to greet me, plopping on the ground before rolling over and gently nudging me to rub his belly. He developed a friendship with our dog, Kirby, sometimes sleeping beside him—both without a care in the world. He would even rub against our dog, giving him the assurance that they were friends. I remember Jedi looking so dapper, wearing his black collar that looked like a bow tie, and his gentle stare made everyone who met him rush to give him a head massage.

Both a charmer and quite a character, Jedi's antics were funny, like often using his tail to swat at flies despite his eyes remaining shut. Because of his size, he looked lazy and slow, but Jedi could zoom past other cats if and when he wanted to. He was sweet, kind, extremely patient, and oozing with charm that made strangers fall in love with him. More than one neighbor asked me if they could adopt Jedi. Of course, I politely declined each time. He brought so much joy and warmth into my life. I had no idea that this would soon change.

One regular evening, just over a month ago, Jedi decided not to eat. I thought he was just being picky because he didn't exhibit any other signs that he was ill. He was more lethargic than usual; when I'd call him, he wouldn't respond, choosing to hide under metal sheets in our basement. I brushed it off and thought he just wasn't in the mood. Two days later, Jedi passed away. It all happened so quickly. He probably had been ill already the previous day.

I was unable to process my grief properly. I didn't want to believe he was gone, and I'd fool myself into thinking he was still there, just out of my sight. My thoughts would meld into an unhealthy mix of regret, anger, sadness, and pain because I blamed myself. It was my fault he had died. I should have known he was sick. I could have brought him to the vet. I might have saved him. If only …

I guess Jedi sensed how bad I was feeling because he visited me in my dreams not too long after. In my dream, he entered my parents' room, and we were all there as he was saying goodbye to us. It was very painful, and I woke up crying, but I needed that. I needed him not to blame me; that dream lent me a small measure of peace. It was the beginning of acceptance; I had to start letting go.

I now understand why our pets have to leave before we do. We're able to handle their passing much better than they would handle ours. If they go before us, we still have a world to live in, battles to fight, family and friends to love. If we go before them, they lose their entire world. And someday, we will be reunited with them.

Roscoe's Journey

By Andrea Williams

Roscoe wasn't just a pet; he was family—a cherished member whose personality was as vibrant as his bark. Originally a foster dog from Carolina Boxer Rescue, he quickly became a permanent fixture in our home. Roscoe's howls and deep barks turned heads wherever he went, especially when he chased his beloved squeaky balls. Despite his imposing size, he had a heart as big as his love for his fur sister, their playful antics a daily source of joy.

Adventures with Roscoe were always filled with laughter. Whether on walks or playing in the backyard, he brought boundless energy to our lives. Less than a year after adoption, signs emerged that something was wrong with his back leg. The faint sound of "step, step, scrape" as he moved upstairs initially seemed innocuous—perhaps just a sign of aging. He would occasionally stand awkwardly on his left paw or scrape it against the carpet. As a boxer, we initially chalked it up to laziness or clumsiness in his old age.

However, during a trip to the mountains for a hike, I noticed a trail of blood. My heart sank as I realized it was Roscoe—his left paw nails were shredded, a sight that demanded immediate attention. Concerned, I scheduled a vet appointment as soon as we returned home, though deep down, I feared what we might discover.

Having volunteered with a boxer rescue for over five years, I was all too familiar with degenerative myelopathy (DM) and its signs. Despite my suspicions, I clung to hope, praying it might be something less severe. The vet initially shared my optimism, cautious about jumping to conclusions without more evidence. We were referred to a specialist, where an MRI ruled out spinal disc issues, and a genetic test confirmed Roscoe carried the DM gene. It was a slow-motion death sentence, a progressive neurological condition destined to rob him of mobility and, eventually, his life. My heart sank deeper into despair, grappling with the reality that our beloved Roscoe faced an uphill battle we couldn't win.

With the diagnosis confirmed, we threw ourselves into action. Our days became a whirlwind of research, appointments, and treatments. We tried everything—special diets, supplements promising to slow the progression, laser therapy, and twice-daily physical therapy exercises. We did it all, hoping against hope to defy the inevitable, to buy Roscoe more time.

We started with protective coverings for his worn-down nails, which no longer gripped the ground. Remarkably, Roscoe took to them without complaint, his patience and gentle demeanor shining through as his left leg grew weaker. We laid down yoga mats for better traction, watching him navigate with a determination that inspired us all.

By February, six months into the battle, his left leg had noticeably deteriorated. The once-strong paw that eagerly trudged through trails now faltered, requiring a boot to prevent further injury. Despite these challenges, Roscoe soldiered on, his spirit undaunted as we continued therapies, exercises, and endless doses of love. He greeted us with slobbery kisses and happy howls, displaying resilience and joy.

Eight months after his diagnosis, we made the decision to get Roscoe his wheels—a customized wheelchair to support his weakening left leg. He adapted with characteristic resilience, racing up sidewalks in his chair with determination, oblivious to obstacles in his path. Seeing him explore beyond our home filled us with gratitude amid the sorrow of his declining health.

Ten months into his battle, DM claimed another victory—Roscoe's right leg began to falter. Walking became arduous, requiring boots on both feet to protect fragile paws. Yet, Roscoe remained determined to keep pace

Goodbye for Now

with his sister and our daily routines, his indomitable spirit a beacon of strength even as our hearts broke with each stumble.

As his condition worsened, eighteen months in, new medications and a second heavy-duty wheelchair aimed to bolster his failing strength. Physically and emotionally drained, we meticulously tracked Roscoe's moods and health, grasping for stability amid the ebbing tide of time.

Then, twenty months into the relentless DM onslaught, a new adversary emerged: cancer under Roscoe's tongue. Rapidly spreading, it signaled further decline. Once filled with activity, his days were marked by exhaustion and sleep, his vibrant presence fading.

The most agonizing decision awaited us—twenty-two months after DM first appeared, we said our goodbyes. Heavy with sorrow, we cradled Roscoe, whispering love and gratitude for the joy he brought. Tears flowed freely as we kissed his furrowed brow for the last time. Amid the anguish, a fleeting smile reassured us he was at peace.

Grief consumed us in the days that followed. Roscoe's absence—his bark, his howl, his unwavering gaze—left a void that seemed insurmountable. Every corner echoed with memories, a testament to the love and laughter that filled our days. Through the torrent of emotions, gratitude flickered—for the privilege of sharing life with such a remarkable soul.

Roscoe taught us resilience in adversity, patience, and love that transcends mortality's boundaries. He taught us that life is a gift, to take more naps, and to howl when you are happy. His legacy, tinged with sorrow, brims with enduring love and cherished memories to guide us through darker days.

If I could have spared Roscoe pain, I would have in a heartbeat. His time with us was a priceless gift, a testament to the unbreakable bond between human and canine. I imagine him now, running free, his legs strong, chasing butterflies where pain is unknown.

My Maggie

By Kelly Vasquez

Maggie was my cancer survivor dog. After a year of cancer treatment with chemo, radiation, and surgery, I was told my cancer was in remission. We had lost a dog at the beginning of my treatment, and I wanted to get another dog to be a companion to my other dog, Kelse. My husband and I love Australian Shepherds, and I wanted to try to find another Aussie. I knew this dog would have to be a rescue like all our other dogs had been.

I searched rescue groups and found an Aussie being fostered in Cleveland, just north of Houston, where we live. I went to see her and see if she would be a good fit. It was love at first sight. She was young and loved to run and play, so I had brought her a squeaky toy, which I threw, and she ran after it. I was told her name was CeeCee and that we could change it if we liked.

When we went to pick her up, she would have her new name, "Maggie." Even the rescuer cried. She knew what a special dog she was, but they could not give her the time she needed. I assured the foster mom that all of our animals would live their best lives.

Shortly after we first got her home, I was walking her one day in the neighborhood. She slipped her leash and just started to run. I was scared to death of her getting hit by a car. I was able to wrangle her back and fussed at her. She did not know any better because she had been living in the country and was used to just running and playing in the pond.

We realized that we needed some other outlet besides walks. We found a great dog park near us, which became a wonderful weekend activity. We would take her off leash, and Maggie would just run and run and run. It was several acres. She played with some dogs, but she just wanted to run. We taught her a few agility skills, like running through the tubes, and she was so proud of herself.

Maggie liked to get in the water, not just dive in. She was a lady, so she would just wade in the water. We did this with her for years; it was so much fun to see that dog enjoy life. She was the sweetest dog and loved everyone. I think she was more of a person than a dog. When my husband and I would get home from work, she would just cry and cry like we had been gone for days. It was so wonderful to be greeted like that every day. She loved, loved us unconditionally. I have never had a dog that dreamed like she dreamed.

One of my special memories with her was when I was laid off from my job and had a lot of time. I took her with me to Galveston; it was off-season, and not many people were on the beach. I was able to let her run on the beach. She would run and run, but she would always come back when you called. She just looked so happy being able to just run free. She provided me with much companionship while I was off from work. Maggie was one of those dogs that would rub her head against your chest because she just could not get enough or show enough love.

Another thing that made Maggie so special was that she figured out there was a long window in the front of our house. Every day, she would wait at the window for us to come home, and then she would run to the back door to greet us with her famous crying, as if we had been gone for days. She had an absolute love for us.

Over time, I noticed that she started having some cognitive issues. She would pace and be restless at night. She was given some meds, but all that seemed to do was make her sleep. Her pacing and circling at night worsened, and she began to lose strength in her hind legs. I put rugs everywhere; I think I was in a bit of denial. She was starting to struggle. Maggie was not in pain, but she was struggling mentally. She was now almost fourteen and struggling to get into the car. I decided to try acupuncture, which seemed to help for a few months, but even this was temporary.

We made the ultimate decision to put Maggie to rest. We had a service called Angel Arms come and administer the injection. Maggie went silently. When I asked the technician if she was gone, I wanted to say, "No, I want her back!" But at the same time, I knew it was the end. After the technician left, I cried, "Maggie!" It makes me tear up to this day. I knew it was the best for her, but it hurt so much. I even joined an online support group for grief to help cope with the loss.

We had her taken so she could be cremated. When we received her ashes, we took some to Galveston so that part of her could always be at the beach. The rest of her still resides on our mantle over the fireplace at home. It's been several years and we now have two dogs, but I have not removed Maggie's food bowl from in front of the fireplace. I don't know if I ever will. She will forever live in our hearts and will never be forgotten.

The Last Meow

By Brandon Markus

I have been around a lot of cats in my life, but none of them entered a room the way Zombie did. She was vocal. She was *very* vocal, no matter what room she was entering and what time of day it was. But she wasn't always loud. Sometimes, she would be gentle with her announcement meows, just letting the world know that she was there and that we should all feel blessed to be in her presence.

It was just one of the many aspects of her personality that felt unique. Of course, nearly all cats meow, but I had never heard one do so with such character. Each of her vocal statements sounded different, as if she was trying to get a point across. She had inflection and tone when she spoke up. At first, I found it bizarre. But a few years later, I found it nothing but endearing.

Why the name Zombie? To be honest, I don't really remember. We found her for sale on a street corner at a local arts fair. A family was selling a litter of kitties, and Zombie's big green eyes just seemed to pop along with her gray, tabby fur. In the heat of the moment, my girlfriend and I tossed around ideas for names, and for some reason, we came up with "Zombie," and it just seemed to fit. Maybe it was because she was already feasting on a snack, or maybe it was just because it was an odd name that no one else would think of. But soon, she was staying at home with my girlfriend, tearing up the furniture and curtains and really living up to her name.

Zombie had an attitude. She had sass, and she wasn't afraid to show it. She would hold a grudge and act out, but she would also become cute and cuddly when she wanted affection. Living with her really was like living with a small child, one who *barely* had control over her emotions.

And she was a lot of fun. I remember one of my first memories with Zombie. I was lying on a couch, watching something on TV, and getting quite sleepy, preparing for a mid-afternoon nap. She hopped up on the couch and lay in the sliver of space between my stomach and the edge of the couch. She didn't have much room but made the most of it and started purring and sleeping beside me. I felt a loving sense of peace at that moment as I felt her little soft body rise and fall with her easy breathing.

But she also loved to go outside when we would let her. She was an indoor cat but occasionally wandered around a yard, sniffing at things, dancing around in the grass, looking for little bugs to devour. You could almost see the excitement in her eyes. Late at night, she'd twitch in her sleep, surely dreaming of her exciting time in the great outdoors.

Every time I came home, I'd hear her before seeing her. She would be lying on the carpet under the window, having found the comfiest spot of sun to bask in. And she would loudly meow before I'd even come around the corner. I'd walk right up to her, look down, and ask if I could help her, and she would look right up at me, refusing to move, and meow back as if she was saying, "Welcome home."

Then she'd lay back down and sleep.

And that is how it was for years … until it wasn't.

One night, my girlfriend was petting Zombie and noticed a couple of bumps under her fur. She was old at that point, about thirteen years, and so we both agreed to get Zombie checked out. She was acting fine, still eating and still active. But a week later, the vet informed us that Zombie had an aggressive form of cancer.

Within days, we started her on chemotherapy. We'd trek out to the clinic, wait for an hour as she was pumped full of drugs, and then take her home. And she seemed to be doing okay. She actually had more energy after a chemo session, and I believed, naively, that she was going to beat her cancer.

But the doctors said the treatment was only prolonging Zombie's passing, not preventing it. And after a month of chemo, she started to weaken. She was wobbly when she walked, slept all the time, and stopped eating. We knew the time had come.

Saying goodbye to Zombie was terribly hard, a moment that still sometimes plays in my mind. She went peacefully, and the vet staff was so incredibly caring about the entire experience. But the loss was enormous and felt crushing. Walking into the apartment without her was like walking into a black-and-white movie after years of living in color. Everything was different, and it didn't feel right.

The weeks after her diagnosis were incredibly emotional and challenging. But they were also rewarding in some ways because they allowed me to feel closer to Zombie and provide her with the sort of care that she needed. I can rest my head at night knowing that she felt loved every second of her life, and even as it came to an end, I don't think she was scared. I take great pride in that and am thankful that her passing was handled well. She was a great cat, and she deserved that.

A lot has changed in the years since Zombie's passing. I no longer live in that part of the country, and I have aged over ten years. But no matter where I go or what I do, I still remember opening the front door, coming around the corner, and seeing my little gray buddy basking in the sun, excited to see me. Wherever she is now, I hope Zombie is as happy and peaceful as she was in those moments.

Snowy

By Mieke Steyn

S nowy was an amazing white and cinnamon show budgie with a tough past. She came to me through the parrot rescue I work with. A volunteer picked her up from her previous owners and came straight to me. Housed in a filthy, small cage with one perch and no food bowl—it was evident that she didn't mean much to her previous owners.

She was a large, quiet, regal budgie, much like the white alpha dragon (the Bewilderbeast) in *How to Train Your Dragon 2*. Gentle and sweet-voiced, she had a tender heart but wouldn't allow herself to be bullied. She cherished her independence but was always open for a cuddle.

She had this way of sitting—always upright with a posture fit for a queen. If she were annoyed with you, she'd give you this half-lidded side-eye. She wouldn't even bother giving you as much as a full head turn in those moments.

When she was happy, that posture would not change, but there was a softness that showed on her face and in the way she ruffled her feathers. She had this way of chatting—closed eyes, fluffed-up feathers, and still body, with her whole head (not just her beak) moving as she spoke.

One of my fondest memories is the day Snowy came into my care. No one knew the condition she would arrive in, but it soon became clear that she had several health issues and disabilities—some suspected to be due to abuse and neglect. Despite this, she hopped onto my hand as if no human had ever harmed her. She sat there, closed her eyes, and fluffed her feathers, immediately showing her trust in me. That was the start of beautiful things.

Another cherished memory is her feeding times. Despite being an adult, her disabilities required a special diet and a separate eating spot away from the energetic flock. She would wait patiently on a specific perch next to the cage door until I arrived with her food. Once I opened the door, she'd happily hop onto my hand for the ride to her feeding place. After eating, she'd lie flat on her stomach next to the food bowl and sleep until I arrived. Then she'd either hop back on my hand to travel to her play area or make me work for it by having me chase her around a bit—just enough for us to screech with laughter. Then she'd hop on again for her daily free travels to her next play area.

Even vet visits were not an issue. It was like she knew I took her there to help her and that the vet was also there to help. She'd go there all chatty and light up the room with her singing, even when she was admitted for a stay. She never bit anyone—not even the vet who gave her those annoying injections.

One of Snowy's main health issues was a deformed crop. The vet suspected that it was due to being fed with a crop needle by an inexperienced person. The needle punctured her crop and tore through it, and although it miraculously healed on its own, the damage was severe. Her body could not digest food quickly, and the crop placement put pressure on the nerves on the left side of her body, temporarily leaving her semi-paralyzed after each meal. Every few weeks, she had to be admitted to the vet for antibiotics and other treatments to deal with crop infection and severe weight loss. This became part of our routine.

Saying goodbye was incredibly hard. Snowy's last bout of crop infection wasn't improving, and it became clear that she wouldn't pull through. The antibiotics didn't clear up the infection like they had in the past. Her body had had enough, although her mind hadn't. She'd lost so much weight. I had to make the call; it was time to let her sleep.

My heart was shattered, but I am grateful I had the chance to say goodbye.

There were two goodbyes: one for her and one for me. I held her fragile, weak body in my hands and whispered that I loved her and that she was the best Snowy-Budgie I could have ever asked for. I gave her some last scritches, a big cuddle, ensured she was warm and felt loved, and we walked into the room.

Our amazing vet made the process easier by being gentle and understanding. This vet had been treating Snowy for years, and everyone at the practice had come to love her. This goodbye was for Snowy—I needed her to sense love and gratefulness, not my brokenhearted panic.

I felt heartbroken but also at peace. Her body was tired, and I knew it was time. Once she passed in my hands, I held onto her all the way home, intent on giving her a sweet little burial spot reminiscent of her personality.

Once I got home, and before burying her, the emotions hit me. I cried on my bed for what felt like hours. I held her small body against my chest and let all my emotions out. She's now buried under a big tree that has a lovely spot in the morning sun. That goodbye was for me.

Settling into a new routine and rhythm without her was not easy. I still sometimes find myself waiting for her to hop onto my hand for that free ride. I still haven't had the courage to remove her soft, padded sleeping perch from the cage. The other budgies miss her, too—no one ever sits on her fancy perch. They're managing and healing, though—we all are. Grief is the price we pay for love.

Remembering Rascal

By Britney Hallmark

The runt of his litter, Rascal was a spirited tiny dog, full of personality and character! A miniature dachshund, he weighed around eight pounds most of his adult life. Short in stature, he was big in personality. Black with tan patches, he was the cutest little fellow.

I received Rascal as a Christmas present our first married year together, and he became my first little baby. He was the last puppy left when we arrived to pick one. He was the one no one else wanted. He had a crooked tail and thicker cartilage behind his ears, so he always looked like he was ready to fly away. The lady selling him told me he was odd and that she would have more puppies in a few weeks, but I thought he was perfect. He fit in my hand when we brought him home, and he grew up as an only child—for a while. He was spoiled beyond belief. He slept in the bed with me, curled up at the foot, and had his own blanket. He had his own bed but preferred to snuggle into his humans. He relished treats and expected them whenever he did a trick to show off his skills, came inside from a potty break, or sometimes just for being so adorable.

While he hated the ridiculous outfits I subjected him to, he never refused them and even grew to love his many sweaters in the winter months. He was quite a fashionista with an impressive wardrobe and a wide selection of outfits. One Halloween, he was a cowboy; another year, he was an inmate, while another year, he went as a hot dog. It was quite fitting. While he hated dressing up, he loved to play. Fetch was his favorite, even if he sometimes forgot to give the ball or stick back to me so the game could continue.

He was fiercely protective of me and, later, my kids. He adjusted to the role of "big brother" like a champ! He wasn't sure about the new, crying, tiny human at first, but he quickly warmed to him and became his fierce protector and even best friend before long. He enjoyed walks and going "bye-bye." He loved visiting his grandparents at the lake. After all, he was free to swim there and chase the ducks. As he got older, he got a life jacket, but not much slowed him down. He loved the beach but could never quite understand sand. He would taste, run, and even roll in it, but he was always drawn to the water.

One of my favorite memories was Halloween, when we had a small gathering of friends and family over. Rascal didn't know what to think of the pumpkins. Everyone brought a pumpkin, and we had a pumpkin-carving contest. There was food and a lot of fun. Rascal was always right in the middle of it all. I remember him sticking his whole body in one of the pumpkins and sniffing all around. While he wasn't a fan of pumpkin, he was still very curious. And he loved people! He would get so excited seeing everyone, getting treats, and all the pets and scratches he could want. He was a very social dog.

Another time, we decided to take him on vacation with us to the mountains. He usually came with us but got to stay with the grandparents if he couldn't go on our trip. He was a big fan of exploring the mountains. He would mark his territory so much that after a while, it was simply a leg lift with nothing else happening. He loved the mountain air and exploring new surroundings but did not love the other animals he would encounter. In his mind, Rascal was a big, formidable, tough dog. Not one to be messed with, he was full of energy and adrenaline. In reality, he was only about eight pounds and the length of a small loaf of bread. When he encountered a family of raccoons, he was intrigued. He decided to inch closer and investigate further. When his powerful barking didn't phase them, he got closer. When the mother raccoon had enough of his nosy snooping around her babies, she let him know that she wanted him to keep his distance. The second she ran at him, he tucked his tail with his ears straight back and ran for his life. He came back to us and hid behind our legs until she went away. With a quick little yap, he let her know not to come back!

As the years passed, Rascal grew older, and his fur began to gray around his muzzle. He was still a young pup in his mind, though. He was never too tired to play and always ready to run. His body began to slow down, but his spirit never did. He stayed healthy, and I am thankful that when he passed, it was because of old age. He went to sleep and never woke up again. So, there wasn't a specific time to say goodbye, but at almost seventeen years old, we knew it was coming. His last few years were slower-paced, and we relished every minute with him, taking extra walks and car rides until he was simply more comfortable resting at home.

After his passing, we created a memorial in our garden for him, complete with a remembrance plaque showcasing his adorable picture and some kind words. We keep his memory alive by telling Rascal stories to my daughter, who only had a few years with Rascal and doesn't remember as much. We miss him daily and cherish every memory we made together.

Dear Hound

By John Ensor

It's strange what can trigger the memory. It might be a piece of music, a certain fragrance, or perhaps a familiar flavor on the palate—taking you back to a certain time or place. For me, whenever I hear the unmistakable happy whimper of a dog in the middle of a doggy dream, that's when I think of Violet. She would doze off by the fireside and, soon enough, her long limbs would begin to twitch and gallop along, all the while accompanied by a high-pitched "Yip, yip, yip." I would smile and wonder to myself, What is she dreaming of?

Violet, or Vi as we called her, was/is a deerhound. I say Vi *was/is* a deerhound because even after all these years, she's still very real to us. We still use her purple-colored leash while out walking her grown-up offspring, and to this day, I often still call out her name by mistake.

Deerhounds are big, but Vi was big—even by deerhound standards. She never failed to make an impression. I once remember her mooching around the garden when a Chinese couple happened to be passing by.

"Is it a bear?" they inquired.

This giant Scottish breed, lumbering (mostly), grey, and shaggy are, to the untrained eye, somewhere between an Irish wolfhound and a greyhound—I think. You see, Nina's the expert. I had never kept a dog before and Vi just happened to be the big, hairy girl-dog I adopted when I met my wife, Nina.

What is it that makes a pet part of the family? Very often, it's the simple, everyday things. And Vi had so many endearing qualities. To get your attention, Vi would utter an earth-quaking bark that made her two front legs lift clean off the floor. Her sheer physical size meant that she found it difficult to sit. In fact, in all the years we were privileged to have her with us, I never once saw her sit; she either stood or laid down. Although, occasionally, we would catch her posing as the Great Sphinx of Giza. She would have probably given her eyeteeth to have been a lap dog. To compensate for this, she would gently rest her head on my knee; if I happened to be standing, she would lovingly lean against my legs to show her affection.

Another of Vi's trademarks was that she hated water. Sure, it was okay to drink, but she much preferred a cup of tea. Her hydrophobia meant that bath time took on a whole new dimension. Nina and I used to plan it down to the last detail with the same precision as a military operation. However, in reality, it often ended up with two soaked-to-the-skin human beings and one partially bathed dog.

I have so many fond memories of our gentle giant—like the time she gate-crashed a neighbor's barbeque; or the time she ran for her life, leaving our ancient toy poodle all alone to bravely tackle a snake hiding in the long grass—but there's one particular shaggy dog story that stands out. My wife, Nina, had discovered a secret place not far from our house.

"It's beautiful. There are hills, and trees, and a lake. And Vi loved it," Nina explained.

We set off early the next morning and finally arrived at the spot. It was a disused quarry that had long since given up its treasure and was now overgrown, wild, and forgotten. For a brief moment you were transported; you could almost be somewhere in the highlands.

Suddenly, out of nowhere, ran a small herd of Roe deer. For a moment, Violet stood stock still, and a strange far-away look flashed in her eyes before she leapt into action. Maybe this was her doggy dream come true! I watched, hypnotized, as they galloped away up the hill. In slow motion, deer and deerhound disappeared into the ether. I knew there and then that we had seen the last of her.

As twilight drew near, we scoured one last remaining field. There, between the ploughed furrows, she lay motionless, her coat blowing around in the strong wind. Without saying a word, I put my arm around Nina as we walked with our heads bowed. As we got closer, we looked up and realized that it was a large, ragged grey bin bag caught in the earth. It was dark when we finally gave up our search and travelled home in stony silence.

We arrived home and, to our astonishment, there was Violet—still panting, tongue like a length of red carpet—but, thankfully, alive and well. Unbelievably, against all odds, she had somehow managed to find her way home. She slept solidly for three whole days.

Six years later, sadly, her generous heart, which had given us so much love, finally gave out. She had developed a heart condition, and despite medication, she could barely walk, let alone stand. In the end, she even lost the simple pleasure of eating, and couldn't even be tempted by her favorite treats. It became impossible to watch her, once so full of life but now so diminished, that Nina, reluctantly, made the difficult decision to give her sleep.

The vet looked on as Nina spent those last few precious moments whispering in Violet's ear and hugging her one last time. For some reason, I stood back and watched; my lasting regret was that I didn't do the same.

Violet was never going to win Crufts, but to us she was exquisite and left us with two wonderful pups. She was the most gentle, simple soul you could ever wish to meet. There was not a bad bone in her body—unless, of course, you happened to sport antlers. I can still hear that deep-chested woof, and I still miss it terribly. I like to remember her, free and boundless, fearlessly running with the deer, living her deerhound dream.

Phantom of the Shadows

By S. Kay Smith

It takes a special kind of person to love an animal. In most cases, we will outlive the animals we love. Yet, we still put ourselves through the heartache of losing them just for the sake of having them in our lives.

I adopted Phantom when I was twelve. My family had just moved away from our little town in Kentucky to an even smaller town in Texas. It was my family's second move in four years, and to soften the blow, my parents promised me a kitten.

Phantom was the only black kitten at the shelter. As a fledgling spooky girl, I loved black cats. Black cats were witches' familiars, and with *Harry Potter* at the height of its popularity, I very much wanted to be a witch. He was the only cat in his cage, lurking in the shadows, visible only by the light's reflection in his eyes. I immediately sympathized with that undersized kitten, and I knew immediately that he was the cat for me.

Early on, Phantom and I were practically inseparable. He insisted on being wherever I was, and I happily obliged by carrying him around wherever I went, going so far as to find a way to stuff him in my hoodie and ride my bike around the neighborhood with him.

As time wore on, I eventually made friends. However, my bond with Phantom never wavered, and anyone who knew me knew Phantom and

I were a package deal. Phantom was fiercely loyal to me and expected the same of me. If I did anything that seemed like a betrayal to him, he was quick to seek retribution.

As much as he loved me, Phantom didn't like anybody else much. He hated the dog with a burning passion. The dog thought it was great fun when Phantom would chase him around the pool, but we all knew Phantom would have shredded that dog if he could catch him.

When the time came for me to go to college, I had to leave him behind. I was going to be staying in the on-campus dorms, and pets weren't allowed. This was the first time I would be separated from Phantom for longer than a week, and the question of who would care for him was at the forefront of my mind. By that point, Phantom was a well-loved member of the family. I had a plethora of volunteer caretakers.

After my first week, I came home for the weekend to do laundry and catch up with friends. My mom was out in the yard when I pulled into the driveway. So was Phantom. He was hiding in the wisteria and wouldn't come to Mom. As soon as I called his name, he sprang from the shadowy branches and ran at me. He had been waiting for me.

Phantom was with me for nearly fifteen years before his health started failing. It started with several small, fatty tumors. The vet said they probably weren't something to be concerned with but suggested they be removed regardless.

Not long after Phantom's second tumor removal, he started losing a lot of weight very quickly. After a blood test or two, Phantom was diagnosed with kidney failure.

I did everything I could to keep him with me for at least another year. I switched him to a prescription diet that was easier on the kidneys, but he refused to eat it. His weight started dropping even more rapidly, and I moved him back to his regular food.

Phantom's condition was worsening daily, but I still couldn't let him go. Eventually, there was nothing more the vet could do for him. The vet's suggestion was to put him down.

I couldn't accept it. He still came to me when I called his name and purred when I pet him. He even jumped in my lap when he could muster the strength for it, demanding pets and attention. How could he be dying if he still did all the things he usually did?

One of the few good memories I have from that time was with Phantom. We were alone in the house. It was late, and I was enjoying a rare quiet night off. The only light in the house was in my bedroom, where I was lying in bed reading.

I heard a noise out in the hallway.

I glanced up from my book and smiled. A pair of green eyes bobbed toward me out of the shadows, and Phantom hobbled into the room, chirping a greeting at me. He struggled to jump into the bed to join me, so I gave him a little help and pulled him into my lap, where he immediately started purring.

Phantom died on April 16, 2018. It happened right after I came home from work that evening. I went straight to my room to check on him like usual. He was curled into a tight ball on the floor in the closet, but he still greeted me with a weak meow. He was waiting for me.

Phantom died in my arms that night.

I will never forget the way his body shook as I held him. Sometime later, I couldn't help but feel guilty for trying to prolong his life—and his suffering. Maybe the kinder thing would have been to put him down. Now, I have no regrets. As tragic as Phantom's death was, I think of it as intimate and beautiful.

Six months after Phantom died, I found another kitten in the holly bushes outside my new apartment in Sugar Land. I knew I would eventually adopt another cat, but I didn't expect to so soon. Regardless of my plans, it didn't take long for me to fall in love with that kitten. My love for that kitten did much to heal the hole in my heart that Phantom left. That cat is no replacement for Phantom. He will eventually die just like Phantom, but the heartache of losing them is just the price I have to pay for having them in my life.

My Four-Legged Duchess

By Linda Bishop

One day, out of the blue, a beautiful black lab showed up at our son's place in the country. She was so well behaved we thought someone must have lost her and was looking for her. But no, two weeks later, we discovered she was pregnant. Someone had dumped her after all.

About two months later, she gave birth to nine pups. My husband found them under the trailer house and moved them to a box on the porch. Six lived, and my husband drove to the country daily to check on them. He'd always said he'd never have another dog because it was too hard to let go of them. So, he never asked for one … but I saw the look in his eyes. When I said, "You can have a puppy," I'll never forget the joy on his face.

"I can have a puppy?" he asked. "Really? I can have a puppy?"

I'd never really raised a pup before, but I was eager to do so. We didn't know what breed the daddy was, but the two produced beautiful pups. We chose the (slightly) larger of the two black and white ones and called her Ziva (yes, after the NCIS character who had just left the show). She was weaned a week before Christmas, and we were ecstatic to have such a Christmas present!

The first thing my husband did after we walked in the door at home was set her on the couch. The couch! Well, that was my fault; we hadn't

Goodbye for Now

discussed it. But it turned out to be a blessing for me when I came down with a sinus infection. Because of the drainage and coughing, I slept propped up on the end of the couch. Little Ziva would crawl up on my chest and snuggle. I'd never had children of my own, but from then on, I was a puppy mama. As far as she was concerned, we were always Mama and Daddy.

Ziva transitioned easily to sleeping in the bed with us at night. While she was definitely a daddy's girl, she also had a special connection with her mama (i.e., me). I liked to read in bed in the evenings, and—even when she got too big to sleep in the bed with us—our special time together was when she jumped up on the bed and spooned with me while I read.

A couple of months later, we wound up taking the other black and white pup from Ziva's litter as well. A little smaller than Ziva, we called her Li'l Bit. Oh, how Ziva loved having her sister with her. But Ziva sometimes adopted a regal attitude, holding her head up high and walking with a grand "I was here first" attitude. At those times, we laughingly called her "Duchess."

Still, the bed—especially when Mama was in it—was always Ziva's spot. If Li'l Bit tried to move in on her territory, Ziva would trick her. Getting a toy (usually a rope they liked to play tug-of-war with), she would tempt Li'l Bit off the bed, then drop the toy and jump up on the bed with me.

They always got a milk-bone in the morning and a bite of human food after our supper. Right before bed, I gave them each a bacon-flavored treat. And I always told them the same thing: "Night, night, baby girls. Mama loves you."

But then, one day, Ziva developed a lump on the side of her rib cage. The vet took a biopsy and said it was just a fatty deposit. So, we sighed with relief and let it go—until another lump showed up. Then another. And another. This time, the vet said lymphoma. We could treat it, he said, but there was no guarantee it would work. And her quality of life would practically disappear.

She was only eight years old. And, though we knew it meant we would lose her sooner, we chose quality of life with our duchess, our baby girl, our Ziva, over longevity.

Getting up on the bed got harder and harder for her as time went on but she let me help her up so we could have our evening snuggles as I read. She could even still play with her sister in the backyard sometimes. She still got up to greet us when we came in the door, wagging her tail, whining, and licking us all over. Still had enough quality of life to delay the inevitable.

One day, when she got her morning milk-bone, she lay down and started chomping on it as usual. But a few minutes later, I saw huge chunks lying on the floor next to her head. That's when we knew. It was time. Before her quality of life got any worse, we needed to do what was right and let her go. With heavy hearts, we made the appointment with the vet.

We had to help her get into the car … and help her get out. But her tail still wagged. We took her into the room; she snooped just a little, then lay down in the middle of the floor. I lay down beside her, hugging and spooning her one last time. It was the most natural thing in the world—yet one of the hardest—for me to hold her as she went to sleep for the last time.

When I finally let her go and moved up to sit on the bench next to my husband, I saw him wiping the tears from his eyes with a handkerchief. Wiping my own eyes, I looked down at the huge puddle of my own tears where I had been lying.

Short as it seemed, we gave Ziva a good life. Night, night, baby girl. We'll always love you!

A Chance on Charlee

By Sara Barnabie

On a cold concrete floor is where he lay his head at night for two long years. Chatter from strangers and barking dogs in distress surrounded him daily. Fellow furry friends were brought in and quickly whisked away to their forever homes. Yet, there he stayed, night after night. This was the life our sweet dog Charlee lived long before we met him.

Found as a stray and taken into the shelter, Charlee was as sweet as he was unsure. He was a mutt sporting a tan-colored coat with distinct features of a Labrador and Shar Pei. There were several adoption attempts over these two years, but each hope for Charlee quickly vanished as he was brought back to the shelter over and over again. The humane society where Charlee resided sent out multiple pleas for help from the community across local towns and cities. It was to no avail until the day my husband came across a flyer for him. He was intrigued and pitched me the idea of giving Charlee a chance. I agreed, and without any kind of meet and greet or video chat, Charlee was brought to our doorstep.

On first impression, Charlee displayed a quiet, calm dog who was just a little awkward. I appreciated how polite he was, having never jumped on us. I took note of the calculated steps he made while sniffing around the house. And I felt a wave of sadness for him when we realized that, at about three years old, we still had to teach him how to climb stairs. This boy had missed out on so much love throughout his little life, but we fell for him instantly. The search for Charlee's forever home was finally over—he was ours.

Charlee quickly became a family member who was with us all the time. When we took him on outings, he would jump in the car, eager to throw his nose in the wind and slobber on the door. When hiking, he would walk briskly and pant happily, no matter the miles we went. Every adventure we took in the beginning was brand new—like he finally got his chance to see the world. He showed his enthusiasm for life with a constant wag of the tail and a goofy grin.

Charlee was a playmate to our rambunctious toddler. Too often, our son would pull on his tail, drum on his soft, velvety ears, or feed him imaginary food with a spoon. Charlee would just sit there, seemingly unbothered. He didn't bark. He didn't move. He was just endlessly patient.

At the first sight of our cat, Charlee tried to chase her around the house. We quickly corrected that behavior, and Ruby established her boss status. She ruled the roost, and Charlee, who was easygoing, succumbed quickly. Ruby loved to cuddle with Charlee and would plop herself real close to him. He never showed much interest in these cuddle sessions, but when she would walk away, his head perked up as if to say, "Hey, come back." She pushed right through his awkwardness, and they became the best of buds.

Shortly after my father passed away, Charlee found me sobbing on my floor. I was alone, six months pregnant, and an absolute mess. It seemed to me that Charlee was unsure of what to do, but he knew he couldn't leave me. He hovered so close, in such a gentle way. He stood staring at the wall while I hugged him, covering his fur in my tears.

As the years went on, Charlee's disposition turned more melancholy. His weight started to drop while his interest in food and activities lessened. We were on alert as his symptoms and accidents grew in frequency. We brought him to the vet, and the hope we had for him to get better grew dim. There was an array of intestinal issues and signs of potential cancer in his stomach. It was the exact news we had hoped we wouldn't hear. The suffering had already begun for our poor boy, and we knew it would only continue.

We took Charlee home for one more night before we had to say good-bye. It was a restless one. I slept on the kitchen floor with him, snuggling close and providing comfort as he winced in pain. The next morning, I watched as his failing body, now so skinny and fragile, walked out of our house for the very last time. Once in the room, we told Charlee he was such a "good boy" and hugged him as he lay peacefully. With heavy hearts and balling eyes, we stayed by his side until the very last rise and fall of his chest. We kissed him goodbye and reluctantly left his room as our new reality set in.

When we arrived home for the first time without our Charlee-boy, his trail of little footprints lay fresh in the snow. When we entered the house and took off our shoes, little pieces of his fur clung to my socks. The doggie bed sat on the floor, a dog bowl off in the corner. I heard the phantom sounds of his paws clinking on the hardwood floors. And a corner of our bed was now vacant—the space where he had slept for six years.

There was now an emptiness within our home. It was loud and apparent. Charlee was more than just a pet. He was a part of our lives, our routines, and our hearts.

This boy, who had been labeled as a misfit, overlooked, and unwanted, filled our lives with so much goodness. We reaped the joys of receiving his love, and I am endlessly grateful we took him into our home. My hope remains that our sweet boy Charlee will look in on us from time to time, remembering the impact four little paws, a wagging tail, and his giant heart left on our family.

The Cat Who Was My True Friend Growing Up

By Vyacheslav Suslov

Serious, responsible, intelligent, well-mannered—words like that don't often describe a person, let alone a cat. But that's what Bass was, my cat, my childhood friend. He came into my life when I was a child and left when I was fifteen. He was there for me as I discovered the world, and like a silent mentor, he taught me kindness and love for life.

Every summer during my school break, my parents would take me to my grandmother's summer house for nearly three months. The trip took about four hours, first by train and then by car. Bass always accompanied me on these journeys, usually in a wicker basket with a soft blanket on the bottom.

So we rode: I would look out the window and imagine a superhero running alongside the train, jumping over all sorts of obstacles, while Bass watched what happened around him through the woven wire of the basket, only occasionally allowing himself to meow.

We spent the whole summer in the garden near my grandmother's house, surrounded by old apple trees, black currant and gooseberry bushes, and restless chickens that always tried to escape. Bass had his own territory, which he fiercely defended, constantly chasing the neighbors' cats away. I used to walk around the house and imagine that it was my little country, and if I didn't protect it, it would cease to exist. In a way, it was. After my grandmother died, we stopped spending summers at her house, and our summer world ceased to exist.

Our last summer—I didn't know it was both Bass's last summer and the last summer of my childhood—was not the same as it had always been. Bass was fifteen years old then—over one hundred in cat years. On his first day, he got into a fight with one of the local cats, fell off a roof, and broke his paw. After that, he moved very slowly, always looking around, waiting for an attack.

I couldn't leave him alone in hostile territory, so I took him out into the yard several times a day to do his cat business. That was probably the first time I realized what it meant to be responsible for someone. I looked at the land of our summer and gradually stopped recognizing it.

The day we went home, I walked around the house and the garden, saying goodbye to each corner. I remember the slight sadness that came over me as I picked up Bass to put him in the travel basket. It seemed as if he knew that my childhood land was gone, that his days were numbered, and that neither of us would ever return to that summer house by the warm southern sea.

After a few months, although Bass's paw had healed and he was walking on his own again, time began to take its toll. He began to have sight issues, and a cloudy film covered his eyes. The vets said there was a treatment, but he didn't have long to live, and it would likely shorten his already short life.

Over the years, Bass had learned the furniture layout by heart and went everywhere by feel, if you can say that about a cat who feels the space around him not with his hands but with his keen sense of smell. We tried to make his life as easy as possible, and our usually chaotic house was suddenly in order. Chairs and armchairs were in their proper places and weren't moved around—even if it was a little uncomfortable. Things weren't left on the floor, and Bass was given the right of way when he went to the kitchen or bathroom as if he moved on invisible rails.

It seemed like this was our new reality and would be the norm for a long time. Unfortunately, life has its own ideas about how things should be.

After a while, Bass's hind legs failed. We took him to the vet again. Then another. And another. One even suggested giving Bass a shot and putting him to sleep.

These were the last days of his life. We knew it, but we didn't want to believe it.

One day, I came home and saw my mom standing unmoving in the hallway, looking down. Bass was lying on the floor in front of her. His breath had already left his body. He was lying there as if he was about to jump over the line between life and death.

He was a good hunter and went out like a real fighter—moving.

I don't know what cats feel. I don't know what happens when they are gone. But I do know that Bass was more than just a pet. He shared some of the brightest moments of my childhood with me. He taught me to love the outdoors, to enjoy the warmth of sunlight, to take responsibility for the less fortunate, and to never—never!—give up. With his big paws, large head, and bright green eyes, he taught me independence and resilience.

Bass passed away, but the real understanding that he was gone came later when I realized he had gone to follow my childhood. I want this tribute to remind readers that true friends do not always take human form, but they play no less a role in our lives.

RIP Bass

I love you.

Gizmo

By Zanandi Botes

When my husband and I uprooted our lives and moved from Johannesburg to Cape Town in the winter of 2012, we were faced with quite a few challenges. Not only did we have to start our lives all over again in a brand new city with few friends or family, but we also received some shocking news: My wonderful mother-in-law had been diagnosed with cancer. To suddenly be so far away from our loved ones wasn't easy, but then one day, Gizmo walked into our new home, jumped onto my lap, and decided that we would be his new cat people.

Gizmo—named after one of my favorite childhood movie characters—was a vocal little furball who'd constantly chat with us and always wanted to be part of the conversation. When people came to visit, he'd greet everyone, making his rounds and sharing his kind and friendly demeanor with any and all willing to pet him. He'd go wild whenever a can of tuna was opened in the kitchen, and he loved eating chicken. He didn't like leaving our side one bit, and we were truly happiest being in his company. Both my husband and I had had cats before, but never one so attached, so wholly dependent on us.

Gizmo was a sea of comfort during the difficult time with my mother-in-law. When she passed away in 2018, he was a refuge for us and gave us family while we were so far away from ours. He was a highly intuitive cat—as many of them are—and he would know when we needed a cuddle, his purring body a salve for a hurting heart.

We moved twice with our little nugget in tow—first to an apartment, where we'd take him for long walks around the block. Neighbors would react, saying he was just like a little dog following us everywhere, no leash required. When we finally moved to a place with a garden, we were so excited and, frankly, proud that we could give Gizmo the private green space he deserved. Little did we know he'd be enjoying it for such a short time.

In May of 2019, Gizmo walked into our living room and collapsed out of nowhere. There was something seriously wrong with his lower body. We rushed him to the veterinarian, who diagnosed him with an infection but couldn't really say what was at fault. He was put on a drip for dehydration and released after two days with a cocktail of medications to treat a broad spectrum of possible prognoses. After a month, we were starting to become hopeful as it seemed like he was on the up—almost his old self again. He was back at his favorite spot on my working desk, soaking up the South African winter sun while I wrote and occasionally stroked his back. We felt relieved. He was going to make it.

In late August, Gizmo took a turn for the worse. A lot of money and many, many tests later, no vet was able to tell us what was wrong with him, simply that his body was shutting down. It broke our hearts seeing our little guy—who, for the past seven years, looked to us to take care of him as much as he took care of us—essentially becoming paralyzed. We felt an overwhelming sense of helplessness seeing his once bright eyes now dimmed with pain. In the end, we had to make the dreaded call that no pet owner ever wants to make. Saying goodbye to him and holding him in our arms when he took his final breath has been haunting me ever since.

I cried for a month, every day, non-stop. I'd walk into the kitchen, and my mind's memory would conjure him right there in my peripheral, following me for a snack. I would turn to look, and he'd be gone, and I would sit on the kitchen floor and sob uncontrollably. It got so bad that I realized I needed professional help. When death's sickle drops twice in a year's time to claim not one but two treasures in your life, it can take a huge toll on a person's mental well-being. It took a lot of time—and a lot of good therapy—for my heart to stop the constant bleeding, even though as I sit here and write this, the wound feels as open and raw as it did the day we said goodbye.

It's been almost five years without Gizmo, and I still miss him dearly. We have a wonderful little cat now, and when the sadness rises up in me, I turn to her, my Mila, grateful that we get to have her. Grateful that, just like Gizmo, she also showed up out of nowhere and chose us to be her new cat people. Grateful that I have these special memories with special animals who trust us to take care of them and might never really know how much they, in turn, took care of us.

Patches

By Chelsea Pinkham

I knew it was coming. But what could possibly have prepared me?

To watch them carry your frail body away, to see you disappear down the street of our childhood home. How it's changed over the years. Your transition from a physical entity—something tangible—to an abstract idea, a story character, a memory—it all happened so fast. Too fast to understand. Too sudden to grieve wholly. One moment, you were there. The next, you were not.

What I wouldn't give to walk together one last time. Anything. If there was something I could do, if there was a possibility of a reunion for even just a moment, I would dedicate my entire life to seeing you again.

Sixteen years prior was the first time I ever cried tears of joy. The moment I held you in my arms. We weren't supposed to visit the pet store that day. But fate is serendipitous. We were ignorant of the evils of pet stores in those days. Still, we hadn't planned on buying a puppy. When our eyes met, I knew we were meant to be together. From across the crowded store, with several looming hands in your display case, you sat down, fixated on me.

It was an instant, deep knowing. As if from a lifetime long past, I knew you. And it was obvious that you knew me too. In that moment, all else ceased to exist. For the first time in my life, I decided that I would not, and could not, leave without you; my vivid imagination was already alive with beautiful visions of our lives together. Before your shiny nose touched my little hand, I couldn't envision life without you.

Maybe what I experienced that day was truly something cosmic and inexplicable. Maybe that's just what it feels like to be a child meeting your first puppy.

You were the "discount puppy" of mysterious origins. In a store full of purebred puppies and the newest puppy mill "designer" mutts, you were a truly random mix. Your marked-down label claimed you were a Shih-Tzu. But the manager knew otherwise. You had arrived with a shipment of puppies two weeks younger than you. No littermates, no paperwork. Your temperament was drastically different from your supposed "siblings." When called and questioned, the Kansas breeder you'd come from denied your very existence. Who were you, and where did you come from? We'd never find out.

Maybe you'd shown up on the breeder's land, and they'd tried to make an extra buck off of you. Maybe you were a child's puppy who turned out to be a handful. Perhaps you'd stumbled onto the side of the road, and some nice old truck driver took pity on you.

What was clear was the fact that this scruffy puppy, with a tremendous attitude and perfect black patches, had managed to be in the right place at the right time. *Patches.*

"You're my dog," I whispered as I felt my eyes begin to well. You were the most beautiful thing I had ever seen, and the realization that you were mine, mine forever, was the most overwhelming emotion I had ever experienced. How anyone could have ever overlooked you was beyond my understanding. How grateful I am that they did.

In your younger days, you were far from a "good dog" in the conventional sense. That wasn't your fault. You knew dozens of tricks and were the reigning champion of the ragtag agility set my dad built for my ninth birthday. You starred as "Toto" in my high school's rendition of *The Wizard of Oz.* The audience loved you.

But I didn't have a clue how to teach you things that mattered, like coming when called. Hence, the seven-mile midnight seagull chase through thick fog. And the swim from the rental boat onto a rancher's lakeside land where you chased cows in over one hundred-degree heat until you collapsed from exhaustion. The "great bakery heist" explains itself. You sure knew how to have a good time.

You were a wild and untamable thing with a deeply kind side. I rescued hundreds of animals during your lifetime; perhaps it was my repentance for buying you from a pet store. Kittens, mice, piglets, lambs—you were so gentle with them.

You were my sidekick in life, seeing me through elementary school, middle school, high school, and college. You took your job seriously. And as it all unfolded, time passed. I didn't realize it because I was growing up too. But suddenly, your eyes were softer, and your muzzle grayer. Time is the stealthiest thief.

Even on your last day, you gave those seagulls one last chase. Although I could see the pain of your aching body behind your eyes, I also saw pride—a fading champion determined to remain dignified even in your final moments, hell-bent on never failing the human you loved most, despite your own weakened body failing you. When you looked back and saw me laughing, I saw a release in your facial expression. It was as if you were seeking reassurance that you had done what I had asked of you. You looked so dignified; head held high, you raised your nose to smell the salty ocean air one last time. After fifteen or twenty minutes—what felt like a lifetime yet was a moment too painfully brief—you looked back at me again, standing and facing inland to let me know that it was time. When I carried you back to the car, it felt like an eternity.

And just like that, it was over.

Four years have passed now. I've grieved deeply. I don't think I will ever "move on." But now, I smile when I tell stories about you. Your collar hangs from the dashboard of my car. I'm even preparing to adopt a puppy. You'd be proud of how far I've come. And with the same cosmic knowing from the day we met, I know I will see you again.

 Goodbye for Now

Achilles the Brave

By Daniel Henriquez

"Is that one of those hairless, skinless dogs?" an inquisitive older woman asked while we walked our Chinese Crested at the beach one night.

"Hairless? Yes. Skinless … well, if that were the case, we'd have a serious problem," my mother quickly retorted.

This Chinese Crested named Achilles—part of a breed that perennially wins the "Ugliest Dog" competition—began his life as a TV celebrity. When he was two years old, the local news ran a piece on this handsome, naked mole rat masquerading as a dog. Our family fell absolutely in love with his sweet disposition and inquisitive personality; the rest is history.

Walking down the street, Achilles loved to take the lead. He would pull confidently on his leash, leading the family from adventure to adventure. No hill was too steep to climb; no fire hydrant was too tall to mark his position in the dog hierarchy. This 20-lb. furless fearless leader walked the walk and talked the talk—that is until a car would pass by and he would hide between our legs, shaking profusely. BUT! When the cars had passed, Achilles quickly jumped out front and led the way as if he owned the road. Again, that is until a bigger dog walked by, and he would pull us to the opposite side of the street. BUT! When that dog had passed, Achilles the

Brave would continue his never-ending mission to mark and claim his territory anew around the city with his family in tow each day.

It wasn't until Lady Godiva, also known as "Diva," came into our family that one of my favorite quirks of Achilles came into full view. Diva, a Chinese Crested/Mexican Hairless cross, was a 40-lb. hairless dog with a sassy attitude. She was number one. She was top dog. She was even *more* naked than Achilles. If Achilles was the original Terminator, Diva was the upgraded model in *Terminator 2* that was physically superior in every way. How would these two figure out who was to be the dominant dog in this relationship?

Both dogs had designated areas in the neighborhood that they would routinely use to lay down their "nightly duties" for us to carry home. Diva was quick and to the point with hers, more of a drop-and-go in a quiet part of the neighborhood. On the other hand, Achilles chose to do his business on a highly trafficked, public thoroughfare leading to the baseball fields by our high school. He would find a patch of grass, take his time walking in circles as if he were surrounding the city of biblical Jericho, and let his business loose. Then, he would proudly stand up, look opposite of Diva, forcefully flick the dirt around his droppings at her one foot at a time, stick his legs out, and leave them shaking in the air for all to marvel. Right foot—*WOOSH*—*dangle … Forceful point.* Left foot—*WOOSH*—*dangle … Forceful point.* Right foot—yeah, you get the point. This wildly weird and wonderful dance would last about thirty seconds or so—an awkwardly long amount of time, mind you, when people walking by are asking if your dog is okay—and then we would be on our way home, Achilles walking victoriously as he showed Diva he was king of the poop dance. This would happen for the next decade as Diva and Achilles vied for the top dog position.

My mother was the administrator of an assisted living facility, where older adults would be taken care of and comforted in their golden years until God took them home. What a fitting way for Achilles to go, too, as he was nearing the end of his years, though his heart was bursting with so much love left to give. With most of his teeth missing, hair going gray, and liver spots all over his smooth, human-like skin, Achilles went from guarding and taking care of our family to guarding the laps of older adults; my mom brought our frail man to work with her every day so he wouldn't be alone in his last days. Shaking with every step in his old age, Achilles would lift his frail body onto the laps of those who needed comfort or warmth and give tender kisses in the special, toothless way only he could. Older adults would describe him as a "hot-water bottle," as his smooth, furless skin would feel 100°, providing immeasurable comfort to those who could no longer provide heat to themselves. Once the brave and intrepid leader for a family of three growing kids (now adults) and innumerable rescued pets, Achilles would be brave in facing the inevitable: the long tomorrow that brings hope of seeing loved ones again when we pass into the horizon into Jesus's arms. What better way to spend the end of his life than helping minister to so many others who were about to embark on their journey away from this earth, too?

Then, one final day, after a kiss on the head and being tucked into bed, Achilles was taken from this earth, to be woken up in Heaven with Jesus and all those who were waiting for him. In Heaven, the lion will lay with the lamb, and I'm sure Achilles will be friends with Sampson. He'll stand brave in the face of cars and chariots, protect every innocent child, and most of all, I'm confident he will be dancing his heart out during that long, everlasting day. Rest well, my friend. Until we meet again, heart to paw and much love from the family.

Milo

By Allison Byrne

"There's fluid around his heart." We watched the rise and fall of Milo's stomach; as he wheezed, each breath cut through the silence in the room. "We'll remove what we can but if it returns, there's nothing else we can do."

Milo's once fluffy red fur, now a greasy, matted mess, tumbled over his sullen golden eyes as he gazed upon his best friend Dane, my 18-month-old son. Steadying myself as tears stung the back of my eyes, I exited the vet, releasing a breath of determination.

"I'll fix you. Not yet Milo."

Red? I never cared for red cats. He's not even cute.

There I was, in a sea of fluff picking out the perfect Persian kitten. The kitten that would ease my nerves on the eve of moving out of my parents' house. The kitten I could place my faith in to make this monumental life pivot. The kitten that would make everything okay. Suddenly, an hour into surveying kittens, the vast mass of fur balls parted to reveal a grumpy-looking, messy-haired cat darting towards me, his golden eyes locked on mine. He released a purr upon meeting my lap, turning clockwise and falling asleep instantly, like a lap dog.

"He is available but he's older and a little quirky—he's also been here quite a while," the breeder offered while shrugging her shoulders. "I have others you might want to look at."

Was this peculiar cat going to be the first big decision I made on my own? Lacking any self-confidence as I stood on the edge of independence, this disheveled, overlooked, and quite frankly, ugly fur ball nestled in my lap displayed a faith in me I wish I had in myself.

Stealing his confidence, I declared, "Yes, this is my cat." Before I knew it, I was shoving the massive red puffball inside his carrier to spend my last night under my parents' roof. The roof I wasn't so sure I wanted to leave the comforting embrace of. But I had my own cat now; we would do this together, Milo and me.

We soon fell into a happy rhythm, and I found myself looking forward to him welcoming me home daily with his grumpy face. His loud purrs lulled me to sleep each night and his loops around my feet as he followed me everywhere helped ease my homesick heart. Milo continued to display an uncanny intuitiveness and puppy-like personality that left me scratching my head in laughter and awe regularly. Stealing household items with his mouth and hiding them under my pillow, or riding along in the passenger seat next to me as his wet nose fogged up the glass were some of his favorite pastimes.

Soon, another life pivot was on the horizon, but I knew everything would be fine: I had my Milo by my side! With Milo in my lap, my new husband carried us through the threshold of our new home, Milo's purr reverberating in tune with my pulse in excitement. With a new roof over our head, the three of us fell into another happy rhythm.

Until there was four.

The day we brought our son, Dane, home from the hospital, Milo was in love. In the background of each picture of our newborn, you would find Milo hovering nearby like a "Where's Waldo," making sure his buddy was okay. When Dane cried, Milo would run to his side. When Dane laughed, Milo's purr would rip through the room like a thunderstorm. When Dane slept, Milo would wait outside his room like a well-paid bodyguard. As a baby, Dane was frequently sick with lung and breathing issues. Each time Dane fell ill, Milo would be glued to him like an appendage, refusing to leave his side. Up all night with us, through the wheezing, crying, and regular breathing treatments, Milo would stand vigil, his focus never leaving Dane—his eyes never shutting to fall asleep until Dane would. His presence calmed not only Dane's soul, but mine as well. Milo had found his person; it was as if he knew Dane would arrive all along. As if he chose me for this reason.

Then one day, he wasn't there—not waiting beside Dane's door, not rumbling his purr at our arrival, not snorting his happy snorts. With hope in our hearts, we took him to the vet.

"He's only ten years old. Plus, cats have nine lives," I whispered to my husband, attempting to hide the fear expanding throughout my soul.

Cancer. That rancid six-letter word. It swooped down and took Milo hostage like a vicious monster. We threw everything at it, but cancer just swallowed up our feeble attempts and spat them back out.

"It's time," the vet said, solemnly leaving the room to gather the concoction that would be the end of our happy family of four. As he did so, Milo suddenly rose to his feet, looking at my husband and I as if to ask us something. His breaths were ragged and his once-full figure was now a hollow shell, his red fur dangling loosely from his emaciated limbs. Yet his golden eyes gazed around the room in desperation, looking for something … looking for someone. He knew it was his time, but he needed his reason for being here next to him. We cautiously brought Dane into the room, and an air of sorrow took hold. Milo relaxed instantly and laid back down, ready for his finality.

In the beginning it was me and Milo, but he knew he was meant for a family. He found that family. And that family surrounded him during his final moments. He left this world peacefully on the wings of our tears, knowing he had served his purpose in this life.

The Good Luck Mutt

By Jennifer Watkins

I'd had an elderly rescue dog, Sheba, for a couple of years; a stunning husky mix with broken teeth and ribs, she was found chained to a picnic table. Hoping to find a companion to keep her company, I brought her to a rescue event and explained what I was looking for to a volunteer. He returned with a young, spotted mutt with perky ears and wide, human-like brown eyes. The volunteer dropped the lead, and the dog calmly walked up and took a seat beside Sheba, never even sniffing her. He looked into my eyes and lifted one paw very slowly, holding it in the air like he was waiting for me to hold it (which I did). Moments later, Sheba relaxed into his side.

My friend took out her phone and said, "Well, we might as well take the first family photo."

I named him Murphy because of his clear bad luck; besides the missing teeth, he had a small moon-shaped scar on the top of his head that never grew hair, a larger one on the bottom of his jaw, and heartworms. Whatever he'd lived through before was quickly forgotten.

As Sheba aged, Murphy slowed his pace to match hers on walks, even though he loved to gracelessly bounce between the flowers he'd shove his nose into. He mourned her for weeks after she passed, laying on her bed and taking deep inhales. He'd rest his full weight in my lap and put his head on my shoulder when I cried over her.

Murphy was wickedly smart, observant, and funny in a way that proved he could read the reactions of the humans around him. Murphy was also stubborn, which I learned when I briefly tried to break him of the habit of offering his paw for holding to anyone he loved. He had a fierce desire to be included, and was at the center of everything that happened in my home, whether he was the star of the party or the comforter of anyone who felt sad.

After a shocking cancer diagnosis during his annual exam, I threw myself into research. I visited holistic vets, consulted with experts via Zoom, found a wonderful oncology team, read every published study, and visited every message board. He'd lay by my feet in the kitchen as I cooked all his meals and dehydrated all his treats at home, eliminating anything that could feed the cancer, occasionally gagging as I blended vegetables and organ meats I'd sourced from online butchers.

I received a grant from a local nonprofit, FetchaCure, that offsets the cost of cancer treatments for owners who can't afford it, and they quickly fell in love with Murphy as well. I meticulously documented every piece of research, every recipe, and every supplement on an Instagram account, hoping that I'd find the magic combination to save him, and that other owners could follow the blueprint I'd laid out. I brought him to volunteer at Fetch's table during community events, and he was photographed and filmed for promos. His oncologists and Fetch team gladly took him to a segment on the local news on a day that I couldn't leave school, and he even went onstage with me at a fundraising gala where hundreds of people smothered him with love and wishes for recovery. In short, Murphy spent his last few months receiving the celebrity treatment he always thought he deserved.

A part of me believed that all of that love would save him. I knew the odds, but I also secretly felt like everything we did was a kind of magic; if I worked hard enough, if I helped other owners, if I proved how far I'd go for him, we'd win. He'd live.

Over a few short days, he declined; I couldn't cook anything to tempt him into eating, he had accidents in his sleep, and on the last day, the jingle of his leash didn't excite him into standing. I brought him to his oncologist and they confirmed that the new tumors were simply too large; he was succumbing to the tumor burden, which had quickly become uncomfortable. I'd planned to end his life at home, but decided at that moment that he'd be more comfortable surrounded by the doctors and nurses who had grown to love the happy patient they'd all given their own special nicknames to.

His doctor carried him in and sat on the floor with me as I held his head in my lap and fought to keep my voice from breaking, wanting him to believe he was simply falling asleep. I told him that he was loved, that he was my best friend, that there would never be another Murph. He passed almost immediately, and I could feel the relief in his body as it went heavy in my arms; he had fought the cancer off to stay by my side as long as he could.

Knowing what was happening inside of him, I'd savored every day that we stole—exactly one year and one week post-diagnosis. I had packed those days with memories and tiny indulgences so there was no possible regret to feel. While I had that comfort, I was still crushed by all of the tiny firsts: the first time in the car without him, the first time I opened the door and my other dog realized he wasn't right behind me, the first time I mistakenly scooped out his dog food, the first time I reached out to pet him in bed and hit an empty pillow. I've stopped listening for his claws on the floor or imagining a paw on my arm, but I still think of him daily. Soon, I'll bring home another bad-luck mutt to love, and I know I'll feel him there—glad I gave my love to another one like him.

Suzi

By Chris de Boer

I met Suzi about twelve years ago when I first visited my wife's family home. At that time, she was around three years old. After realizing that I was with my wife and smelling me, Suzi accepted me immediately. Our relationship became more intense when we moved into my wife's parents' house three years ago.

Unlike most people in rural Thailand, my wife and I view pets as companions. We treat them well, educate them, and train them to listen. We started to give Suzi and her daughter, Soso, good food instead of bones and rice. Unsurprisingly, the dogs liked us.

Suzi became an even more determined guardian of the house, the garden, and us. She was an expert at chasing and killing lizards, mice, and rats that wanted to come into the garden, the car, or the house. As a good mother, she taught Soso how to hunt, too.

When the rice grows in the fields behind our house during the rainy season, there are plenty of harmless, nonpoisonous, relatively small snakes that only eat mice, rats, and frogs. But sometimes, a dangerous snake, like a king cobra, would appear. While Soso would keep some distance from the cobra, Suzi always attacked. In the last five years, there were two instances when a cobra spit poison in her eyes, and she could not see anymore. Her sight eventually came back after a paste of special herbs combined with coconut milk was applied to her eyes.

Suzi was a very nice dog to those she liked, but not so nice to those she disliked. And she had a very good memory. She would run to the gate and bark loudly when one of the village dogs, who had been mean to her in the past, walked by.

About two years ago, I started offering English classes to poor children in the village on weekends. Suzi was not used to children, but she never barked at them when they were at the gate—she welcomed them. We told the children that Suzi was already old and the mother of Soso. The children called her "Kuhn Ya Suzi," which means "Grandmother Suzi." In Thai society, aged people are very much respected. Suzi would sit at the open front door during class, looking at how the class went.

Suzi got cancer. I had the impression that she was never in pain. You could touch her everywhere, hug her, or lift her up. We found no reason to take her to the vet to be put to sleep. Besides, nearly all Thai veterinarians refuse to perform euthanasia because of religious reasons. According to Buddhism, life is suffering. The solution to this suffering is through prayer and meditation.

On Monday, July 15, 2024, I woke up at 5:30 a.m. My morning routine consists of turning on the living room light, starting the coffee machine, going to the restroom, and feeding our two cats. Then, I open the kitchen windows and the back door to let the fresh morning air come in. But that morning, the back door was blocked. I walked around the house to see what had happened. I remember hearing some noise in the middle of the night, but I had thought it was not serious because Suzi and Soso did not bark, so I went back to sleep.

In front of the back door was Suzi. I could see that she was not sleeping—her eyes were open. She was dead. It was not unexpected because I knew she had cancer, but when the moment arrived, it still took me by surprise. I closed her eyes and stood still in silence—sad and happy at the same time. Sad because she was a good companion for many years. Happy because I had known her and had given her an extra hug before going to bed the night before.

Later that morning, we buried her in the garden. Suzi was not my dog. She was my in-laws' dog; but emotions do not care about ownership.

Some of my in-laws believe Suzi's soul belonged to a monk in a past life—a monk who had made some mistakes. The monk's soul reincarnated in Suzi, with the promise that it would come back as a human if it was a good dog. I believe that the soul that lived in Suzi for fifteen years will return as a human in due time. She deserves it.

Part VII

Sibling

A Promise Kept

By Jack Maher

I'll bet most readers don't spend much time thinking about the dedications that precede most novels. Maybe after you read this, you will. You see, the one I placed at the beginning of my book fulfills a promise made decades ago to a troubled young man I loved dearly—my only brother, Chris. Chris was the primary force and spark behind my book, which recounts the legacy of our grandfather, a Native Arts expert and early Denver Art Museum pioneer. The rich and colorful life he led was a stark contrast to ours.

Growing up, our little family was afflicted with mental illness and alcoholism. There were many long nights that included anger, violence, and police calls. We had separate rooms in the basement, and I remember calling out quietly to each other to make sure we were doing okay. We often went to school on very little sleep, pretending everything was fine when it wasn't.

We outgrew the chaos and moved on with our lives, forever sharing a bond of survival. I went to college, married a beautiful redhead named Becky, built a career in broadcasting, and raised a family. Chris remained single, decided against higher learning, and spent quite a bit of time trying to find his true calling. He was a talented artist, excelling in portraying human anatomy in high school and using this skill to draw a superhero strip for the school paper. During his period of self-discovery, he ended up working in manufacturing, specifically electroplating. He left art behind.

One morning, while at work, a mentally ill man who had been our former neighbor came to my brother's workplace with a handgun. He shot Chris several times, left, and went on to murder my brother's best friend within minutes. That day, I was working graveyards at a Denver TV station, producing a morning news show. I remember the assignment desk telling me in my headset that we were sending our news helicopter to cover a breaking story of a workplace shooting. It was a brief report—there weren't many facts. I had no idea that the victim was my brother.

It was only hours later, at home, when I got a call from a police detective. He tried to tell me as gently as he could that my brother had been shot several times and was in critical condition at the hospital. I was numb with shock, and I'm not sure I heard much of what he said after the first few minutes.

I'll never forget visiting Chris in the hospital, wrapped in bandages and hooked up to machines. The doctors told me he was in bad shape but that they were doing everything possible and that I could only stay for a minute or two. He was pretty much out of it, but I remember leaning in and trying to encourage him.

"You're strong," I said. "I know you're going to make it through."

Somehow, he had the awareness and the strength to move his head slightly, raise his right hand, and give me a thumbs up. That simple gesture gave me hope.

Chris survived physically, but he never recovered emotionally and psychologically, especially when he learned of his best friend's death. The man who shot him was deemed mentally incompetent to stand trial and was institutionalized. Chris tried his best to get back on track but increasingly turned to alcohol to get rid of the trauma and the pain. He thought moving away might help, and for a time he was very successful at a sales job in California. But his alcohol intake increased, and he kept slipping further into darkness. He eventually lost his job and became homeless. I knew nothing of this. Every time we communicated, he was upbeat. We'd learned how to hide ugly truths from our chaotic childhood.

He lived on the streets for months until one night, he finally called me—collect—and told me everything. I can only imagine how hard that call was for him and the humility it required. I sent him money for a bus ticket and had him stay with me. It was difficult on our young family. He was clearly damaged, and we weren't equipped to properly deal with his challenges. I got Chris into rehab, found him a small place downtown, and he found another sales job. Things appeared to be looking up.

Our last time together was in the front seat of my car when I was dropping him off at his place. I told him how proud I was of him for trying to start over. He cried, hugged me, and told me he loved me. I did the same and reminded him not to forget how much he'd overcome despite all the darkness. I repeated the words I'd said after he'd been shot.

"You're strong. You're going to make it through."

We talked for quite a while. He asked me what I thought I'd be doing in the years to come. I told him I hoped that one day, when my broadcasting days were over, I'd write a book about our grandfather and his contributions to the Denver Art Museum and the world of Native American Art. At the time, neither of us knew much about our grandfather Poppy—just enough to know he was an interesting, important figure. But for now, my main focus was getting the next day's morning show on the air, picking up the kids from school, and spending time with Becky. We said goodbye.

A few days later, I got a call. This time, it was from the coroner's office. Chris was dead. He'd taken his life at just thirty-two and left a handwritten note. The person from the coroner's office cautioned me against reading it, but I had to. There were tear stains across it. In it, Chris said he was just too tired to fight anymore. He closed by apologizing, by telling me again how much he loved me. And he closed with these words: "Someday, promise me you'll write that book."

Here I am, more than thirty years later. The book is done, and the dedication reads, "For Chris: A Promise Kept."

Ode to My Big Brother

By Catherine M. Finger

My brother Dave was one of my fiercest advocates until the day he died at sixty-two. We shared a love of cooking cultivated by many a "cook-off" in our teens. His passion led him to study at the Culinary Institute of America, and his love for excellent food and sharing it shaped his life professionally and personally. The love of his life was his son, and they shared many happy hours hunting, fishing, and cooking—passions my nephew enjoys deeply to this day.

Our childhood was marred by alcoholism and disarray, framing a shared early experience that featured nearly every "adverse childhood experience" you can muster up. Still—we shared a deep love for nature, humor, and an unbreakable family bond. My brother engaged with the recovery community in our area for many years, and his death was a severe blow.

My brother beat up the first boy who kissed me. He lectured me endlessly on the perils of boys, booze, and Democrats. And he proudly stood in the audience when I was the first in our family to earn a doctorate long ago. And like everyone in my family before or since—he struggled with addiction and bore its constant mental health assaults with perseverance, faith, and grace.

My brother taught me that there are many ways to live a life. He taught me about being there for someone else and what never giving up on someone looks like. And ultimately, he taught me that there are battles we are not destined to win on this good earth. Or maybe he is still teaching me that there are many paths to victory—and some are hidden.

My brother died on June 13, 2021—five days after I was sworn in as a law enforcement chaplain in our little hometown—our little shared corner of the world. His death involved many first responders, and it threw me into an intimate world much faster than I'd planned. And while I was able to rush to his side with our other brother moments before his death to share a final prayer and as much love and peace and presence as our broken hearts could offer—the aching absence of what could have been remains.

The short piece I share with you reflects the tension of love and loss and the unsettling nature of tragedies suffered and shared. In my work as an executive and health and wellness coach, my clients present with a range of mental health challenges and desires sitting below the surface of the issues that bring them to my table. My brother's life and death empower me to listen beyond what is said and offer a light and supportive presence as others struggle down their own sometimes rocky paths. I share with you what I think of as an ode to my big brother as it sits presently, lightly in my heart, and I offer it as one woman's experience with tragic loss and the shadowy walk through grief we all must bear.

Ode to My Big Brother

I miss you, Dave.

And I'm sorry I wasn't there more.

Sorry I wasn't able to race home to you that final time you reached out to me in your desperation—asking for cigarettes and whiskey the day before you died. Sorry that you found someone else willing to pick you up a gallon of Jim Beam when I would not. I'm sorry that you died angrily—sorrowfully—in your desperation, in your chosen solitude.

I'm sorry for your final night and your final morning of agony … when I was in Nebraska, Pete was in Missouri, Dan was in denial … and you died. Alone. Tragically.

I'm sorry, Dave.

I'm sorry I couldn't offer you a better—stronger—faster reason to stay. I'm sorry I couldn't wrap you in arms of love warm enough to keep you tethered to this family, grounded on this earth, encircled in love on this planet.

I'm sorry.

And I love you from afar—through the galaxies of heavens and earths and spirit worlds between us.

I hope your face is shining, bright and beautiful. Eyes alight with the sheer love of nature, a good mushroom hunt, and a raucous, off-color joke—the brother I remember and miss every day still.

The fierce love and abject sorrow with which you held your son, your grandsons, and your place in their lives.

Your sacrificial parting gift of financial security.

Your sacrificial spirit of departure—clouded though it was. Your loneliness, your despondency. And while I wish—still—I could've lifted the weight of that sorrow, that pain, that generational curse from you, so too do I delight in your freedom from it.

I see you now—celestial. Your beautiful self, surrounded by lush green forests, hunting, fishing, luxuriating in all of your great loves. This good earth and her bounty. Your dear son and his dear sons. The rest of us who loved and love you still remain—holding you close in our everydayness, our hearts forever entwined with yours.

I miss you, Dave—and I'm sorry.

My Big Sister

By Amy Reeder

I never understood how any girl could grow up without a sister. Sure, there are friends—even best friends who become part of your family—but a sister is a built-in best friend who never has to leave—or so I thought.

When we were little, Jen did the talking. To say she was outgoing would be an understatement. As my big sister, she saw fit to take the lead, and I was more than willing to let her. Someone would ask me my name, and she would proclaim, "This is my little sister, Amy! She's four! She's really shy, but she's very pleased to meet you!"

All of her sentences were marked with frenzied exclamation, a trait that stayed with her throughout her lifetime. She never stopped talking, even in her sleep.

Jen wasn't just my keeper in childhood. She continued to be my person for life. She was insanely intelligent. If she didn't already know the answer to something, she would do extensive research to find it. She was creative and a jack-of-all-trades, which was evident in her hobbies, education, and career choices.

Jen was great at knitting, crocheting, quilting, baking, singing, playing piano, art, photography, and political science. She was an exceptional hair-stylist, known for her ability to create the most beautiful hair colors. This sparked her interest in the chemistry behind formulating those colors, so she returned to school and became a chemist. She taught chemistry at the collegiate level.

Jen had a way of breaking things down and making ordinary minds understand the most complex equations, and my gosh, she would get excited about it. She'd say, "Sit down! I wanna show you my favorite equation!" Having no interest, I would tell her I didn't want to learn an equation. How could anyone have a favorite equation?

Unphased by my objection, Jen would pull out a chalkboard, direct me into a chair, and teach me anyway. I ultimately went along with it because I knew anything she was involved in was going to be the most fun thing happening all week, even if it was learning a six-page-long series of numbers and letters that I'd never need to know.

Jen wasn't just *my* person. She was everyone's person. Everyone depended on her for guidance, strength, wisdom, love, and entertainment, and she never missed an opportunity to deliver.

Growing up, we did all the things sisters do. Over time, our relationship transformed a bit. We still talked several times a day, but Jen moved two hours away, and our focus shifted to our own families. When we did break away without all the kids, it was always fun.

I just didn't know that our last shopping trip would be our *last* shopping trip.

It was the day Jen and her husband, Adrian, brought baby Arwyn home from the hospital. She had a very rough pregnancy, so Arwyn's birth marked what we thought would be a turning point. The last couple of months of pregnancy were extremely painful for her due to having a blood clot in her groin. She could not walk. She could barely eat or sleep.

Jen had expressed concern several times that the issue was something worse, but nothing was found. We were thrilled that day when she suggested a trip to the mall. Before we left, while everyone doted on the baby, I made Jen lunch, and we sat and talked. She was relieved that she had survived the pregnancy and delivery. She was unbelievably excited to now be a mother of four. Her son JJ was just shy of his fourteenth birthday, and her twins, Laurel and Xander, were two. Just like everything else in her life, she excelled at motherhood.

When we finished lunch, Jen, Mom, and I made a quick trip to the mall. That whole day felt magical somehow, and I remember telling my parents that on our drive home after our visit. That was the last time I saw my sister alive.

Ten days later, Jen went to the hospital for a small procedure to break up the blood clot. Adrian and my mom were there with her. Prior to her surgery that day, I kept meaning to call her, but I was busy at work and regretfully did not make the time. On the way home from work, I called my mom a couple of times for an update, but she did not answer, which seemed strange.

A bit later, as I was changing clothes, I answered a call from my mom. She interrupted me mid-sentence, the tone of her voice sounding a way I had never heard it. "Amy," she said, followed by a long pause. "She didn't make it." I felt my heart sink as I made her repeat herself. Weeping uncontrollably, I fell to the floor in a pile. Jen had never awoken from surgery.

It was determined to be a rare condition called disseminated intravascular coagulation. That was March 17, 2014. Jen was thirty-eight. Arwyn was twelve days old.

By the next morning, word had spread, and thousands were mourning with us. The line of people at Jen's viewing circled all the way around the building and down the street. Everyone showed up for her just like she always had for them. It was an amazing testament to how much she was loved. Many spoke at her funeral, and the stories perfectly captured her essence. There were a lot of tears and a lot of laughs.

I can hardly recall the months that followed, and all things related to St. Patrick's Day continue to trigger overwhelming emotions. So many lives were affected by Jen's death, as they were by her life.

All of Jen's children are well-adjusted and thriving, and all of them inherited many of her great qualities, talents, and beauty. She was a big ball of scatterbrained quirkiness who provided enough love and entertainment to last an eternity. Everyone wanted a piece of her, but for some reason, God chose me to be her little sister. I will never feel worthy of such an honor. She was, and will always be, the wind beneath my wings.

The Endearing Legacy of a Devoted Sister

By Linda Hawkins

In the vibrant fabric of our family, shaped by Sylvia Pearce and James Hawkins of Two Mountains in Quebec, Donna, the second-born daughter, emerged as an unforeseen force. Brimming with infectious laughter and a considerably loving heart, Donna thrived amidst her three sisters, embodying innocence as a child while exuding unparalleled kindness and authenticity, which she carried for her entire life.

After our father's untimely departure at the age of thirty-seven, Donna's life trajectory took a profound turn. She centered on a deep connection to both family and her community. She was often by my side in church and felt a deep conviction in embracing others and providing support.

As a child, one of the delights of my relationship with my sister was the ease with which I could sway her thinking. Her innocent nature, bordering on overly trusting, provided ample opportunities for me, as the older sibling, to playfully manipulate her beliefs. Our shared bedroom, where our differences in room temperature preference became apparent, served as the canvas for many lighthearted schemes.

We had contrasting preferences; I enjoyed a crisp and cold environment, whereas she was fond of warmth. When she requested the bedroom window be closed, I seized the chance to weave an imaginative tale.

With a mischievous redirect, I would tell her that in my ideal scenario the entire wall would vanish, leaving us enjoying sleep in an open space. I argued that since the open window only granted half of my wish, she had already received half of what she desired, rendering my open window arrangement a fair compromise. Remarkably, as a naive younger sibling, she would often succumb to whimsical logic, often agreeing to these one-sided compromises.

As children, our paths often mirrored each other, as Donna had an uncanny desire to engage in similar pursuits. When I joined a majorette group, she quickly followed suit. However, she excelled in her craft, wielding her baton for the Montreal Alouettes' majorettes, showcasing her talents and garnering our family's admiration. Her commitment to our bond remained unwavering, even when I took on the role of a mother's helper for a family up north during the summer months. Donna joined me by working in a nearby summer cottage, thus ensuring our continued companionship.

Reminiscing about quieter moments brings me to my younger married days when I often perched atop the stairs in my home after putting the kids to bed. Coffee and cigarettes within reach, phone in hand, and feet casually propped up on the wall, I would spend hours on the phone with my sister, sharing stories, catching up on our days, and reveling in laughter. Her off-colored jokes and infectious loud giggle had a way of brightening the days.

Donna was a cherished sister and a favorite aunt to my children. We frequently orchestrated visits between New Brunswick and Quebec, creating simple yet lasting memories. Outdoor bonfires, camping, motel pool adventures, small boxes of breakfast cereal, park picnics, trips to the beach, and her rendition of "Two Little Dickie Birds" or the favorite, "My Grandfather's Clock," all contribute to the treasure trove of memories for my children from our family bonding and time enjoyed with cousins.

If asked to describe my sister, Donna, it would prompt accolades of her selflessness from those who knew her best. A devoted participant in The Immaculate Heart of Mary Catholic Church and the Ladies Society Church, both in New Brunswick, she could always be relied upon to volunteer for any community function. Alongside her life partner Peter, my sister committed herself to nurturing their three boys—Jimmy, Ron, and Larry. She was a devoted advocate for her eldest child, born with severe cognitive and physical impairments and developmental delays. She ensured that love and laughter filled the home, focusing on inclusivity, acceptance, and caring.

After her retirement, her community involvement continued to blossom, with joint efforts in volunteering at the Albert County Food Bank, participating in community theater, and extending the warmth of the family home to young billets from the Moncton Wild Cats hockey team. An ordained minister, Donna focused on her church knitting club, infusing each stitch of her prayer shawls with heartfelt prayers for the deserving recipients.

Reaching the milestone of her fiftieth wedding anniversary with her husband on June 24, 2017, Donna and Peter's enduring love stood as a testament to their unwavering commitment to each other. Their journey was one for the storybooks. Describing the occasion as "remarrying the love of her life," Donna and Peter, with the beloved Father Phil by their side, renewed their vows as she humorously reflected on her wisdom as a seventeen-year-old who foresaw their enduring connection.

Even with her battle with squamous cell carcinoma, a cancer of the tongue and lymph nodes that put her through months of endless pain, surgeries, treatments, and medications, she focused on connection and laughter with others.

Grieving her loss has been an ongoing process since her passing in 2018. I miss her voice and I miss sharing stories with a sister who always shone brightly and provided much. Seventy-one years of life were enough for her to make an incredible difference, rippling positivity in each encounter. She was my sister and best friend. In a world that can sometimes have dark times, she was that light that guided and comforted me. Her memories continue to do so.

A Brother's Pride

By Leya Hunter

Remembering Aaron, my big brother. He was funny, witty, and unfiltered. He was always up for a laugh, and banter was his specialty. I often claim the "funny sibling" title, but now I see I must have got it from him. He was three years my senior and the oldest of four, so naturally, he got first dibs on my nickname, "Bubby Stubby," which no one knows the origins of. Perhaps I had some puppy rolls about me when I was a toddler. Either way, the name has stuck and remains a mystery all these years later.

Aaron was always first to find the comical, no matter the circumstance. I have fond memories of his wild storytelling and ability to make others laugh. In the late 1990s, I was nervous about entering high school, but in true big brother form, Aaron made me feel protected and at ease. He was a few years into high school and considered popular, with friends in every corner of the neighborhood. It wasn't long before I became known as "Aaron's little sister." Unlike many older siblings, who would shutter at the thought of being seen with their siblings at school, Aaron always made sure I was okay and welcomed me into his group of friends. He made that chapter of my life much easier, and it showed the type of character he possessed.

In the early 2000s, Aaron became a father, devoting much of his life to his new role. In his early fatherhood days, I visited him every week, and my two other siblings and I would share laughter, banter, and a type of sibling humor that is hard to describe. It is a type of humor I carry on in his memory.

Aaron was an old-school millennial with a disdain for modern technology. Throughout his twenties, he preferred to ride his bike, read the newspaper, and carry his vintage wireless radio to listen to his beloved horse races rather than drive a car, watch the news, or use the internet. One family gathering in the mid-2000s is etched into my memory. Sitting in my father's backyard, Aaron proudly boasted about me getting my first job and commended me on my hard work and dedication. His words were a reminder and assurance of his protective nature and warm big brother heart.

The last Christmas we spent together was at my five-acre hobby farm. I was cooking up a storm in the kitchen when he came in, and—in true big brother style—took over, telling me I was doing it wrong. His strong but respectful demeanor was hard to argue with, so he got to cooking the "right" way. His two sons joined us for the weekend, and we shared many laughs, light-hearted debates, ATV rides, and backyard cricket games. He relished the view from my living room, gleaming at the valley with the sun shining over the ocean. He once again told me how proud he was of me. It reminded me of the pride he felt when I got my first job—his pride seemed to only get stronger as we got older. Perhaps a quality and sense of pride was inherent in him.

Fast-forward to Father's Day 2022, I was getting ready to go out and spend the day with my husband and son when my husband received the fateful call that Aaron had passed away. The look on my husband's face said it all—tragedy had struck. I sat numb on the end of the bed, thoughts racing, body frozen, a feeling that no words could describe—shock perhaps? How could my big brother be gone?

I had never faced grief like this, and I didn't know how to deal with it or even how to "feel" it. The seven stages of grief followed, but one thing remained: the inability to grip onto something tangible, where mourning is concerned at least. It was an intense feeling of something foreign—something I wanted to rip out of my body. But it never left; it became a part of me. I thought of it as a type of frustration that had to meet surrender if I were to live any type of fulfillment.

It's strange how it is usually only when we reflect on a person who is gone or a moment that has passed that we shape and unify the memories into something more meaningful and grand. In hindsight, I wonder if I should have said something more encouraging rather than the comical jargon I thought he wanted to hear. Life weighs us down; "resilience" is arguably the only defense between us and how we deal with our dreaded fate. The last phone call I had with him was a conversation about accelerating my writing career. He was once again so proud and had a heightened enthusiastic tone. This memory propels me further into writing, and I now carry around his sense of pride in me whenever writing is involved.

As I look back on the type of big brother he was, I am now "the proud one," proud to have had a brother like him. His loss is a reminder of my place in this world, a fleeting moment in the space-time continuum, a reminder of my mortality, a recognition of opposites, a readjustment to purpose, and a reimagining of the future. I can see through the loss that it's not so much about the length of time I have but to what degree I fill it with meaning and purpose. I had things left unsaid, so now I hope to say the things sooner!

One Last Dance

By Heather Schuller

My baby sister came into the world like a beautiful, angelic disaster. My mother delivered early, and the little peanut weighed 1 lb. 12 ½ oz. Her teeny, tiny fingers were almost translucent when she held onto my fingertip from her incubator at Toledo Hospital's Pediatric Intensive Care Unit.

We had the privilege of living at the Ronald McDonald House in Toledo, just outside the hospital doors, because every other night was going to be her last. Countless times, the hospital told us to say "Goodbye" because it didn't look like she would make it through the night. The Ronald McDonald House was a dream come true for a teenager like me, with two kitchens stocked with food and ice cream freezers at every entrance. The basement was a huge game room.

After a year, Tiffany finally came home from the hospital, and we had a huge celebration waiting for her. She was slow to develop—she didn't start talking until age three or walking until age four—but once she could stand, she was ready to dance. As a teenager, I always had the radio on, listening to Casey Kasem's Countdown of America's Top 100 songs. Dancing and cracking jokes with the DJs was one of the funniest moments Tiffany and I shared. She fell in love with all the Toledo DJs like they were the gods of all creation.

When they played Bette Midler's "Wind Beneath My Wings," she would go into flight, and I would dance her in the air like she was flying in the sky—arms stretched and a smile so bright you could see it on the other side of the country. As she grew, she constantly got herself into a pickle, had a very rebellious spirit, and picked up curse words as soon as she knew they caused a reaction.

In the summers in Ohio, we have Cedar Point, arguably the country's best roller coaster theme park. I took her for the first time, just she and I. Her favorite DJ was Denny Schaffer, and on her first roller coaster ride, she screamed, "Denny Schaffer will save me." It became our motto after that. I always took her to events where her favorite DJs were, and she knew them all. They began attending her birthday parties and integrating her into their radio shows.

She had an enduring love for babies and animals, which was the cutest thing I had ever witnessed. Anytime we went somewhere and there was a baby or an animal, she just wanted to care for and love it. We made up funny songs for whatever situation we found ourselves in.

She was everyone's favorite because, regardless of the time of day, when the music came on, she was always ready to dance, laugh, crack a joke, or hurl a curse word, depending on her mood.

When she became ill, the doctors told us her organs were shutting down. It was so disheartening. When my daughter and I went into her room, she lay there and couldn't move. We walked in singing her favorite song, and we'd get a smile but nothing else.

Then she heard Denny's morning show, and he said, "Get up, Tiffany, it's time to dance. You must get well. You have to get better." She wanted so badly to get out of her bed and dance. And for a moment, I thought maybe Denny Schaffer could save her. A caregiver and I got her in her wheelchair, and I danced with her one last time, spinning her wheelchair around the room. She was so happy, but I could see the pain in her eyes, and her body just wouldn't move anymore. That's when I knew it was time to say goodbye.

That was my last dance, my last moments with my sister. I was working in Texas that year. As I left, I heard her singing, "Dancing in my wheelchair, man, like the muffin man." My heart soared, knowing that although she couldn't move, she was still making up songs in a positive way. That knowledge helped me get on that plane.

She passed away near my birthday that year, and my heart broke into a billion pieces. I always ask her to visit my dreams, and although I've only dreamed of her once, at least I got that one last dance. The smile through the tears was worth every wheelchair spin. I find solace in knowing I gave her the best memories a sister could. I miss her terribly and look forward to the day we can dance our first dance in the sky.

The Loss I Could Never Prepare For

By Shoshana Gardiner

D o you think of death? This is a question I often ask my friends, family, and significant others. My answer has never wavered: I think about death every day. I lost a father at an early age, and my grandparents on both sides followed not long after. Understanding that I could lose a loved one when I was a child prepared me for the other heartbreaks of my life. However, I could never have prepared for the one I experienced at nineteen years old—the passing of my brother Jacob.

I was the baby of five, a surprise to my mother at forty years old, which meant the age gap between me and my siblings was significant. Because of this and many other reasons, I never felt the camaraderie many experience in a large household. My family was comprised of my sister and three brothers. My sister was closest in age to me, and Jacob was next. I understood quite early on that he battled demons, specifically heroin, and was in and out of my mother's house, not often or coherent enough for me to truly form a connection. Yet each time, he left me with the briefest blips of hope. Then the jail would call, and I would lose him again. I didn't realize then that these month-long stints resulted in an uptake in correspondence. I still have all his letters, remember each phone call on my birthday, and would savor the knowledge of his whereabouts and current health status. I would take that for granted later on.

Jacob was business-savvy. He grew a business that provided him with the funds to shower everyone he cared for with expensive gifts and had enough left over to indulge himself as well. And, oh boy, did he. His favorite indulgence? Shoes. There was a whole room dedicated to his collection. My memories of him during his most lucrative moments as a drug dealer all contain a man with impeccable style. He would show up at my mother's house dressed in designer shirts, Gucci sunglasses, embroidered jeans, and his prized diamond earrings.

I was in awe of him, not only for his style. His generosity went far past material; he truly would do anything for the ones he loved. He was loyal—sometimes to a fault—but I understood the impact he had on those around him and how valuable he was to all who considered him a part of their life.

Anyone who was in Jacob's presence long enough fell in love. There would be girls who showed up unannounced at our doorstep when he was still in school, all requesting to catch a glimpse of him. He was charismatic, loving, and incredibly fun to be around. The drugs dimmed the best parts of him. But my family never gave up, and he never gave up on us.

My favorite memories of him all include his laugh. It was infectious. One could not help but smile when they heard it. He was funny, too. He would tease relentlessly, calling me a lumberjack when he saw me with a flannel shirt on once and taking a jab at my broad shoulders, but I never minded. Anytime he singled me out, it felt like the touch of the sun.

For my eleventh birthday, he brought me to a Stanley Cup playoff game, Red Wings vs. Penguins. We sat behind the goalie and cheered at the top of our lungs. He bought me a jersey—which I wore the whole time—and taught me how to trash talk the man with the Penguins hat on in front of us (we were Red Wings fans). It's a memory I will cherish forever.

He died on September 26, 2016. Despite the previous overdoses and warning bells, I never could have prepared myself for this. I had already experienced the loss of a parent and a grandparent, but I never expected the toll the loss of a sibling would take. My world collapsed in so many ways. We weren't close; we had only recently reconnected the month before, but I assumed he would be there. I assumed he would see me through my biggest milestones: a career, a marriage, perhaps a baby of my own. But at age twenty-nine, he was gone. How did he not even reach thirty? It wasn't fair. He deserved a sober life. He deserved to see his three girls grow and reach their own milestones. He deserved to laugh again and again. We deserved a life with him—one untouched by the evils of drugs and the unrepairable damages they inflict.

The truth I had to forcibly come to terms with to preserve my own sanity was that no one deserves a single thing. Life plays out, and we choose how to handle it. This may mean only we have our fathers—our siblings—for a short time. We may regret the moments we chose not to spend with them, even when they hurt us unintentionally. I know I will forever hold on to that. I will look back on the missed phone calls and the times spent with friends instead of him, and I'll yearn so vividly for the briefest moment back in his presence.

But I also think of him as with me always. I know if he were still alive, he would be proud of the woman I have become and the milestones I have accomplished—none of them actually involved a career, marriage, or kid. I look back and realize the amount of pain he was dealing with and under-stand that his actions never meant his love for me had diminished. He was dealing with life the best way he could. If only it didn't take him so soon.

Nikolet: My Sister, My Best Friend

By Nikolai Andre Alexander

At four years old, I decided I wanted a sibling. More specifically, I told my mother that I wanted a sister.

"If you have a boy, leave him at the hospital. I do not want him," was apparently what I said to her. I do not remember this, but it is likely I actually said that because I had always gotten along better with girls than boys. As providence would have it, a year later my mother brought home a baby girl and I loved her from the moment I saw her, eyes closed and swaddled.

My sister, though five years my junior, quickly became my favorite person and we were inseparable. Well, she followed me everywhere and wanted to do everything I did. I didn't mind much though; she was my close companion. When she was still a toddler, I would lie beside her in her bed and pat her back until she fell asleep. If she woke up before morning and I was not there, she'd come find me in my own room and ask to stay with me because she couldn't sleep, only to be fully asleep again five minutes after I laid my hand on her back again.

As we grew up together, we only grew closer. I went from playing alone to having someone to watch TV with, play hide and seek or cards with, and go exploring in the neighborhood. Over the holidays, we visited and stayed with our dad on the family farm; our time was spent playing with our cousins, grumbling about hard chores, and eating every ripe fruit we could pluck from the trees until we were too full for dinner.

In our late teenage years, we held each other's secrets, whispering about girlfriends and boyfriends out of earshot of our mother. Eventually I moved out, and she went to live with my grandma, which created distance between us for the first time since April 1994 when I first peeked at her little face in those blankets. As a young adult, I moved around a lot, trying to figure out life; she always called and worried and questioned and made sure I came to see her often.

Then, before I even realized she was really an adult too, she got married and moved out of my grandma's house to live with her husband. A year later, I got married and moved to Canada.

Thankfully, before my wedding, our mom invited us over for a family weekend, the first we'd had in a very long time, and we spent the whole time talking and catching each other up on anything we hadn't talked about over the phone. Then when I knew I was leaving for Canada, we spent another evening just chatting about everything and nothing. She jokingly begged me not to leave her behind. We laughed about it and shared a heartfelt goodbye filled with what I—at the time—thought were way too many tight hugs.

I'm glad for those hugs now, those conversations, and those memories. I'm glad for all the times she invaded my personal space to kiss my cheek or demand I kiss hers. I'm glad for all the requests to just come spend time with her, with no objective other than that she missed me.

Six months after I landed in Canada, my sister was taken from me suddenly. We had talked on the phone a week before she died and it had been a normal, "Okay, I love you. Bye," before I hung up the phone. Then, the next call I received from family was one telling me that she and her husband were gone. My world shattered. It was too sudden: she was too young—it couldn't be true. The times we'd had weren't enough and the goodbye we had shared felt woefully inadequate. I had never experienced that kind of pain before, like the ripping apart of my very soul. Pain as though my heart was on fire. I wept bitterly for months afterwards.

Five and half years later, it still hurts. I will grieve her for the rest of my days. And I will celebrate her life. I'll tell my son stories about her when he is old enough to understand. I'll dedicate my first novel to her. I'll love those close to me the way she loved me: honestly, openly, and without judgement. My final goodbye wasn't meant to be truly final, but rather a goodbye for now. But I am grateful that it was as tangible a farewell as people often share with someone they're departing from. The light of her life and the joy she brought to mine outshines the pain and darkness of her passing, and I'm eternally thankful for the fact that I was able to grow up with her. I merely wanted a sister; instead, I received a best friend. I will treasure that forever.

For Evan

By Hayley Charles

You said something funny and I couldn't stop laughing—the kind of laughter that is so intense you end up making no noise at all—your body simply convulses with joy. Usually, we were doing nothing and that's what I loved about being with you.

Evan passed away in 2020 after battling depression and using substances as a numbing agent for that pain. It had been a longer battle than I realized; before he died, I thought we told each other everything, but I found out the hard way that that wasn't true. I've had my own struggles with mental illness but Evan and I felt that we were somehow different from the rest of the family. We joked about it—that our older brother turned out well while we were busy trying to stay alive. We also spoke candidly about our struggles and relied on each other for support that was often unspoken, but never unknown.

I really wanted a little brother. Something about being the only girl in my family was appealing to me and meant that every day, with brothers, would be an adventure. As adolescents, Evan and I were the same height and often shared clothes and shoes. I have drifted away from most of those tomboyish tendencies, but growing up with two brothers did not lend itself to being a girl who played with Barbies and wore makeup.

By the time he graduated from high school, Evan was 6'8" and towered over me. He played basketball, loved disc golf, and mastered any skill he decided to learn, including how to hand-toss pizza crust. He also possessed an uncanny and impressive ability to recite quotes from television shows or movies after seeing a scene just one time. I remember him perfectly delivering lines from the movie *Tommy Boy*, making my brother, dad, and me laugh until our sides ached.

One of Evan's best friends avoided me after his death. After some prodding, she admitted that she had a hard time talking to me because I reminded her so much of Evan. I felt honored to be likened to him because Evan had never met a stranger. He was incredibly kind, engaging, and funny, with a dry wit that sometimes meant you walked away from a conversation before you processed the punch line.

We spent many evenings on various porches, banished because we wanted a cigarette. Sometimes, we talked about benign things, and sometimes we talked about the mire of being an adult. I struggled with my mental health for many years before I knew that Evan was also battling something unseen.

Four years have passed and my grief moves in and out of the stages because healing isn't linear. I know that Evan didn't talk about his pain because he didn't want to burden others. I find myself wondering if he felt alone and know that this is a question I will never get the answer to. Part of accepting that someone is gone is accepting that there will be things we do not know. I do know that my deep love and admiration for my brother were not secrets to him or anyone else.

Sometimes, I still talk to him; I don't know if he can hear me, but I like to imagine that he can. I tell him that I miss him. I tell him that I need one of his big hugs that will wrap me up in the feeling of being known. I tell him that, some days, I am happy and I wonder if that's okay. I tell him that I'm not mad at him—I'm mad at the sweet escape of addiction and the harsh world that looks at us with judgment and tells us who we need to be. I tell him that I've been in recovery for three and a half years, and that every time I accomplish something that I thought was impossible, he's with me.

Though Evan is no longer here, I feel him all the time; when that happens, I stop what I'm doing and take a long, deep breath. The future

 Goodbye for Now

without him stretches ahead and if I look too far in that direction, I am afraid I might get lost and exist in the space between until someone reaches out their hand to pull me back from the edge. Sometimes, I hang out on that edge and consider it a gift to see the chasm and not want to fall in anymore. I talk about Evan as much as possible; not because I am afraid that I will forget him, but because others will experience him through me now—and I will not deny anyone that gift.

Echoes of Her Voice

By Gabrielle May

I was traveling in the Canaries when my sister, Andrée Anne, announced her brain cancer was in remission.

I spent that day in an expectative state, straining to metamorphose my unrelenting panic into hope. I thought if I had faith in her healing, I could manifest it. Had I listened to her doctor's recordings, which explained that it was the type of tumor that always crept back, I would've known better.

Andrée Anne was a natural talent; any art form she dabbled in, she instantly excelled at. She was an inspiration, but the gap was inexorable. She had a unique sense of style, rocking a rooster-like bob, checkerboard slip-ons, and music band t-shirts. Once, as I was driving us to visit our grandmother, I put on a scratched disk of Jason Mraz. I was an avid fan, and although she hadn't heard any of his songs in years, Andrée Anne sang along with effortless pitch, remembering the lyrics far better than I did. She told me how lyrics were the most important component of music to her; nowadays, especially, all the lyrics of the songs I compose are made with meticulous attention. And all of my songs are dedicated to her, their sad undertone hinting at my loss.

Andrée Anne was kind and funny. At my worst jokes, she'd at least fake a laugh. She never had to fake one for my mom; she found her hilarious.

They were besties and were planning on moving to Gatineau. I'm the one staying with mom now, both of us aware we will never have something resembling that friendship.

A couple of months after the good news, while I was traveling to Morocco, a sense of impending doom started to loom over me. We soon got the call—the cancer was back.

Despite the slow and excruciating process of her body losing response, resulting in a dizziness that escalated into her inability to stand, hear, and move, Andrée Anne still retained her sense of humor. Deep in my denial-manifesting-faith, I played "catch the seashell" with her, using a decorative conch from the table, to work on her motricity. As we played, she laughed and sang the goofy tune, "Go on, touch the seashell!"

Eventually, she lost her hearing. I visited her one day and played her a song I had written for her. Suddenly, she interrupted me.

"Gaby, I can't hear you. But go on. You're beautiful."

Through my tears, I did.

The sight of it all traumatized me. I had to leave the house. I hate myself for this; no one could judge me as harshly as I do. I left her decaying with our mom.

Fast-forward a couple of months and she'd been put in a facility. Once a day, we'd dress her up in winter clothes, go outside and hold a cigarette in her mouth, pinching her lips together for her so she could inhale the cancerous smoke.

I was the only one able to understand her speech. She couldn't hear that the slurred sounds she was emitting had nothing to do with what she was trying to express. On December 21, 2019, a man came into her room, and through laborious translation I found out she had requested assisted suicide on New Year's Eve. But there was an awkwardness in his eyes. I didn't understand at the time that he knew she wouldn't make it that long.

Three days later, my mom called me. Andrée Anne had not woken up and was having a hard time breathing. I came over in my pajamas. It was just before the pandemic so all the family was there. Her biggest fear was to die alone, and we made sure that didn't happen.

I played all of my songs on a ukulele to drown out the noise of her groans, numbing the sharpness with the Km12 gin she had requested for us. When I finally sat beside her, she opened her eyes. I reached for our mom, but she was talking to someone else and never turned around.

Andrée Anne mumbled, "Gaby, I did it …"

"What?"

She looked confused. "I achieved to …"

She never finished her thought. She closed her eyes for the last time, although she was still breathing.

Around 7 p.m., while heating up a warm compress down the hall, I imagined a conversation with her. At this point, denial was gone. Faith was gone.

"Andrée Anne … Will you keep us here all night? It's so painful …"

"I'm trying … but it's so hard."

"I know … But it's also very hard for us."

The microwave beeped. I started walking back, and then ran.

Andrée Anne's eyes were open. The groans had stopped. My other sister, Marie Julie, had just come back too. Andrée Anne had waited until we were both out of the room.

Mom kept repeating, "Touch her … She's still warm."

I had to tell her to stop. Those words … I can't express how soul crushing they are.

But Andrée Anne kept whispering to me, from within. Every time I had a smoke, she would nag me: "Cigarettes give cancer!" I thought she'd always be there, ghosting my steps, but ten days later, half-asleep before sunrise, I saw her moving to the right. When I woke up, she wasn't around. I had lost her again.

I miss her, almost as much as my sister.

Part VIII

Spouse/Partner

I'll Be Seeing You

By Anna Burks

Young love can be so cheesy. Ours was as gushy as the bubbly cheese clinging to the slippery sauce of a piping hot pan pizza. Talk about cliché; our first date was like a scene from a movie. We played video games and sipped soda pop in the lobby of the local Pizza Hut while waiting for our food. I was fresh into adulthood and barely eighteen when we met. Who knew I'd be a mom and a widow before I would be thirty?

Patrick was, and still is, the love of my life. Our first hello, and our not so final goodbye, both took place in the springtime; in the month of May, to be exact. I was out for an early morning walk when he eased up beside me in his silver Volkswagen Scirocco. He cruised beside me, with the perfect combination of gas and clutch, for several yards. Despite his efforts, I turned my head away to let him know how utterly disrespectful it was to talk to a lady while hanging from the window of a car. He switched gears and sped off with a slight jerk. That was the end of that, or so I thought. He paused for a long minute at the end of the block, then made a left into a parking lot. The next thing I knew, he was standing directly in my path, his arm stretched out, clutching a business card between his fingers.

"Patrick Burks," he said. "Pleased to make your acquaintance."

On January 18, 1992, we welcomed our son, Pat's namesake, into the world. Ironically, he is named after his father because his mother wanted a girl. In the face of three ultrasounds, all pointing towards a boy, I stood firm in the faith that God would grant me a girl. I was so sure, in fact, that I refused to pick out an alternate name. I was in active labor when Pat asked, "Don't you think we should pick out a boy's name?"

"You can if you want to," I said, "but I'm having a girl."

How do you tell a nine-year-old that his daddy isn't coming back home? More than twenty years later, that is still the hardest question that I have ever asked myself or had to answer. In the face of seemingly insurmountable hurdles or decisions, even now, I remind myself of that very conversation. It is, by far, the hardest thing that I have ever had to do. If I can do that, then I can do anything.

I could see it in his face the moment I came through the door; he knew something was wrong. The atmosphere was heavy, and the television was off. Our television was never turned off. But he needed to hear this from me, not a newscast. I didn't know all the details of the accident yet, but for this conversation, they wouldn't matter.

Struggling to hold back my own tears, I took his hand in mine, and we walked toward his bedroom. I sat down on the bed with my son cradled on my lap and began to rock. I just rocked slowly, back and forth, like I had done when he was little.

"Do you remember when Papa left?" I asked in a whisper. "I told you that he moved to heaven to live with Jesus and the angels. Your dad is going to go live with them now too."

"Is my dad dead?" He looked up and asked me bluntly.

"Yes," I choked and began to stroke his head. His body went limp in my arms, and he began to wail at the top of his little lungs. The sound pierced my soul like nothing I've heard before or since. He sobbed, and he wailed while I cried and rocked. I'm not sure how long we stayed there, but it must have been a while. Reality came with a subtle tap on the door. I lifted my eyes to the silhouette of my aunt, my mom's baby sister, in the doorway.

"It's time to come out," she said. "He needs the rest of his family."

She was right; we did.

 Goodbye for Now

The funeral procession stretched down the expressway for as far as my eyes could see. I gazed at it emptily, through the mirror of the limo, without even turning my head. I could feel my son's hand cupped on top of my thigh underneath my own. It was in that moment that I threw myself, even more fully, into being his mom. Some kids dream of being doctors or lawyers. Not me; I only ever wanted to be a wife and a mom. Now, being a great mother was all I had left to define myself by. I never wanted to be known as a widow—still don't.

After the funeral, I put my most precious memories into a decorative grey box and tucked them away on a shelf. I didn't touch that box again for a little over a year. I came across it one day while packing for a move. I just happened to be home alone that day with a chilled bottle of wine on hand. With a glass of wine and my box, I took a seat on the sofa and braced myself to say goodbye, at least for now.

The snapshots of our life together actually brought me great comfort. I could almost hear the laughter and smell the food as I strolled down memory lane. I realized then that I had spent the past year shielding my son from the memories that would bring both of us the most peace. I picked out a few of my son's favorites and arranged them in a little blue booklet. He slept with that album for the longest time, and cherishes it to this day.

Two Souls Who Saved Each Other

By Cindy Mich

My Michael was not someone I searched for but rather the one I wished for years ago. I asked God to bring me a man who would give me happiness and good mental health. A guy who could bring out the best in me and compel me to see my own self-worth. A soul that scared away my demons but also protected me from myself. Heaven must have heard me, as he found me in July 2018.

A short film was submitted to my film festival that starred this funny, intriguing, and talented actor named Michael Gentile. After watching the movie, I reached out to Michael to share how much I loved his performance. We then agreed to meet at my birthday party in New York City to discuss a film role. At this time, I was neither attracted to nor interested in him. What a difference eight hours can make between two hearts. Michael and I would end up staying until the bar closed; then, we had breakfast at the diner and a long walk through Washington Square Park. I left New York to head home to Wisconsin with some wonderful memories.

It took approximately four months, and I was in love. I found myself so attracted to him that sometimes, I could not stare directly at him because I blushed all the time. My heart leaped with excitement each time we had a conversation. The sound of his voice brought me such contentment.

Moments apart felt like an eternity, and together, they were divine. We had a rule that we would not go longer than three weeks without time together; however, he was in my heart every day. I had never met a man with such class, distinction, loyalty, and respect. I had also never dated anyone who drove me that crazy. Sometimes, I literally wanted to shake some sense into him. He was funny, intelligent, and interesting. He was engaging, insightful, maddening, and handsome as hell. He was also stoic, strange, and, at times, his own worst enemy. His love left me feeling so incredibly content, calm, and confident. He made me feel beautiful and blissful. I no longer needed to wear a dress or be all dolled up because he desired me as is. Despite knowing all my dark sides, he still wanted me. He helped me with my career and, at times, did things he hated. Yet, he rarely ever refused my requests. He was loyal and loving, and he never left. I loved every side of this soul.

Besides a beautiful love, what else did we earn from this union? We partnered together on a t-shirt line, a black and white film festival, film screening events, two films, and a TV series. I constantly attempted to get him cast and his films seen. I was constantly wracking my brain to find ways to be with him, both personally and professionally. We were best friends and partners.

With most great love stories, there are always some downsides. It was difficult to maintain a relationship between two states. Actors have like six personalities, and at times, their work hours suck. We were passionate when arguing, which led to many hurt feelings. Two breakups were not fun. His lack of prior relationship experience was rough. Also, I repeatedly ran from him instead of to him. Despite this, we kept love alive. The most difficult and heartbreaking downside was that we only got three years of good.

He began to lose weight in December 2020. He finally gave in to getting checked by a family doctor. In May 2021, he was diagnosed with diffuse large B-cell lymphoma. He and I clung to the belief that the six chemotherapy treatments would heal him. Love then started looking different. Love was sitting on airplanes going to New York for treatment, sleeping in hotels, and bringing him back home sick. Love was cooking and caring for him, researching cures, and praying. Love was crying and hoping he did not see me. Love was attending doctor appointments and treatments and being his voice and stern advocate when needed. Love was clinging to him as they said, "You now also have stomach cancer," and realizing that this would mean a second battle against sickness. Love was watching him having a heart attack at home and then being forbidden from seeing him in the ICU for eight days. Love was holding his hand while he was on a breathing and dialysis machine, and asking him to marry me. Love was sitting alone with him on December 2, 2021—now bald, 135 pounds, and no longer breathing—and still seeing him as beautiful. Nobody told me true love would look or feel like this. I loved us so much and lost half of myself when he left.

I know that society would say that my goodbyes came within his two memorial services. Others would claim it happened while donating his clothing to a theater, passing on his valuables to loved ones, or through the thousands of tears I shed for him. The day I saw his death certificate, I could no longer dispute that he died—and I had to say farewell. However, I believe that true love means you *never* fully say goodbye. He will always remain a part of me and in my heart.

Fancy Face. I love you.

—Dearest Mich

Saying Goodbye

By Wayne Rapp

The match seemed implausible from the start. She was too short for me. I was a hodgepodge of ethnicities from a border town in Arizona, and Anne was a full-blooded Italian from New York. She had never eaten tacos or enchiladas; I had never heard of gnocchi or braciole. And yet, after meeting at the mailbox of the apartment complex where we lived, we were spending time together. She had left home to accept a teaching job in Southern California, and I to work in the motion picture department of an aerospace company.

Thinking about the attraction later, I couldn't miss her nice figure or those dimples that made her that much cuter. Anne was an extrovert, natural and easy around people with a great smile and laugh. Besides the physical attraction, it was her love of family and strong Catholic faith that attracted me. My own faith lagged during my college years, and her religious commitment uplifted me. We started attending Sunday Mass with my father's relatives, whom she quickly charmed. When she made lasagna for all fourteen of them, they were won over. One aunt pulled me aside and said, "Wayne, you better grab that girl," and that's what I did.

From the beginning, our married years were kind to us as God gifted us four beautiful, intelligent children. After I was transferred to Columbus,

Ohio, Anne and I filled our lives with our children's activities but tried to remember each other's needs and let our own love continue to grow. A typical outing might be to a play or poetry reading. We also enjoyed spending time with our friends and watching the latest movies.

Anne was a teacher, an excellent one who had been honored as Outstanding New Teacher in the California school district where she first taught. When we moved to Ohio, she continued teaching as a substitute, allowing her to devote more time to raising our family. Between teaching assignments, she volunteered at Children's Hospital and her church. Always a lover of words and their proper spelling and use, she also worked as a freelance editor for McMillan, McGraw Hill, AT&T, Paul Werth—a marketing and PR agency—and Rockwell International. She worked for Bob Taft when he was the Ohio Secretary of State and then in his campaign office when he ran for governor. She was also the operations manager for the Spirituality Network. In 1999, Anne and three friends started Respite, a program for low-income single mothers so that they could get a break and be pampered for a change. The program is still operating today.

Anne was a busy woman until an autoimmune disease called inclusion body myositis (IBM) began taking control of her life. This progressive muscle disorder, characterized by inflammation, weakness, and atrophy, robs a person of strength in their lower extremities. We first noticed the problem when it became increasingly more difficult for her to climb the stairs to bed each night. Lifting her foot high enough to move up to the next stair became almost impossible. Eventually, she had to drop to her knees and climb that way. I could neither lift nor push her because of the pain she experienced. I could only listen to her agonizing groans as she moved slowly, step by step. Fortunately, members of a card club Anne belonged to learned of her plight and came to the rescue by donating a stair lift. What a wonderful gift!

Our life together was dominated by canes, walkers, and wheelchairs. As the IBM progressed, Anne also began having trouble with dysphagia. This difficulty in swallowing meant she was not eating as much and had more trouble than usual in taking her medication. She began to waste away, and we all knew that there was no cure for the autoimmune disease.

With Anne's condition, good days could change into bad days in an instant. They did for us in late September 2017. One minute, we were talking about her getting out of the house for the first time in ages; the next, I was following an ambulance to the hospital. Anne had suffered a stroke. The doctors managed to remove enough of the clot in her brain to restore some blood flow, and the family was hopeful at first. However, as the days in the ICU wore on, the impact of her autoimmune disease began to overshadow the stroke. It became increasingly difficult for her to swallow the excessive saliva she produced. She was literally choking on it and had to be resuscitated continuously. Our family was faced with the horrible reality of what lay ahead.

Anne was restless and slipping in and out of consciousness. She kept scooting from the center of the bed to the side, and one of our daughters asked her why.

"I want to be next to Wayne," she said. "Because he's my guy."

I hadn't heard the remark, but when my daughter relayed it to me, I was overcome with emotion. The thought that she was thinking about me in her last hours was overwhelming. How do you say goodbye to such deep love? In the end, I knew I could not say goodbye to this wonderful woman God had sent to greet me at the mailbox in Downey, California, so many years ago. Instead, I would say goodbye to her pain; I would say goodbye to her suffering. I bent over her and whispered in her ear that I knew her spirit was still with me and that her smile and laughter would forever have a special place in my heart until I came to join her.

Johnny Angel

By B. Del Rossi

There's an old song called "Johnny Angel" by Shelley Fabares. It's a beautiful song, but to me, it has a different meaning. My husband, John, is now my Johnny Angel. What seems like a different lifetime was the best one I have lived so far. It was short and sweet, but if that was all the time I could ever have with John, I would choose it every single time.

My husband, John, was everything I had hoped for—charming, handsome, smart, witty, extremely creative, and most importantly, the greatest father any kid could ask for. Together, we had five children and wanted a sixth, but the universe had a different plan for us. He loved our children deeply. We had four girls, and our fifth was a boy. He played everything imaginable with them. He would take our oldest daughter's teddy bear and Little Tikes people and play out Jack and the Beanstalk for them; they'd go nuts over the teddy bear being the giant. He would do magic tricks, like tossing up an imaginary ball in the air and catching it in a Dunkin' Donuts bag, and somehow the ball would make a noise as if he actually caught it. The children were mesmerized by him, as was I. He did everything for us, making sure everyone felt special in their own way. You could tell how much love surrounded us in our family and how much love we had for him.

John had battled kidney cancer; first, in 1996, one kidney was completely removed. Then it spread to the other kidney in 1998; the doctors removed just a piece of his kidney that year and thought they had caught it in time.

On a bright summer day in August 2001, we all headed to the Hamptons to stay over in Montauk. We did this each summer at my sister's house. A few years earlier, we had stopped at the FYE store in Bridgehampton where John bought a CD by Donna Lewis. He then played "I Love You Always Forever" on repeat for the rest of the drive. This song became a key connection to John after his passing, often playing as a sign from him. Halfway through our trip out this time, John began clutching his side in severe pain, which was unusual and alarming for him.

Shortly after that, we spent a lot of time in doctors' offices. We found out he had gallstones and needed them removed. On September 10, 2001, John went in for surgery. The following day, from his hospital bed, chaos ensued in New York when the 9/11 attacks happened. I remember him recalling the panic and fear he felt in his hospital room alone while nurses and doctors were scrambling and screaming. He thought there had been an attack on the hospital. The following day, we were given a very hard pill to swallow. His cancer had spread; somehow, they had missed this. How could the doctors have missed this? That is why we had been going for follow-ups annually—to avoid this, yet it happened.

The following three months were a blur of radiation and chemo. There were many horrible nights where he was so sick, my kids would wake up crying, and I would have my sister come pick them up to spend the night with her. We were losing him before our very eyes, slowly yet rapidly.

Friday, December 7, 2001, was our final day with John. I decided to keep him home so he could be comfortable in his own house, in his own bed. Hospice had delivered a few things to keep him comfortable, like oxygen and other items. He was tired; you could see it in his eyes and his body—what used to be a broad, six foot two muscular frame was now frail, weak, and gray. I picked up my children from school early so they could be with their daddy. He lay in bed, and our oldest daughter sat in the dark bedroom with him. They took a nap together, and after they awoke, family came in to see him. He could no longer speak at this point; it was heartbreaking.

My mind was scattered; I couldn't process a single thought. Later that evening, my sister took our four younger children with her to my niece's basketball game to keep their minds off the utter sadness at home. I had called hospice, asking for a few beds to be delivered so we could all sleep together in our bedroom one last time. We used to have the kids sleep in our bedroom in the summer months since we only had one A/C unit in the house. I thought it would be a nice way to spend our last moments with John. Unfortunately, he didn't make it that far.

Around 7:40 p.m., you could tell he was struggling. Desperately, I tried to save him. I sponged his lips with the tiny sponges hospice had provided and then cried out for the oxygen. My oldest daughter, who had stayed home, ran out and got the oxygen but it was too late. At 7:45 p.m., John took his final breath and made his way up to heaven. His body was no longer fighting. I screamed and sobbed, holding him and weeping. My daughter was removed from the room by my brother since she was in the same state I was. I put on our wedding song and lay there with my husband, the greatest person to ever be a part of my life, and held him tightly. Our song, "Evergreen" by Barbra Streisand, played softly throughout our room. Since then, there has been this hole in my heart, and when I think of John, it hurts the same way it did twenty-three years ago.

The Rondo

By Mara Farrell

The dream I like to play in my head is one where I escort my cured husband from his hospital bed. We gather up his things, leaving the teeming city blur behind. Driving north along the Hudson, we arrive home. In our kitchen, we uncork the premier cru Burgundy that has been aging in the cellar and quietly sip the red liquid. My husband sleeps by my side that night and all the sorrow falls away.

There's a Mozart rondo, "Rondo in A Minor," that I used to perform when I could really play the piano decades ago. My husband, Josh, only ever heard me play fragments. But when he died last September, and grief approached like the storm it is, I gravitated to the piano again. And that's the piece I resumed.

I first met Josh in 1990, when I was thirty-four. After a series of bad romances, I was starting to think marriage was not in the cards and I'd have to face the world alone. But shortly after meeting, we became inseparable. Married in 1992, we had our beautiful daughter, Daisy, the next year.

Josh had the most exquisite tenor voice but made a career in the wine industry after discovering he loved that world too. I was also in the wine world and that's how we met. But our passion for music was constant. Though I played the piano less and less, Josh kept up his vocal work.

We had this precious life together. And I had my partner by my side for three decades. Josh knew all about the turbulence of my childhood; the stories of my father, his terrible mood swings from the trauma of a youth spent in wartime, and my utter fear of him. I knew all about Josh's chaotic childhood, and his brilliant father's steady decline from renowned lawyer to shattered alcoholic. We knew each other's secrets and emotional histories. Laughter would bounce between us on a daily basis.

On a perfect September day after thirty years of marriage, we flew to France for a week in Paris. But days into the trip, Josh felt his stomach was troubled. We called for a doctor at the hotel but he simply wrote it off as a bad reaction to rich food.

We never entertained the serious thought that something might be really wrong.

When we returned to New York, he still felt lousy and met with a gastroenterologist. Scans and tests were ordered immediately. Soon we knew it was stage 4 pancreatic cancer.

Exploring options was heartbreaking as we quickly learned that there was no real cure at his advanced stage. But Josh was accepted into a promising clinical trial in Manhattan, led by a brilliant oncologist. For a time, the trial went smoothly. Then bacterial infection after bacterial infection robbed his chances for any level of remission and he fell behind on the treatment schedule.

By late summer, the advancing cancer gripped his stomach with pain and my stylish husband could only wear overalls. One day, posing in his latest pair, he stood before the door of our 1927-era home and told me I was the love of his life. He was dearly mine. There he was, gray and weak, but lighting up my world with the sweetest smile on his face. And he carried this calmness within, a superior level of humanness that was majestic in its acceptance of what was to come.

Shortly after, we left for the hospital ER on the Upper West Side of Manhattan, never to return home together again.

During Josh's final weeks, I would only leave him for morning cups of Starbuck's dark roast, found in the vast lobby, or quick trips to the hotel. On the last day, our daughter, Daisy, her husband, Bryan, and I were all on his left side. Josh's bed was facing the Hudson River, the river he loved so much. We wanted to create a forest of green in his room and brought in many large palms, ferns, and flowering plants. We played his favorites, like the duet from *The Pearl Fishers* sung by Jussi Björling and Robert Merrill.

Witnessing his last breath remains, to this day, incomprehensible. Forever and final. September moved on to October, and winter approached. The leaves that Josh had seen as he lay under our redbud tree, months past, were now gone.

One frigid afternoon, during a particularly bad day of raw pain and loneliness, I lifted the lid of the fifty-year-old Steinway grand and attempted the rondo. And I would continue to muddle through it over the next few months. Around March, my son-in-law had a session with a medium in Ireland. They talked about many things, but at one point she paused to tell him to give a message to me: "Tell your mother-in-law her husband is enjoying the piano playing. And he is always with her."

No one knew I was playing the piano again; only me. But my beautiful husband, now on the other side, clearly knew and could hear me. And there was this incredible thought that he was with me during every waking moment, and as I slept and dreamt. And as I figured out this new life—not the life I wanted, but one I had to navigate.

The pain of losing Josh is still piercing. But perhaps this tremendous loss has not cruelly returned me to the place of loneliness I inhabited before Josh entered my life. I'm edging toward the belief that our two realms can merge, sharing many mysteries, which suggests that the glowingly happy dream I spoke of earlier is happening somewhere in time and space.

The Love of My Life

By Irena Nieslony

How do you say goodbye to the love of your life? Nothing can be more difficult, but I had to do so on January 12, 2019, when I lost Peter, the funniest and most loving man I had ever met.

I wasn't a believer in soulmates. In fact, I had just about given up on love. I was thirty-two years old and had experienced too much heartbreak. However, they say when you're not looking for love, it appears out of nowhere.

I was an actress but was temping in an office between jobs when I met Peter. He was the sales manager, and I was a lowly office worker, but when he came and talked to me, I knew he was special. There was something about him that made him seem different from other men. Yes, he was handsome, but when he talked to you, he made you feel like the most important person in the world.

It wasn't long before Peter asked me out on a date. We barely stopped talking the whole evening and found that we shared a lot in common like motorbikes and boats. He had a small boat on the River Thames, and when we got married three years later, we lived on a steel barge.

The next couple of years were wonderful, but then I got sick with Crohn's disease and was seriously ill for over two years. Peter proved his immense love for me during this time. He looked after me completely self-lessly and never complained. Often, I couldn't even get out of bed, and he would do everything at home. I couldn't have asked for a more caring and compassionate partner. I will always be grateful for his love and support during this difficult time.

Our wedding day was halfway through this ordeal. It wasn't ideal because of my illness, but I felt honored that he still wanted to marry me even though I looked as if I would waste away at any minute. I managed to get through the day but collapsed in bed in the early evening. Peter was understanding and didn't complain that it wasn't the ideal wedding night. We honeymooned in Mauritius, and I think God must have been looking down on us as I wasn't quite as sick. We even hired a motorbike to tour the island, which I coped with. Peter was in his element, maneuvering the bike around the beautiful island.

One year later, I had an operation, and I was well again, so we were able to enjoy our lives to the full. It was also the beginning of our new careers. We took over the cafe bar at the marina where we lived, and I cooked while Peter ran the bar. The regulars loved him, and I think he was one of the main reasons they came to us rather than the pub down the road. He told great stories, listened to all their problems, and made them feel special.

In October 2018, Peter started to have pains in his left side. He couldn't lie down and slept in an armchair. A shadow was found on his lung, and after Christmas, he went into hospital for a biopsy. We thought he'd be out the day after, but he wasn't discharged. I closed my eyes to the fact that he was never coming out even though it was staring at me in the face.

Peter deteriorated quickly and was in more and more pain. The doctors were going to give him morphine, and I knew that he was going to drift away. We had to talk while he was still able. He lay in bed, and I took his hand. He was a shell of the man he had been a few months before when he still looked fit and healthy. Now, he was thin and drawn, but he was still the man I had loved for the past twenty-seven years. He wasn't that coher-ent, so I did most of the talking. I talked about all the adventures we had shared, the exciting countries we had visited, the fun we'd had living on a boat. Peter didn't say much, just smiled and squeezed my hand. However, one of the things he managed to say was that I had to continue having adventures and not give up on life. I felt the tears welling up but tried to hide them from him.

The following day, the morphine kicked in, and although Peter was there physically, his spirit wasn't. I sat with him for another week until he slipped away. Although I knew it was going to happen, I was still numb with shock. I felt that my life was over, and I didn't know how I was going to manage without him. The love of my life and my best friend was gone. I would have nobody to confide in, nobody to laugh with, nobody to share special occasions with. I felt that my heart was breaking. Why couldn't we have had more time together?

Five and a half years later, I still miss Peter, The house is empty without him, but I am getting on with life, though perhaps not having the adventures we used to have. I haven't met anyone else. Peter was the best and is irreplaceable, but I have settled into a routine and am happy to live with the wonderful memories of our lives together.

Vibrant Sam

By Jennifer Simpson

Sam was the man every woman dreams of and every man aspires to be. He could light up a room with his smile. He had an undeniable charm and a presence that captivated anyone fortunate enough to cross his path. With the charisma of a movie star, he exuded a warmth that made everyone feel at home and cherished. His unique blend of fun, irreverence, and classic sophistication made him unforgettable.

When I first met Sam, we were college students, thrilled to join the exclusive orchestra that warm April evening. Apparently, I caught Sam's eye immediately, but to me, he seemed too accustomed to female attention. I wanted a quiet, studious man and had sworn off dating for a while. I had previously committed to God that He was going to have to knock me down before I would date again.

With commencement three weeks away, Sam and I were asked to play the trumpet march. I remained focused on our daily practice and was intentionally aloof toward him. Sam, ever the charmer, was determined that I would see his true side and took this opportunity to woo me. His enthusiastic heart began to break through my defenses as I saw his strong love for God and people.

After a continual three-week rebuff, Sam determined to give me one last chance at the single's late skate game night. Later, the announcers called an impromptu speed skating race, which he dominated with flair, and my heart fluttered. I, on the other hand, got knocked down and bruised during a trio skate. Afterward, I surprisingly accepted his offer to couple skate even though I had previously turned down his advances. As he skated backward, holding my hands, I unknowingly stared him down. He kept looking away, and my heart broke a little. Later, when I left, I parked my new Camaro next to his rundown Buick. He walked out, puzzled as to why I would be parked next to him. I shared how my heart hurt that he wouldn't look me in the eyes during the couple's skate. He responded that I had looked at him in a different way than I ever had before. Without realizing it, my heart had softened when I got knocked down. Softly, our love story began, filled with a warmth and connection I never saw coming.

Three months later, in August, I was telling friends about how I had committed to God that I wouldn't date until He knocked me down. I recounted the skate night and showed them the bruise still visible on my leg. A lightning bolt hit me as I realized my heart had changed the moment I got knocked down.

Another night, another memory etched in my heart. As Sam raced down the highway, I pondered the raindrops on the windshield. The rain could not dampen our excitement as our first child was on the way. Our anticipation was palpable. As our son was born at the hospital, Sam's eyes welled with tears. When he handed me our newborn, his voice cracked with emotion, overwhelmed by the profound love he felt in that first moment holding his son.

Nine months later, I again found myself looking through the car windshield, my vision blurred by raindrops and tears. I was in the depths of despair. Friends were driving me to pick up our son, and I was reeling from the news that had shattered our world. Sam had been diagnosed with brain cancer. Only hours earlier, surrounded by our friends and family in the emergency room, we believed Sam was battling a stubborn sinus infection. When the doctors finally took him for a CT scan at around 10 p.m., he began having a seizure. At midnight, the neurosurgeon performed emergency brain surgery to relieve pressure, and the devastating diagnosis followed: stage four brain cancer, with a prognosis of only three to six months. The news hit like a freight train. Sam's older sister, standing nearby, collapsed on the floor in shock. Our vibrant Sam, who had always been a pillar of strength and joy, was now fighting an unimaginable battle.

Thirty days later, our family gathered around Sam, clinging to each other and to the hope of a miracle. As he lay there in a coma, we sang "Turn Your Eyes Upon Jesus," our voices blending in a bittersweet harmony. In those final moments, as his spirit began to leave his body, I heard his voice in my spirit, faint but unmistakable: "I love you, baby." The words echoed in my heart, growing softer as if carried away on a gentle breeze out the window behind me.

Sam's passing left a void that could never be filled. His radiant presence had been the center of our universe, a beacon of light and love. Every memory of him, from his infectious laughter to his tender moments, was a testament to a life lived fully and beautifully.

Josiah became the embodiment of Sam's spirit. Every time I looked into his eyes, I saw a reflection of his father's unyielding zest for life. Sam's memory lived on in our son's laughter, his curious questions, and his boundless energy.

Sam's legacy continues to inspire all who knew him. There was and will never be anybody like Sam. He was a man who loved deeply, lived fully, and left an indelible mark on the world.

A Once in a Lifetime Meeting

By Lori Wigsten

It is only once in a lifetime that you meet someone who changes your whole life. Rob was that person for me.

During my college years, we met while I was working at a laundromat where he would come in to have his clothes washed. He was an attractive, short guy with a hefty build and sandy-blonde hair. I usually went for tall, dark, and handsome men introduced by friends. He was friendly and out-going. I had no idea he had a huge crush on me until the last day I worked there. He came in to drop off his clothes, as he did every other time. Then, he left. At the night's end, the phone rang and I answered. Rob asked if I remembered him. He explained he wanted to ask me out earlier but felt awkward. Looking back, it seems unbelievable—Rob formed friendships everywhere he went. It didn't matter if the person was a janitor or a CEO. People always liked Rob. His exuberance for life was catchy. You could not help but get caught up in it. I said I would go out with him, which was unusual for me. I would break the rule just this once because I was return-ing to my hometown once classes ended.

Well, that first date led to nineteen years of marriage. I should have known when our waitress asked us how long we had been together; we laughed as we told her that this was our first date. Six months later, to my family's surprise, I moved in with him—they were happy for me, though, knowing that it must be love.

Rob came into my life at just the right time. I had lost my mother a year earlier and had been living with my older sister before leaving for college. I knew my time in school was limited, and I was unsure of my future. Then, Rob showed up, and that all changed. I moved to South County to be with him, and Rob gave me the emotional security and confidence I needed to believe everything would work out. No one else I had dated had made me feel that way. Rob did this by just being himself. He was the most dedicated and loyal partner I could have asked for. He had proven he loved me long before I knew I was in love with him. Once this realization hit me, I knew I had found a soulmate in him.

Our life together was not always easy. Although Rob was highly intelligent, he chose a different route than his Cornell-educated mother would have wished. He decided to spend his life on the sea as a New England lobsterman. For us, that meant the ups and downs of seasonal work. With two young children, we had to watch our pennies. This never stopped Rob from enjoying life. He always found a way to have fun, from second-hand bookstore hunts and launching rockets to building wooden toys for our children. Rob was always filled with interest, surprise, and knowledge. Life with Rob was never dull, and his outgoing, friendly personality brought in friends from all different walks of life. As his family, we got to share in all of his crazy adventures. Life was never dull with Rob around.

However, at age forty-five, Rob was diagnosed with colon cancer. It was a shock to all of us because, as Rob would say in his usual humorous way, "I am pretty healthy, except for the cancer." This truly was the case. He had not had any serious health issues until then. Rob did not give up the fight easily. For two and a half years, he amazed his doctors. As someone with stage 4 colon cancer, they told him they expected him to be dead within six months. He surprised us all. He dealt with chemo treatments like they were just a part of everyday life, and when people commented how brave he was, his joking response was always, "What choice do I have? It's this or die." Humor aside, he was a brave person to us all, even before the cancer, as he was always willing to take risks and try something new.

This is why I think it was difficult for us to believe when, three years in, the doctors told him he was at the end of the road and his liver was failing. Rob had accepted his fate at this point and made me promise to find love again once he passed.

"How can I do that?" I asked. It would never be the same.

Within a month of this final diagnosis, he passed away in our home; I had reassured him that it was okay to go, that the children and I would be all right. After his passing, I felt lost. I questioned who I was without him. Why did he die when he had fought so hard for so long to live? His death felt unfair.

Rob requested his memorial service be a celebration of his life, not his death. It lived up to his expectations. At the service, people stood up to share stories of how Rob had touched their lives. It truly was a celebration of a man whose exuberance in life even followed him after he died. After his service, I began the most difficult year of my life. Slowly, I realized that to honor him and our life together, I needed to focus on what I had to be grateful for and find a way to live a happy life. With Rob's memory as a guide, I learned to find the fun in life again. Being able to do this was his parting gift to me. As a result, a part of him will always be with me.

About the Contributors

Nikolai-Andre Alexander is a Jamaican who migrated to Canada in 2018. An avid reader from a young age, Nik has always loved words and stories. He lives with his wife and son in Kitchener, Ontario, and is pursuing opportunities in freelance copyediting while working full-time in supply chain management.

Toshi Allan Alibudbud is a high school teacher, a ghost writer for online platforms, and a staunch advocate for strays. Having fostered and rehomed over forty cats, he has no plans of stopping anytime soon. He lives in the Philippines and takes care of his senior parents and a sister with cerebral palsy.

Chris Angelis has a PhD in English from the University of Tampere, and his research focuses on Gothic fiction and time. Besides a stint as a university teacher and a journalist, he has worked as a content editor. He is a published writer, visual artist, and musician. He also programs interactive fiction games and web apps focusing on texts and literature.

Shahana Arain is an educator with eighteen years of experience in various roles, including principal. Her most recent role was as EDI learning specialist at Toronto's SickKids Hospital, and today she leads as the inaugural director of equity, diversity, and inclusion at the Faculty of Social Work at the University of Toronto. As a community advocate, she co-founded Ontario's first Muslim Educators' Network and she currently sits on the board of directors for Durham Youth Services and Frontenac Youth Services.

Olubukola Awodamila, is a writer and sister to Tofunmi, who had the privilege of calling Ruth her soul sister and friend. Olubukola witnessed the profound impact of their friendship on her sister's life and was inspired to share their story. Through her writing, she hopes to honor Ruth's memory and celebrate the transformative power of friendship and love.

Sabrina Bachert is a freelance writer and bookworm based in Colorado, USA. Her work has appeared at the Ent Center of the Arts Film Festival, on Société and The Pylon Journal. Sabrina has a background in military and mental health counseling and loves to consider psychological concepts in her work. Outside of freelancing, she is an avid creator of topical articles, screenplays, historical fiction, and fantasy. Get in touch with her on Instagram @themightybean.

Sara Barnabie lives in upstate New York with her husband, two children, and their cat, Ruby. She is a homeschooling mom, a lover of words, and enjoys capturing candid moments with her camera. Her favorite place to be is anywhere with her family, whether they are on a fun adventure or simply snuggling together over a good book.

Charlotte Bennardo lives in New Jersey with her family and writes both fiction and non-fiction. Her novels include the middle-grade trilogy *Evolution Revolution: Simple Machines, Simple Plans, and Simple Lessons.* She co-authored the young adult novels, *Blonde OPS, Sirenz,* and *Sirenz Back in Fashion.* Currently, she is working on several speculative fiction and romance novels and short stories. She still has her father's toolbox.

Linda Bishop has a bachelor's degree in mass communications and theater arts and master's degrees in education and communication. Starting in publishing, she later transitioned to education, teaching mostly speech classes at the high school and college levels while continuing to freelance as a copyeditor and proofreader for the first few years. She is married and has one son.

Zanandi Botes is a professional writer and published playwright. She has written screenplays, comic books, and hundreds of online articles for various internet publications, including Cracked.com and BunnyEars.com. She is currently writing short documentaries for a YouTube channel called Good News that focuses on social and environmental issues.

Myriah C. Boudreaux writes, edits, and proofreads Catholic content through her company, Pax Proofreading. Primarily a mom and homemaker, she has homeschooled her seven children for more than two decades. When not wielding or whittling words, she enjoys baking goodies, taking nature walks, creating picture books, and watching family movies.

A southern California native, Myriah has appreciated raising her family in Cajun country, Louisiana, since 2001.

Glenda Braganza was born in Halifax and raised in Ottawa. Glenda is a first-generation Goan-Canadian with a BFA in theatre performance from Concordia University. Glenda has performed on stages across Canada with established companies and produced a range of independent work. Her ability to play varying styles and a broad scope of roles has earned her several accolades. Striving for positive representation on screen as well, Glenda's twenty-five-year career also includes film, television, voice, commercials, and video games.

Anna Burks is an author, speaker, and publishing coach. She has a BA in communication and professional writing. Anna is the founder of Christ in Real Life, a ministry that helps aspiring writers fulfill their dreams. She is also the author of the book *The Devil Doesn't Want You to Read This: Unraveling Your Strongholds*, which originated as a letter to her adult children.

Allison Byrne is a mother of two and devout wife to her high school sweetheart of twenty years. Although she had a major in journalism, and was a lover of the written word, she relinquished that career path in order to help her family with their struggling business. Now, however, she is pursuing a career in writing, her original passion. Allison continues to pursue her passion for philanthropy by hosting fundraisers for families in need.

Hayley Charles is originally from Hays, Kansas, and currently resides in Springfield, Missouri. She has a BA in journalism, is a candidate for an MS in clinical mental health counseling, and is passionate about spreading awareness, increasing education, and reducing stigma related to mental illness. When she isn't in class or writing, Hayley can be found talking about her feelings on the poetry stage or rollerblading around town.

Shannon Coburn is a fiction writer and mother of three from South Dakota. After the loss of her middle child, she dedicated her life to researching mental health issues and has since started on a path toward a degree in neuroscience in an attempt to prevent others from making the same decision he did. *Ocean Man* is her first publication.

Anna Frances Conway is an artist from rural Northern Ireland. She's a writer, actor, and stage manager fascinated by the art of storytelling and what it can achieve. Anna has worked as a stage manager for several productions, including *Monster*, written and directed by Nathan Martin. She's always itching to perform and most recently played Ophelia in Bright Umbrella's all-female adaptation of *Hamlet*. In her writing, themes of mental illness are strong, as well as identity and sexuality. She also enjoys comedy, in particular terrible puns.

Eileen Antoinette Cullen is a Boston-based writer and editor. She holds a BA in English from the University of Massachusetts Boston, where she was awarded the James William Fay Prize for Outstanding Work in British Literature.

Angelique Davies is a graduate of OISE/UT. Her career in the field of early childhood education and care has included various roles: educator, blogger, course instructor, curriculum developer, and project manager. Her interests include writing, reading, knitting, music, cooking, thrift shopping, and volunteering. She and her husband live in Toronto with their adopted pet budgie, Willa.

Naomi G. Davis is a first-generation American from the Bronx, New York. Naomi's career in television began as a writer's PA on *The Get Down* and writer's assistant on *P-Valley* and the first Emmy award-winning season of *The Marvelous Mrs. Maisel*. Naomi received her first credit on Netflix's *Dash & Lily* and quickly followed that up with NBC's *The Endgame*, by writing episode 106, "Judge, Jury and Executioner." Naomi has written two episodes of the upcoming Netflix animated action-adventure *Splinter Cell*.

Chris de Boer is a retired university teacher in marketing and management in the Netherlands and Thailand. He lives in northeastern Thailand, in Udon Thani, in a small village up-country.

B. Del Rossi is a mother of five children who lost her husband to kidney cancer twenty-three years ago. Since then, she has raised their children on her own. She honors his memory each year on his birthday and on the anniversary of his passing. She cherishes her children and her six grandchildren and the time she gets to spend with them. They bring so much joy and love into her life.

Dr. Debbie Donsky has been an educator for 30 years and lives in Toronto, Ontario. Outside of work, Debbie is a voracious reader (and listener) of books. She can walk for hours along the streets, parks and waterways of Toronto, and draws/writes her feelings. Debbie loves exploring the city and world with her loving husband and her two wonderful *adultish* children.

Johanna Douglas is an author who was born and raised in Montana. She graduated with a bachelor's degree in creative writing from the University of Montana in Missoula. Johanna spends her days working at her local library and spending time with her two dogs, a cat named Bojangles, and her partner. Her life is centered around coffee, books, and her family.

John Ensor is originally from Yorkshire, England. After spending much of his life working in an office, he relocated to Galicia, in Northern Spain, along with his wife, Nina, and their four dogs. After producing articles for an English-language newspaper in Spain, he now works freelance as a writer and copy editor. He is passionate about short stories, animals, current affairs, music, and cycling.

Anita Ellerington is a devoted mother of two teenagers who lives in a small town in New Zealand. Anita gained her degree in psychology in 2019 and uses this knowledge in her support role. Writing is a passion so she spends her spare time writing poetry and using writing prompts. Anita loves swimming in rivers and being with nature; this is her happy place—where she can detach from life and reconnect to herself.

Mara Farrell is based in the beautiful Hudson Valley region of New York and has spent decades working for legendary family-owned wine estates in Europe. Her essays have appeared in *The New York Times*, *Poughkeepsie Journal,* and the Cultural Landscape Foundation. A graduate of Sarah Lawrence College, she received her masters from Columbia University.

Joseph Ferrier is a full-time dad, aspiring writer, and cancer survivor, living in Oregon. He received his undergraduate degree in psychology and community studies from the University of Maine, Machias. He enjoys Tolkien, Le Guin, and the absurd comedy stylings of Gen-Z.

Catherine M. Finger is a retired high school superintendent and multi-certified award-winning coach offering transformational coaching in leadership, health, and life. She also serves as a mentor coach and offers coaching supervision for practitioners. When she's not coaching, engaged as a chaplain, or writing, you can find Catherine riding her horses, traveling, and sharing Cabi fashion experiences with friends near and far. Learn more on her website, www.CatherineFinger.com.

Shoshana Gardiner was born in the Upper Peninsula of Michigan. She has lived nomadically throughout most of her adult life. Currently, she is traveling the Pacific Northwest in her vehicle, immersing herself in the abundance of nature and building a community with others who cannot seem to keep still, documenting every step along the way.

Abriana Gardley is from St. Louis, Missouri, and splits her time between Austin, Texas, and home. She has a background in computer science and IT writing. Some of the things she enjoys for leisure are traveling and cooking for her loved ones. Although her inner family circle has been cut smaller, it has only grown them all closer together. If she's not seeking the next fashion statement to rock, you'll most likely find her at the library, Barton Springs Park, or off to Italy just for fun.

Brooke Gero was born and raised on the East Coast of the United States. Despite her natural affinity for writing articles and journals as a child, she finds it difficult to write about past memories with her beloved aunt. It's almost as if there are too many moments and memories to single out and write about. In her story, we get a glimpse into her trying to do the impossible.

Bijaya Giri is an Indian writer. With a degree in environmental science and English, she is a high school teacher who primarily teaches English. She writes short stories and poems that have garnered significant appreciation. She is currently working on a collection of poems which she plans to publish soon. Apart from writing, a hobby that turned into a passion, Bijaya is an accomplished artist. She is also actively involved in social work.

Lyra Goga is a teacher, writer, and literary translator based in Kosovo. She holds a BA in English language and literature, an MA in English literature, and is currently a PhD candidate in literature. Lyra believes that art can change the world and make it a better place.

Brian Gurnham is a retired teacher, having taught grades four to twelve over a thirty-nine-year career. Originally from Montreal, Quebec, Brian now resides in Edmonton, Alberta, with his wife Diane. They have two daughters and four grandchildren, also living in Edmonton.

Karl Gruber is a lifelong runner from Columbus, Ohio. He became the ninth man in the world to successfully run fifty-two marathons in fifty-two weeks in 1996–1997. Gruber is also the author of six books, a certified life coach, a former professional radio disc jockey, and currently the host of the podcast *World Awakenings: The Fast Track to Enlightenment*.

Sarah Hahn is a writer and teacher from Ontario, Canada. Her writing has appeared in *The Northern Miner*, *Relevant Magazine*, and *Canadian Mining Magazine*. She previously worked in communications at a non-profit organization. Like most writers, Sarah is a coffee addict. When she isn't writing, she enjoys organizing spaces in her home and watching legal dramas. Sarah has a bachelor's degree in journalism from Ryerson University and a master's degree in teaching from OISE. Visit her online at <ins>https://hahnsarah.com/</ins>.

Brittney Hallmark is a national board-certified teacher specializing in English and language development. She has a son and a daughter and enjoys being outdoors, reading, and writing

Susan Hartzler's debut non-fiction narrative, *I'm Not Single, I Have a Dog: Dating Tales from the Bark Side*, follows her through the ups and downs of finding unconditional love. Her next title, *The Peace Puppy: A Memoir of Caregiving and Canine Solace*, is a personal roadmap for those facing the daunting role of caregiver. Both books are available on McFarland Publishing and Amazon.

Mary Haralson is a Maine-based writer whose diverse life experiences infuse her work with depth and authenticity. A former combat engineer in the US Army, Mary later channeled her leadership skills into entrepreneurship, founding a successful massage therapy practice. Her writing explores the intricate tapestry of human experiences, from loss to resilience. A graduate of the University of Maine with degrees in anthropology and history, Mary is embarking on a new adventure by pursuing maritime archaeology at Southampton University.

Linda Hawkins was raised in the Two Mountains (Deux-Montagnes) area of Québec and later settled in Dunany in Wentworth, Quebec, where she raised her three children. Cherishing family memories and actively participating in her community have always been central to her upbringing and parenting philosophy. At seventy-seven years old, her greatest joy is spending time with her grandchildren, reinforcing her commitment to strong family ties and community involvement.

Daniel Henriquez is from southwest Michigan. He loves playing guitar and is a creative genius in the kitchen. He loves learning new things and is a deep well of wisdom and a knower of random, fun facts. He married his wife, Janice—a whirlwind, God-ordained love story—in March 2024. They love to serve the Lord together in ministry.

Maryem Hmayed is an English teacher at the British Academy of Tunis. Born in Tunisia, she has collaborated with German writer Raimund Pousset on a published work. Writing is her passion and her favorite way to express her feelings and thoughts. Currently, she is working on her own book, which explores the diverse stories of her family. Alongside her teaching, Maryem pursues freelance writing, allowing her to continuously practice and nurture her craft.

Jennifer Holmes-Dziuba retired from employment as an elementary school teacher and speech-language pathologist but remains passionate about using her skill sets in volunteer roles in her community. She has enjoyed working on her own schedule as an historical interpreter at a local museum, as an amateur actress, and as the director of a vintage car club. She is married and is the mother of two adult children who were deeply loved by their Grammie.

Dr. Jimica Howard is the principal of Shelby Academy in Louisville, Kentucky, where she lives with her husband, daughter, son, and four-year-old service dog. In her twenty-one years as an educator, Dr. Howard has been a teacher, counselor, and assistant principal in both middle and elementary schools. She is passionate about social justice and equity in education and is devoted to providing every student with the access and opportunities needed to achieve excellence. She also loves to bake, read, sing, and write poetry.

Leya Hunter is a versatile writer and blogger, known for her philosophical fiction and poetry. As the author of two thought provoking eBooks, Leya's work often explores deep psychological introspection and invites readers to engage with open-ended interpretations. She has been featured in online literary magazines, and her latest work will be featured in two upcoming anthologies. Currently, she is working on her third book, further enriching her literary repertoire.

Aiza Claire P. Jamisolamin was an overseas Filipino worker from 2019–2020. After her contract ended, she decided that she had to go back to school for herself and, most importantly, for her son. She is a single mom-witha six-year-old son and is currently studying for her degree, a bachelor of secondary education with a major in English, at Southern de Oro Philippines College.

Dr. Lincoln Johnson is a professor of special education at the University of Nevada Las Vegas. He dedicates his life and career to working with students with disabilities from high risk, urban areas. His commitment to multicultural education, global and international research, and diversity, equity, inclusion, and belonging are evident through his work with urban school districts, worldwide research and collaboration, and his never-ending quest to meet students where they are.

Dr. Darian Jones, founder of The Jones Edge coaching and consulting firm, is a keynote speaker, executive coach, and healer with over twenty years of experience in education and leadership. Known for empowering leaders through transformative racial equity and anti-racism work, his coaching and consulting create lasting change in organizations. Dr. Jones' dedication to leadership, diversity, and holistic healing has made a profound impact on individuals, schools, and companies nationwide.

Carol Kay, born in St. Louis and raised in the San Fernando Valley of Los Angeles, is a retired university professor who now writes and edits with newfound pride and joy. Having moved from Phoenix a decade ago, she currently resides in Beverly Hills with her husband and two cats.

Dr. Kay Keiser has been an educator for over forty-five years, first as an Omaha teacher and administrator. At the University of Nebraska Omaha, Dr. Keiser teaches educational leadership. Receiving UNO's Outstanding Teacher and Outstanding Graduate Mentor Awards, she served as department chair. A native of Nebraska, she has traveled to all continental United States and Canadian provinces. She has written several articles and books and enjoys crafts and playing the harp.

Kumanan Kunaratnam is a dedicated teacher with the Toronto District School Board and a passionate community activist. As a strong advocate for social justice, Kumanan works inside and outside of schools to ensure children have access to a fair and equitable education. Kumanan holds a master of education from the University of Ottawa. Kumanan has also been actively involved in seeking justice for the victims of the Tamil genocide in Sri Lanka.

Steve Ladd is an experienced physical education and English teacher of twenty-eight years. He loves sports and spends a lot of his time volunteering in various sports, especially athletics and rugby. Steve leads an active lifestyle with his wife and two sons and is always searching for the next challenge.

Jim Landwehr is the author of four memoirs: *At the Lake, Cretin Boy, Dirty Shirt*, and *The Portland House*. His non-fiction stories have appeared in publications such as *Main Street Rag, The Sun Magazine*, and *Story News*. Jim was the 2018–2019 poet laureate for the Village of Wales, Wisconsin. He is retired and lives with his wife, Donna, in Waukesha, Wisconsin. For more information on his writing, visit https://sites.google.com/view/jimlandwehr/home.

Jo Lavender is a writer and editor who has had a long-standing love affair with literature and wrote her first book when she was nine. Encouraged by amazing family members like her grandma, she has enjoyed a wonderful, adventurous life, both on the written page and in reality. She loves cats, gardening, video games, and baking, but her favorite thing is to sit in the garden hammock and write.

Timothy Law is a writer of fantasy, children's stories, and general fiction who comes from a little town in Southern Australia called Murray Bridge. A happily married father of three children, family is important to him. Currently working at the Murray Bridge Library as library manager, he has dreamed since early high school of becoming a full-time author. Many of his short stories and general musings can be found on his blog, http:// somecallmetimmy.blogspot.com.au/.

Rochelle Lazarte has taught college-level English courses, and has years of experience in product training and communications training. She currently lives in Madrid and works as a language assistant. A spoken word poet under Words Anonymous, she is an advocate for mental health awareness and LGBTQIA+ rights. Her first work of long fiction, *Maty's Mixtape for Moving On*, is available on Amazon.

Heather Lewis-Barchue is a writer who regularly shares on Medium and will be published in *Rat's Ass Review* in Fall 2024. She is the wife of a lawyer, the mother of two young women and three boys under six—one who resides in heaven. Heather is an accomplished triathlete, expert sea glass finder, avid indoor gardener, and lifelong learner. She enjoys listening to the river running through her backyard in Silvermine, Connecticut, and reading anything and everything.

Jelena Lukic is a skilled writer and copywriter celebrated for her engaging and persuasive writing. Her work spans various genres, showcasing her versatility and creativity. Jelena's ability to craft compelling narratives and persuasive copy has earned her a reputation for excellence in the literary and marketing fields. Her insightful and impactful writing continues to captivate readers and clients alike.

Jack Maher, historical novelist, is a proud fifth-generation Colorado native and grandson of Denver Art Museum pioneer Eric Douglas, the subject of Jack's book *Poppy: A Novel About A Colorful Colorado Life*. A four-time National Television Arts & Sciences Heartland Chapter Emmy winner,

Jack worked at NBC affiliate KUSA-TV in Denver as a multimedia journalist and executive producer.

Brandon Marcus has been creative his entire life and has wanted to be a writer since before he even knew his ABCs. Today, he spends his days writing and editing about sports but still loves to explore his creative side via short stories and essays. From sci-fi to fantasy, horror, and more, there is no genre Brandon doesn't want to dive into.

Gabrielle May is a creative writing graduate, songwriter, and traveler. At twenty-one, she hitchhiked across Europe carrying nothing but a backpack and her trusted ukulele. She was unaware of her connection to the spirit realm until Christmas Eve of 2019.

Kelly Mack McCoy is a writer and ghostwriter from the beautiful Texas Hill Country. He lives there with his wife, Miss Emily, and two Yorkies, Dixie and Dolly. McCoy is the author of *Rough Way to the High Way* and *The Sojourner's Road Home: A 40-Day Journey to the Heart of God.*

Caitlyn McMorrough is a dedicated student at UCF, pursuing a degree in nursing while balancing a passion for writing and community service. She has volunteered over three hundred hours at animal shelters and hospitals. In her free time, she enjoys creating educational content and sharing stories that inspire and uplift. She continues to honor the memory of her cousin, Michelle, by helping others and spreading awareness about the struggles and triumphs of those dealing with addiction.

Selena Mell, enriched by family gatherings, laughter, and creativity, has developed strong community values and cherished memories. With decades of experience in education, she focuses on fostering learning and inspiring creativity in young minds while guiding educational leadership teams across four continents. Committed to family, heritage, and personal growth, Selena is deeply dedicated to nurturing the next generation with passion and care. She credits her childhood roots and foundational years with significantly shaping her values.

Lizbeth Meredith is an award-winning author, speaker, podcaster, and true crime interviewer living in Chattanooga, Tennessee. Her memoir, *Pieces of Me: Rescuing My Kidnapped Daughters,* is now a Lifetime television movie,

Stolen by Their Father. A contributor to anthologies like *Chicken Soup for the Soul* and *A Girl's Guide to Travelling Alone,* Lizbeth's second book, *Grounded in Grit: Turn Your Challenges into Superpowers,* is available now wherever books are sold.

Cindy Mich is an award-winning journalist and media personality who founded the New York City-based independent film festival, Art is Alive. She is the creator of her own publication, *Elegant Expressions Magazine.* Mich is regularly called upon to cover film premieres and festivals, events, product launches, and so on. Her made-for-TV series on medical misdiagnosis is premiering soon. Finally, Cindy's public-access TV talk show, *Cin's Chat Corner*, has more than two million subscribers in eleven states.

Dr. Lesli C. Myers-Small is a senior executive leader, educator, influencer, storyteller, and advocate known for her impactful community focus and servant leadership. She delivers engaging keynotes, workshops, and presentations locally, regionally, and nationally, including a "TedTalk" at TEDxRochester. Her humorous, straightforward, and sincere style inspires people of varied backgrounds and ages to use their talents creatively to serve others.

Lisa Muldoon is an elementary school teacher and resides in Hamilton, Ontario, with her husband, Tim. She has a Master of Education degree from Brock University. When she is not at school, she enjoys volunteering in the community, spending time with family, and participating in sports. Her favorite activity is snowboarding, but she enjoys a variety of outdoor adventures and exploring all over the world.

Tiffany Neal is a published author and poet living in Delaware, where she enjoys a fulfilling life with her partner and family. Her works often explore themes of love, loss, and resilience, resonating deeply with readers. Beyond writing, Tiffany cherishes traveling and spending time with her adult children and grandchild, finding inspiration and joy in their shared adventures and experiences.

Irena Nieslony has a BA Honors degree in English and drama and worked as an actress, puppeteer, and voice-over artist for several years before becoming a writer in 2008. She has had fourteen novels published, as well as a non-fiction book, short stories, and many articles. She married Peter Fletcher on November 5, 1994.

Michelle Ann Patrovani, EdD, is a writer, educator, former school leader, and mom to two phenomenal young men who live with incurable, progressive, life-threatening illnesses. She considers her sons her greatest gifts and teachers in life. She writes mainly about education, overcoming childhood trauma and incurable illness, relationships, and life balance. Her articles have been featured in the NYAPE Journal, Cystic Fibrosis Foundation (CFF) Blog, and various online publications.

Jarvis Ottum writes middle-grade horror. His favorite authors are R.L. Stine and Stephen King. His works have appeared in the anthologies *Balm: Poetry for Beautiful Broken Souls* and *The Gift: Your Gift is Inside*. His works have also appeared on LinkedIn, TripAdvisor, and the Agape Review.

Chelsea Pinkham is a professional dog trainer, animal advocate, and writer based in the San Francisco Bay Area. Over her lifetime, she has personally rescued, transported, or fostered over one thousand animals of a wide variety of species. She credits her deeply intelligent childhood dog for inspiring a love of canine behavior and training. Her goal is to strengthen the bond between dogs and their caregivers, training with compassion, connection, and empathy.

Justo Quiroz Chilcumpa, a Chilean from Santiago, developed an interest in language learning after living in Australia. Now settled in Canada with his wife and stepchild, he enjoys exploring diverse cuisines and embracing new cultural experiences. His journey reflects a deep appreciation for global perspectives, enriched by connections with family across Chile, Australia, the USA, and Spain.

Talha Raja is a creative writer with a deep interest in music and art. Known for a profound love of literature, Talha is currently working on his debut novel, *Abyss*. Drawing inspiration from personal experiences, including battling mental health issues and striving for self-improvement, Talha's work reflects a journey of resilience and growth.

Wayne Rapp has written two books and numerous short stories, essays, and nonfiction pieces for publication. A collection of short stories, *Burnt*

Sienna, was a finalist for the Miguel Mármol Award. A short story, "In the Time of Marvel and Confusion," was nominated for a Pushcart Prize. His creative writing has twice been honored with Individual Artist Excellence Awards from the Ohio Arts Council.

Amy Reeder is a behavioral health specialist whose professional background includes social work and business development in the field of behavioral health. She focuses on the behavioral health needs of long-term care residents and treatment for substance use disorders. She enjoys writing in her spare time. She resides in Wheelersburg, Ohio, with her fiancé, Justin, and her three daughters, Lyla, Adelyn, and Catherine.

Chuck Reid is an educator who has a strong belief in lifelong learning and service leadership. His past has included being a public school teacher, special education consultant, elementary and secondary administrator, superintendent of schools, associate director, and director of education. Currently he is providing consultancy support to a private international educational organization in Cairo, Egypt, as their director of schools.

Kevin Roberts is a fifty-eight-year-old horticulturalist who lives in East Tennessee, USA, with his wife of twenty-two years. He relocated from the UK to America in 2003 and worked as a native plant propagator for a large native plant grower. He is an enthusiastic amateur writer in many subjects.

Terra Sanders, a native of Madison, Wisconsin, currently resides overseas working as a digital marketing specialist and writer. Her hobbies include reading, exploring new cities, and learning all she can about entrepreneurship. She uses her experiences to craft thoughtful and engaging articles and writes in a way that appeals to a broad range of people.

Kevin A. Sawyer began his career in education in 1975, although his work with youth began in 1968. Over the course of his career, he has served as a paraprofessional, teacher, coordinator, assistant principal, principal, area director, state department of education assessor, adjunct professor, national consultant, and motivational speaker. Mr. Sawyer has spent his entire adult life in the service of youth and continues to do so today as a national educational consultant.

Heather Schuller is a poet, author, animal activist, and student of the world. She loves to travel, cook, and study the effects of natural medicine, making tinctures, and how food is medicine and medicine is food. She loves to share recipes, walk her dog Gizmo, and provide photography and videography services. You can find her at https://heatherleeschuller.com/.

Tom Seaton is a retired elementary school principal who has been a contributor to several Word & Deed publications in the past. Given the reflective and deeply personal nature of Goodbye for Now, Tom embraced the opportunity to share his writings on love and loss in this departure from past submissions. Tom enjoys exploring reading and writing in the areas of educational leadership, spirituality and mindfulness.

Harun Šehović is a student and freelance writer from Sarajevo, Bosnia and Herzegovina. He spent his childhood, and currently resides, in Sarajevo, where he is studying philosophy and sociology at the University of Sarajevo. He is also a board member of the university's annual student magazine.

Jemimah Silas is a creative writer with a deep passion for exploring life experiences, psychology, and relationships through her work. Family-oriented and driven, she finds inspiration in the world around her. Jemimah enjoys staying active, working out, hiking in nature, and spending time with her two beloved cats. With an optimistic outlook and adventurous spirit, she approaches both life and writing with curiosity and enthusiasm, always seeking new perspectives and stories to share.

Jennifer Simpson, a life and success coach, has created a peaceful life in a cozy cabin by the river, surrounded by friends, family, horses, and dogs. After the loss of her husband, Sam, she devoted herself to raising their son, Josiah, who has grown into a wonderful young man. Jennifer, with a background in corporate training and business development, inspires others through tailored coaching and community involvement, continuing to honor Sam's memory and staying close to his family.

Creshonda Smith is a clinical social worker hailing from Cleveland, Ohio. She has four beautiful children and has been married for a decade. Her favorite hobbies include traveling to anywhere there's a beach, reading, writing, and playing UNO! Above all, she loves to create lovely memories that she can cherish forever.

Gigi Smith, an author, speaker, and educator with a master's degree in social work, is dedicated to promoting mental health awareness and well-being. As a popular content creator in mental health and social justice, she educates and uplifts her community. Gigi, a community organizer advocating for justice and systemic change, lives by the quote, "May the rising tide uplift us all." Her work reflects a passion for making a positive difference in the lives of others.

S. Kay Smith isn't happy unless she's the scariest person in the room. Her love for ghost stories, vampires, werewolves, and all things spooky inspired her to become a horror writer. She has several short stories published online, and she runs the blog "Playing With Demons," where she explores her love for literature and horror. She enjoys spending time at home with her fiancé and their cat, Thorn.

Mieke Steyn is a passionate parrot enthusiast from South Africa with over twenty years of experience. She cherishes her family, faith, and parrots and is actively involved in parrot rescues. When not with her family or cycling, Mieke tends to her parrots and educates others on proper care. She has cared for various species, including those needing rehabilitation.

Vyacheslav Suslov was born and raised in the South and now lives in Eastern Europe with his family, a dog, a cat, and two parrots. Between taking long walks around the city, learning languages, and trying to figure out what is going on with this life, he somehow finds time to write a little.

Halid Tarakčija is an eighteen-year-old senior student at Elci Ibrahim Pasha Medresa College. Born in Bosnia and Herzegovina, he is a remarkable student who values tradition and is devoted to his faith. He learned to speak English and enjoys spending his free time writing and discussing various topics with others. While surfing the internet, he stumbled upon different freelancing applications and decided to further improve his writing skills while working with others on different topics.

Dr. Charles Taylor is the author of over a dozen books and the producer of award-winning documentaries. A retired professor, Dr. Taylor is also a national consultant on diversity and his seminal work, *Juneteenth: A Celebration of Freedom*, was the official book used in the campaign to make Juneteenth a national holiday.

Cynthia "Susan" Thompson is a high school English teacher, ghostwriter, and editor. She is married to the love of her life, Trey, and together, they are raising two wonderful daughters and their beloved dog, Chevy. In her spare time, Susan can be found running, hiking, or lifting weights. Yes, she's the girl who considers exercise fun! In her writing, she often thinks of her dad, who always inspired her to follow her dreams.

Kelly Vasquez is an analyst for an oil and gas company in Houston, Texas. She enjoys nature and all animals—great and small. She has worked at an animal rehab facility and rescued many animals. She enjoys her butterfly garden and small vegetable garden. She and her husband currently share their lives with two dogs, Kaycee and Jackson, and two cats, Lowrider and Max.

Charlize Venter is an avid writer of various genres with a preference for freeform poetry. Recently coming out of remission, she has focused on rebuilding her strengths and creating a new version of herself from what remains. Growing up in rural Mozambique, she lived a full and beautifully adventurous young life. Charlize hopes to honor those she has lost by living a little bit louder.

Katrina Voshall was raised in San Diego and has lived in the Northwest for thirty years. She was a single mom who waited tables to get her bachelor's degree. She has lived abroad, teaching English in Thailand and Colombia. She loves to travel, hike, and do yoga. Family is the most important part of her life. Since losing her child, her spirituality has been growing stronger each day.

Jennifer Watkins developed a love of animals growing up on a small farm in Virginia where her first word was (to the disappointment of her parents) "dog." After a few years of writing and editing in Los Angeles, she returned to her hometown to pursue her passion for teaching English, which has been her focus for over a decade.

Goodbye for Now

Sharon Wells has a passion for sharing stories and connecting with others through words. She is a dedicated wife, a loving mother, and a proud cat mom to two fluffy feline friends. In her downtime, you can often find her indulging in her two passions: all things *Wizard of Oz* and *Star Wars*.

Lori Wigsten, educator and freelance writer, holds an English degree from the University of Rhode Island and a liberal arts degree from Community College of Rhode Island. She enjoys spending time in nature and with her two grown daughters as well as with family/friends. After losing her husband, writing a blog called *Survivor Benefits* became a way of coping with his loss and helping others on the same path. Learn more about her journey at https://survivor-benefits.com/.

Lloyd Wilkinson is a husband, father of five, and grandfather of eight. Family and church family are his life. He has had a forty-year career in the IT business and is the pastor of a small church in Atlanta, Georgia. He enjoys reading, writing, and the occasional bourbon and cigar.

Andrea Williams, based in Charlotte, North Carolina, is a seasoned writer and marketing professional. Passionate about animal welfare, she serves as the director for Carolina Boxer Rescue, advocating for and rescuing boxers in need across the region.

Ronda Williams grew up in Northern Indiana but now lives in Ironton, Ohio, with her husband of forty years. They are blessed with a son, daughter, and grandson. She is a graduate of Kentucky Christian University (BS) and Peru State College (MEd) and works as an English language arts middle school teacher and a freelancer. Ronda enjoys reading, music, singing, nature, photography, kayaking, taking walks, teaching Sunday school, and spending time with her family.

Dr. Catherine Zeisner is a proud Canadian and educator working as a professor at a university. She got to meet her son after a long search and enjoyed the time she spent getting to know him as an adult. Sadly, he died in 2020 from natural causes. Catherine is very appreciative of his adoptive parents and the incredible love and support they showed him during his life.

About the Editors

Sandre Griffiths is an associate editor at Word & Deed Publishing Inc. In addition to her BA in communications, she gained extensive experience in writing and editing during her thirty-two-year career in the civil service. Sandre has a passion for writing and credits the *Nancy Drew* book series for inspiring her love of reading and writing. In her spare time, she enjoys hiking, afternoon tea with her friends, painting, and spending time with her husband and their blended family.

Darrin Griffiths, EdD, is an associate editor at Word & Deed Publishing Inc. He also works as an assistant professor (limited duties) at Western University and is a sessional instructor at OISE/University of Toronto for the Master of Education degree. Darrin is a retired elementary school principal who worked in numerous schools in Hamilton and Toronto, Ontario. His research interests are connected to educational leadership and equity and social justice.

Made in the USA
Middletown, DE
19 November 2024